Boo

Body Panic

Gender, Health, and the
Selling of Fitness

Shari L. Dworkin and
Faye Linda Wachs

NEW YORK UNIVERSITY PRESS
New York and London

NEW YORK UNIVERSITY PRESS
New York and London
www.nyupress.org

Library of Congress Cataloging-in-Publication Data
Dworkin, Shari L.
Body panic : gender, health, and the selling of fitness / Shari L.
Dworkin and Faye Linda Wachs.
    p.   cm.
Includes bibliographical references and index.
ISBN-13: 978-0-8147-1967-1 (cl : alk. paper)
ISBN-10: 0-8147-1967-8 (cl : alk. paper)
ISBN-13: 978-0-8147-1968-8 (pb : alk. paper)
ISBN-10: 0-8147-1968-6 (pb : alk. paper)
1. Body Image—United States. 2. Advertising, Magazine—United
States. 3. Culture—United States. 4. Gender identity—United
States. 5. Physical fitness—United States—Periodicals. 6. Exercise
—Psychological aspects.   I. Wachs, Faye Linda. II. Title.
[DNLM: 1. Body Image—United States. 2. Advertising as Topic—
trends—United States. 3. Culture—United States. 4. Gender Identity
—United States. 5. Periodicals as Topic—United States. 6. Physical
Fitness—psychology—United States.   BF 697.5.B63 D939b 2009]
BF697.5.B63D86 2009
306.4'613—dc22   2008038249

New York University Press books are printed on acid-free paper,
and their binding materials are chosen for strength and durability.
We strive to use environmentally responsible suppliers and materials
to the greatest extent possible in publishing our books.

Manufactured in the United States of America

c 10 9 8 7 6 5 4 3 2
p 10 9 8 7 6 5 4 3

Contents

Acknowledgments

After ten years and a tremendous amount of work, it is difficult to remember each and every person we wish to thank. There have been many research assistants and volunteers such as Isabel Howe, Nancy Zheng, Lorraine Lothringer, Alyssa Sankin, Margo Weisberg, Rivkie Elbaum, Erin Winter, Kristen Nelson, Lori Ottaviano, Alicia Van Nice, Samantha Wolsky, and Dustin Hamm. All of these individuals were just extraordinary with their help, and we thank them. A lot of people commented on conference papers related to this work, including Mike Messner, Dan Cook, Cheryl Cooky, Jenny Higgins, and others. We also received comments on drafts of some of the chapters, so it is important to especially thank Linda Blum, Christine Williams, Kari Lerum, and Mike Messner, although there were others.

The intellectual inspiration that academics derive from others' hard work deserves a lot of special gratitude, and we rank the works of Mike Messner, Margaret Carlisle Duncan, Gary Dowsett, Toby Miller, Raewyn Connell, Susan Bordo, Leslie Heywood, Don Sabo, Mary MacDonald, Mary Jo Kane, Patricia Hill Collins, Jennifer Hargreaves, and Michael Kimmel as being the most influential. Mike Messner has mentored both of us in generous, consistent, and wonderful ways for many years, and we thank him enormously for that. Thanks to NYU Press for their patience, ease, and professionalism, and to Ilene Kalish for being a supreme editor. More special thanks go to Isabel Howe (yes, again!) for being such a pleasant and dedicated perfectionist and for helping us to get to the final stages of this project.

I (Shari) offer a lot of thanks to the coauthor of this book, Faye Linda Wachs. I have worked with Faye for over ten years, and her intellectual contributions, energy, fast mind, and steady hard work continue to amaze me. Thanks to her for lengthy discussions and the research and writing time she put into this project. Additionally, the way she boldly added consumption and consumer culture into the bodies/health/gender analysis also helped the manuscript enormously. I reserve my final thanks for Kari Lerum, who has been a true inspiration. She is also endlessly supportive of all of my work, life, and dreams. The peace, contentment, joy, entertainment, challenge, and presence I receive from her helps me to find meaning in the words that drop (or don't drop) on any given page. I wish that writing was as easy as being with her is, even though writing always feels quite good.

I (Faye) would like to thank Shari Dworkin. She truly transforms work into an enjoyable experience. Her humor and spirit kept us going throughout the project. Moreover, her work ethic is unbelievable. I hope this book is only one of many we will produce over the years. I would also like to thank Gene Kim for his support throughout the writing process. He patiently endured many theoretical brainstorming sessions and assisted in innumerable ways. His willingness to spend many weekends playing golf while I worked on the manuscript was also greatly appreciated. My family also deserves recognition for their patience and support. My parents, Helen and Martin Wachs, and my brother, Steve, and his wife, Shirley, were always there when I needed them. I would also like to thank my two faithful companions for their patience and support. Bobo greeted me warmly at the door and then ran to the computer to take his customary spot at my feet, while Briggs proved invaluable as lumbar support.

1

The Nature of Body Panic Culture
Image and Popular Culture

A quick stroll past any newsstand will reveal a plethora of magazines devoted to health and fitness. "Healthy," "fit" bodies are draped across covers. Serving as advertisements, cover models beckon, enticing readers. Take a closer look. Choose a magazine. Pick it up, and your eyes will undoubtedly peruse the finely tuned form on the cover, communicating the meaning of the words "health" and "fitness," singing it to you through rippling muscles. As if they could speak to you, cover models' eyes look back at you with pride. "Hard work," you hear the implied whisper. All of you can do it. The uniformity of bodily appearances that stretches down the wall of magazines stands in silent, sharp contrast to the cavalcade of bodies in all shapes and sizes moving past the bustling newsstands along such streets as 42nd Street in New York City or on the Third Street promenade in Santa Monica, California.

Invariably, men's health and fitness magazines feature an athletic man posing in a tank top, or shirtless. Usually he is white, has a "healthy" tan, and his vascular, cut form implies the successful engagement in and cumulative repetition of a variety of bodily practices. Bulging biceps, defined broad shoulders with rippling striations, cut six- or eight-pack abs, and wide, pumped chests merge into a singular ideal. Nearby, a second character awaits. Women's health and fitness magazine covers "flesh out" this being in detail. She is "perky" and inviting with a coy smile, she leans, lilts or languishes, displaying a lean, tight, compact body beneath monochromatic smooth skin, in tight, revealing clothing. Frequently she wears a bikini. Also usually white, she is tight and toned, but lacks visible rips or cuts. Her muscles are long and lean, and certainly not "too big," while her body possesses a subtle dose of curvaceousness.

The differences between the two bodies are striking. Big. Little. Wide. Narrow. Bursting. Contained. Massive. Toned. Gender seems to permeate every aspect of bodily presentation. But look again and think about it. Complex social and contextual factors get us here, to these images. Ideologies of gender difference, the exacerbation of a "culture of lack" where consumer capitalism steps in to improve you, the reality of changing gender norms in postindustrial society, a wave of women who "made it" into sport, fitness, work, and the military—only to be remade out of the office, gym, or playing fields. The images reveal men experiencing a loss of certainty around gender norms, a cultural resurgence in the importance of sport for making boys into men, new emphases on the large male body in what some call a "crisis of masculinity" (Gillett and White 1992). And, for (some) women, challenging traditional gender norms of inferiority through sports and fitness has marked the new millennium. These forces *are* redefining idealized bodies and are making and naming the boundaries of difference. Like a siren's song, the viewer is drawn in, not noticing what lies beyond.

We began this project ten years ago as graduate students at the University of Southern California in Los Angeles, and we are now both professors—in San Francisco (Shari) and Los Angeles, California (Faye). Endless sit-ups and bench presses aside, we were workout wonders and publication partners, perusing health and fitness magazines for workout tips, noticing what we thought was an acritically produced trend: the silent trope that we call the conflation of "health" with the maintenance of narrowly defined gendered bodily ideals. Students in our classrooms noted contemporary trends when they raised their hands to earnestly tell us, "It is healthy, right, to not have any extra fat, you know . . . extra . . . stuff . . . on you? Isn't that . . . well . . . unhealthy?" Others told us about their gendered plights on treadmills or the stairmaster: "You know," the women told us, "you're not supposed to have anything that's jiggling nowadays." Some of our colleagues even added their own observations: had we noticed that women and men in the gym are changing roles? "The men are looking in the gym mirror and grabbing their extra body fat much more than the women, so . . . what's up with that?" We hadn't even put our ideas together yet, nor a book contract, and the mantras were there: The current cultural choices in the terrain seemed to be dichotomized around jiggly and disgusting, or firm and unable to detect any traces of body fat. Did this hold for both women and men? Was it truly health—or was it the image of health—through an idealized image of gender that was for sale? Are these really the options? We weren't sure just yet. We had some work to do.

The differences between the two bodies show how, within fitness discourse and imagery, gender seems to permeate most aspects of bodily presentation. (*Exercise & Health*, Fall 2001)

Examining the literature on these topics offered some options to explain contemporary trends on fit, gendered bodies in the media, but these were neatly packaged into overarching assumptions that led to the creation of our main positions in this text. That is the purpose of this first chapter: to trace these theoretical arguments, note our own and others' criticisms, and arrive at our methods and framework for the chapters that follow.

Gender, Bodies, Media, and Fitness

Feminist analysis, both broadly and within sport and fitness, added substantially to the emerging arguments on gender, media, bodies, and fitness. Much feminist analysis (second wave, 1970s–1990s) had long claimed that women's bodies had been objectified and trivialized through imagery and content in representations. The basic thrust of these works was to underscore that physically strong and competent women pose a threat to ideologies of male physical superiority and that, in order to contain this threat, the media tend to erase such women from view (e.g., by disproportionately presenting women who are engaged in sex-typed activities such as tennis, light weights, aerobics, and not featuring women in more powerful activities). The argument continued throughout the second wave of feminism, and it lasted for decades. Media didn't simply erase strong women from view, but offered a complex politics of inclusion, whereby strong women were often trivialized for their corporeal contributions through sexualization, deviant markings, jokes, or ambivalence about their accomplishments (Birrell and Cole 1990; Duncan 1994, 1993, 1990; Duncan and Brummett 1993; Duncan and Hasbrook 1988; Duncan, Messner, and Cooky 2000; Kane 1995; MacNeil 1994; Messner 2002). While our current analyses press beyond these claims in a number of ways, we do not deny that these basic trends do appear in contemporary culture, not only in sport and fitness media, but outside of it as well. For example, in a recent letter to the editor of *Business Week* (January 6, 2006), the author was repulsed by the fact that a list of women "business leaders" had been subject to the politics of erasure and trivialization:

> I want to congratulate you on our backward slide into the Dark Ages with "Best Leaders" (Cover story, December 19). Of the 21 leaders you recognized, only two are women: Catherine Fake of Flickr and Marissa Mayer of Google, Inc. I'm especially delighted to see that you chose to depict Mayer as a leggy blond cartoon character. Nicely done. As a business owner and a woman, I want to thank you for allowing my invisibility to remain intact in 2006.

Similar to sport and fitness, it is not that successful women business leaders aren't there, but they are largely erased, while men are disproportionately featured and included. When women are included, they are trivialized and sexualized. Voilà. Strong. Gone.

This argument returned through a more thorough and groundbreaking analysis of representations from Mary Jo Kane at the University of Minnesota in the mid-1990s. She underscored how media tended to reproduce some very specific cumulative cultural mechanisms to provide continuity for an ongoing categorical myth that all men's bodies are bigger, stronger, and more powerful than women's. She argued that an analysis of sport and fitness media clearly revealed a disjuncture between material reality and image, where reality offered a continuum of overlapping strength, size, and performance by gender (Kane 1995). In other words, there is a range of performances among women and men and not simply between them, but current media mechanisms present imagery and events as if there is one muscle gap between (all) women and (all) men. The strongest man may be stronger than the strongest woman, but there are numerous strong women who are stronger than many men, and there are many men whose strength does not approach the strongest women or men. Treating average difference as categorical difference for viewers allows the public to create an erroneous consciousness about the remaining women and men who likely overlap a good deal in strength.

Kane went on to describe the specific media mechanisms that work to contain strong women and reproduce categorical differences (she calls these "binary enforcements") by gender through: *sport and fitness typing* (e.g., featuring women in more feminine sport and fitness activities and featuring men in more masculine-identified ones, even though women frequently participate in so-called men's sports and fitness activities), *erasure, selective comparisons* (e.g., going to a men's event and then flipping to a women's event), and *marking strong women as deviant* (e.g., sex testing powerful women or calling strong women lesbians) or *marking strong women as "like a man"* (e.g., erasing them as women in the public eye altogether).

Contemporary toy trends reveal some of the same tendencies to dichotomize gender and erase evidence of a continuum. For example, if Barbie were a "real woman," she would stand 88 inches tall (7.3 feet) and have a 36-inch bust, 33-inch hips, and a 15-inch waist. Barbie's counterpart Ken would be 82 inches tall (shorter than Barbie, paradoxically), with a 30-inch waist, 43-inch chest, and 29-inch hips.[1] Given that masculinity is relationally defined to femininity, psychologists Pope et al. also traced the development of GI Joe and what his muscles would look like over time were he a "real man." In the 1964 version, if he were a man standing 5 feet 10 inches, he would have a 44-inch chest, 32-inch waist, and 12-inch biceps. The measurements since his introduction have become far less realistic. The 1991 Salute to GI Joe doll features what would be a 29-inch waist with 16½-inch biceps. The GI Joe extreme introduced in the mid-1990s features what would be a 55-inch chest and 27-inch biceps, almost as big as his 29-inch waist. This trend was not simply found across Barbie, Ken, and GI Joe, but was also found across many children's toys (see Pope, Phillips, and Olivardia 2000 for a complete discussion; also see Pope, Olivardia, Gruber, and Borowiecki 1999). Male centerfolds have also been found to be much more muscular over time, and anyone's own observations of male basketball players, baseball players, and football players reveal increases in size and muscularity over time (Leit, Pope, and Grey 2001).

Extreme gender display seems to codify as a genuine trend just as gender differences in the larger culture were being called into question. As women began entering previously male-dominated professions, increasing numbers of women entered into military service, and Title IX demanded greater opportunities for women and girls in sport (Reskin and Phipps 1988; Boutilier and San Giovanni 1994), traditional gender ideals were called into question. Some argue that "expanding" definitions of women and men may provide fodder for the increasing muscularity of the male body.[2] At the same time, though, we will argue that within health and fitness discourse and imagery, there are trends of convergence between women, men, consumption, and bodies (this is the main focus of chapter 2).

Why would it be so important to reiterate the cultural imagination around gender difference through iconography (according to those who argue that the expanding male body is a specific reaction to changes in gender relations and women's status)? Is it really as simple as the idea that men are just threatened by being beaten by a girl? History, including contemporary evidence, bears some repetition of this suggestion, but there is much more to the story.[3] Academics have generally argued that most works that relied on second wave feminist thought either explicitly explained suppression of a continuum of overlapping bodies between women and men through (1) some aspects of hegemonic masculinity, male hegemony, or male dominance; or (2) men feeling threatened by strong women, or uncertain about rapid shifts in gender relations and therefore experiencing a "crisis of masculinity" that we will soon discuss and update (see chapter 3). With subtlety, however, such works also tended to rely on the assumptions contained in Gayle Rubin's 1975 analysis of sexual divisions of labor within what she and others might call a gender and sexuality order.[4] This argument is covered next, as it has relevance for one rationale for why difference is embraced, especially during times of rapid transition in gender relations.

The Gender and Sexuality Order—Sameness and Difference

Rubin stresses that divisions of labor (or the fact that women and men will be called on to do different things in the world) represents less of a biological order than a cultural taboo against the sameness of men and women. The reason for the taboo on sameness is twofold: if there are privileges associated with what men do (e.g., higher wages, building stronger bodies, assumptions of efficacy and success, valuations of importance), and men's tasks are more culturally valued, men will have an investment in retaining their tasks while separating women's tasks as exclusively female, and as something less valuable. Second, dichotomous gender difference (seeing masculinity as being attached to the activities and practices of men, femininity as attached to the activities and practices of women) is not just part of a gender order but simultaneously, a sexuality order where adherence to gender norms helps to produce a myth of heterosexuality. When men are "masculine," there are fewer discerning questions about their participation in a heterosexual order, and when women are "feminine," the same holds for their participation in the "normal" sexuality order.[5] Some even argue that the more feminine-appropriate institution of fitness developed out of the emergent fears of masculinization of the female body in the institution of sport (Hargreaves 1994; Giulianotti 2005).

Indeed, some researchers find, especially within a sociology of sport and fitness, that strong women are assumed to be lesbians, despite decades of movement in a gender, sexuality, and cultural order that some would characterize as more "at play," fluid, flipped, contested, trans, or containing a rather large multiplicity of meanings.[6] According to the former arguments, it seemed that men expressed their dismay over women's entrance into male domains through "body panic," given the symbolic power that ideologies of the body have for the constitution of hegemonic masculinity and emphasized femininity (Connell 1987). In this instance, scholars argued that "crises of masculinity" resulted and the ensuing threat led to "controlling representations" of women in media. However, researchers find that men, too, are constituted as bodily objects. Men are increasingly dissatisfied with their bodies and increasingly display symptoms of body dysmorphia in postindustrial consumer culture. Poststructural understandings of the embodied and constructed subject, along with multiracial feminist critiques of second wave essentialism, soon challenged scholars to understand gendered bodies in far more complicated ways.

Men's Bodies and Consumer Culture: Equal Opportunity Exploitation?

As the body becomes a negotiable commodity for men as well as women, and multinationals seek increasing profits, males are increasingly being sold bodily problematization which can be soothed through continual purchases. Thus, some might argue that all bodies, including men, pregnant women, adolescents, children, and older women and men, are subject to surveillance and objectification.[7] This is one of the facts of life for everyone in a postindustrial consumer culture (Bordo 1999; Heywood and Dworkin 2003; Pope, Phillips, and Olivardia 2000), where even President Bush quickly noted that consumption and shopping were a "patriotic duty" following the 9/11 attacks on the World Trade Center.

The production of gendered bodily ideals that require daily practices and purchases to cumulatively form and sustain them is part of the shift to perspectives of the body as consumer in the postindustrial period (Featherstone 1991a). Just as a host of ideologies and institutions arose to bolster gendered ideologies of privilege during the transition to an industrial economy, gender insecurities in the changing postindustrial workforce called into question a range of beliefs about what it means to be a man or a woman. That is, as more women entered the professional world, as evidenced by women's entrance into college, medical and law schools, as paternity testing solidified the legitimacy of child support, and as women's sports moved toward parity with men's, gender roles were in a state of flux. Scholars point to a host of responses to the industrial crisis of masculinity. Sports, boy scouts, and other all-male environments quelled fears of social feminization and provided suitable forums to "turn boys into men" (Kimmel 1990). They further provided visual displays that offered "proof" of the "naturalness" of emerging ideologies of gender difference. Some argue that as a postindustrial crisis of masculinity solidifies, the body becomes the surface on which the ideal of difference is inscribed. Male body panic joins female pathologies of imperfection, self-esteem troubles, and loss of control in the postindustrial landscape.

Research across disciplines finds that men are in fact more concerned than ever about their physical appearances. Focus group research on men underscores the importance of being muscular, acritical conflations of muscularity and health, fears of being fat, social pressures to be slender and muscular, and links between looking good and feeling powerful in social situations (Bordo 1999; Frith and Gleeson 2004; Grogan and Richards 2002). Research also finds that men are nearly as dissatisfied about their bodies as women, and experience depression and self-esteem problems that are, in part, due to gendered cultural standards, some of which are produced by media (Grogan 1999; Olivardia, Pope, Borowiecki, and Cohane 2004). But numerous scholars present the impact of cultural standards on men, including media, as if there are no differences between the impact on women's and men's health—except that women's eating and body dysmorphic disorders lead her to want to eat less and be smaller, while men want to be larger and more muscular.[8] The addendum to the much-needed correction—that research had focused too much on women and the body—is that *we're all stuck now and we're all negatively affected by imagery and cultural ideals.* Is this really the fate of the literature and of individuals? We think this is simplistic, and therefore we devote much of chapters 2 and 3 to fleshing out whether these debates adequately capture contemporary trends. In chapter 2, we show that within our ten-year sample of health and fitness magazines, there certainly is convergence in consumptive bodily practices and prescribed norms, and this trend increases in our data set over time. However, textual analysis of men's magazines in chapter 3 reveals that even as men are increasingly subject to new objectifying shifts of bodywork under consumption imperatives, they definitively retained subjecthood in a number of important ways when compared to iconography of women. These trends included a resurgence of explicitly masculinist and antifeminist links to male-dominated occupations such as sports, the military, among other tendencies. As we will argue, male body panic is not simply an individualized state of anxiety that men as a group have, but rather must be understood as part of the larger tapestry of changing gender, race, class, and sexuality relations and as part of the broader structure of contemporary socioeconomic structures.

Such approaches move us beyond the common claims of relativistic oppression that can seem to all-too-quickly make women's and men's experiences of objectification fully parallel. Second wave feminist stances and theorists of masculinity in the health, sport, and fitness literature were not the only groups of academics that fell into a partly totalizing stance of oppression around gender, bodies, and fitness. Others also viewed the body as subject to domination within fitness regimes. Drawing on Marxist perspectives, individuals become alienated from their own bodies through fitness regimes designed to restructure the body as capital. The body then becomes a fetish or sign, often a moral signifier for viewers to see and judge, rather than an integral part of the actual identity of the self. In consumer culture, an endless array of goods and services become critical to self-construction and display. Through goods, services, and rituals of display, each body is part of an endless process of marketplace definition. In such an environment, the consumer begins to see his or her body as an alien object that must be constantly managed through consumption to preserve position and identity.

Consumption and analyses of consumer culture certainly advance debates on fitness, bodies, gender, and media, and these analyses had been overlooked by some feminist analysis and critical masculinity studies for many years. The addition of consumption is vital to understanding "masculine" and "feminine" bodily ideals because advertisements, dominant cultural trends, and contemporary health and fitness practices merge to form the popular assumption that fitness ideals "speak to all" while quietly and inevitably including some bodies and excluding others.[9] Once gendered ideologies are internalized, the resultant sexed body frequently gets tagged as "natural" instead of as produced and policed through the effects of purchases and practices (Butler 1993; Dworkin 2001; Lorber 1993). Assuming that women and men have "natural" preferences negates the role that cultural and market forces play in constructing and shaping social locations, healthism (to be defined next), morality, and what one believes is necessary to be desirable and moral.

Consumption, Healthism, and Bodily Surveillance

It is particularly vital to keep in mind that in a postindustrial economy, media serve primarily as a vehicle to produce audience-viewing time for advertisers (Jhally 1989). This means that within fitness media texts, advertisers have a captive audience to transmit messages to readers who might be stimulated to purchase products. Readers employ the messages provided by texts as they learn to self-surveil with respect to the cultural ideals promoted. Coupled with a more diffuse orientation toward power than was typically held in the objectification thesis, some viewed the ensuing bodily self-surveillance that results from an emphasis on consumption as inevitable given that the body can be viewed as a text onto which cultural prescriptions could be overlaid.[10] Thus, media forces in particular, and advertising specifically, conspire with more diffuse notions of power in contemporary society to simultaneously produce a "culture of lack" and an endless array of products to assuage the lack, or at least the stigma of possessing it.[11] Transforming women and men into the right kind of objects is the goal for multinationals, as this produces ever-expanding profits, and there are real, material benefits to collecting signifiers of feminine or masculine success.

As noted by Giulianotti, "Consumer culture is in fact constructed out of the interplay between disciplined/objectified bodies and governed/ subjective bodies" (2005, p. 118). Hence, it is vital to uncover the types of objective and subjective discourses, imagery, and practices that are produced for both women and men simultaneously. Our analysis in this book, then, will attempt to move beyond an objectification thesis by underscoring how bodily subjecthood and objecthood are *differentially and relationally* created for women and men in mainstream health and fitness magazines. Existing and emerging relations of privilege and oppression construct current racialized, classed, sexualized, and gendered ideals. Social practices, such as those prescribed in health and fitness magazines, reify these ideals to a certain degree. The right kind of body reinforces not only privileged social locations, but types of moralities and the performance of citizenship.

It is here where the important concept of healthism must be introduced, as this book centrally combines an analysis of consumer culture, bodies, and social inequality with the concept of healthism from public health and medical sociology. Healthism was first introduced by Robert Crawford in his influential 1980 work, "Healthism and the Medicalization of Everyday Life" (1980). In this work, he discussed the ways in which contemporary capitalist culture is infused with notions of "health" and health promotion that reveal assumptions about normality, well-being, and morality (and are not necessarily healthy). "Like medicine," he argues, "healthism situates the problem of health and disease at the level of the individual. Solutions are formulated at that level as well" (1980). Within such a system, a lack of health begins to be associated with individual "moral laxity."[12] As we will argue, the singular focus on personal responsibility within the text and imagery of health and fitness magazines reproduces discourses of healthism and operates to promote neoliberal ideologies that obscure the impact of government and structural contributions to health disparities.

Thus, in the process of advertising and selling the right kind of bodily object through consumption, the bodies of the privileged are legitimated and idealized as moral actors. This is because the right kind of bodily object—the cumulative effect of one's purchases, social practices, and the ensuing surfaces of the flesh—is always out of reach by some and attainable by others. Those at more privileged social locations have a distinct advantage in attaining ideals, and roadblocks similarly hinder the less advantaged. Cause and effect have been reversed, and the invisibility of one's cumulative social practices make the flesh seem natural and the right kind of flesh more moral (Butler 1990; also see Spitzack 1990). The resultant body you see on the surface is a result of individual and collective expressions of pleasures, purchases, cultural ideals, social positionings, and self-surveillance.

Few sociologists have empirically linked processes of consumer culture to healthism and the body despite the fact that media play a central role in the dissemination and circulation of discourses about bodies and health.[13] Scholars within the field of public health have underscored the ways that healthism was "an undesirable but inevitable consequence of political ideology, dominant in the late 1970s, which couched many health problems in terms of individual acts and omissions rather than the acts and omissions of politicians and policymakers of the deficiencies of the welfare state" (Greenhalgn and Wesselly 2004). As will be noted below, a more Foucauldian analysis of power might see individualized forms of power found within consumer culture as part of a broader shift in power from "mass, punitive external repressions to becoming internalized within the individual and located within the moral category of guilt and reproof" (Kirk and Colquhoun 1989). Hence, the appearance of the fit body, rather than the reality of fitness, has become a critical determinant of social status and a factor that is self-policed by individuals as they negotiate social positions. Scholars such as Crawford and others ultimately saw healthism as part of the project of neoliberalism where it is "an ideologically insidious force, which by elevating health to a super value a metaphor for all that is good in life . . . reinforcing the privatization of the struggle for generalized well-being." Analyses of media and the body have been well theorized yet are not often empirically linked to an analysis of healthism —but should be, as much theory has argued that "body shape is a corporeal metaphor for health," and body shapes and sizes come to mean "not just medico-scientifically 'good' but also morally 'good'" (ibid., p. 430).[14]

As we will argue, then, contemporary media produce body panic not only through idealized imagery that invokes individualized feelings about the body, but also through a process of what is included as content inside of media text and representation—what signifiers are used—and what is, by extension, left out. The resultant effect of these processes of meaning-making[15] is to simultaneously displace critiques of social structures onto individual bodily failures and onto marginalized categories, while stigmatizing those who fail to participate and succeed in the existing system. Body panic marshals resources to a morally valued but socially depoliticized project: the endless quest for bodily perfection. This project is further individualized by discourses of healthism. Thus, individual energies remain focused on personal pursuits for fitness, rather than broader solutions that produce a wider range of health and fitness options for all.

In *Body Panic*, we pay special attention to how healthism operates through the preferred meanings and imagery in health and fitness magazines that focus not only on the fit body but also on discourses of gender, race, class, sexuality, crime/terrorism, family, and nation. We extend previous work on this topic through the analogy of "confessionals," or processes of sin and redemption that we have previously found particularly useful to explain the relationship between bodies, surveillance, and social practice. In this work, we will rely at times on the concept of the confessional, which is, according to Bordowitz, "the story of a sinner who is asking some higher authority to take the burden away through a disclosure" (Foucault 1978; Bordowitz 1994; Wachs and Dworkin 1997). Far from simply being a religious, cathartic, or caring modality, confessional mechanisms have been found to be widely secularized in contemporary society through the disciplines of psychiatry, demography, medicine, and public health (Foucault 1979; Rubin 1999; also see Spitzack 1990). We would argue that the same holds true for health and fitness discourse. Whether a media figure makes public announcements on television about his or her HIV status, patients make weekly statements to a mental health practitioner about their relationship problems, or a woman or man shows us or declares how much he or she ate or exercised (or should have), the practices of seeing, telling, listening, marking, defining, judging, and changing behaviors is well integrated into the fabric of contemporary U.S. culture. Media in fact become a popular forum in which to structure everyday confessionals for the reading public and to lay out the parameters for redemption (e.g., cutting calories, hitting the gym) (Wachs and Dworkin 1997). Health and fitness magazines, in particular, have been noted as a means for confessional bodies to receive instruction and feedback (Baudrillard 1998; Giulianotti 2005).

In his work *The History of Sexuality: Volume I*, Foucault remarks that the confessional is not a neutral ritual, but rather, one which "unfolds within a power relationship, for one does not confess without the presence of a partner who is not simply the interlocutor but the authority who requires confession" (1978, p. 61). The "agency of domination," he argues, "does not reside in the one who speaks but in the one who listens" (p. 62). The one who listens "exonerates, redeems, purifies, unburdens, liberates, and promises salvation" (ibid.). A single listener does not own the power to repress and dominate another during a single confession, but rather the process of confession (in conjunction with institutional processes whereby experts mark, define, and/or change behaviors) becomes a call to participate in the broader task of surveillance that is carried out through "the infinite task of telling" (ibid., p. 20). Those who hear the confession (audience or self who reads about (un)healthy eating or exercise practices) and structure its practices (health and fitness experts) set the parameters for redemption (stopping "unhealthy" behaviors), thereby shaping the confession into specific narrative frames, problems, and solutions.

However, not all bodies have equal access to the redemption associated with the confessional process. Previous work on confessionals, bodies, and health has focused largely on the out of control and sinful female body who confesses her "excesses" (Spitzack 1990), but it is vital to keep in mind that confessional bodies are those that are financially able to employ technologies of the self to aid in self-analysis and improvement, and are able to engage in the process of confession and redemption. Foucault labels these bodies as "bourgeoisie" or middle class. By contrast, docile bodies (working class, poor, and other marginalized categories) are subject to the "biopower" of experts who impose upon these bodies judgments that explain their pathologies and failures. While middle-class bodies are able to use fitness magazines in the process of confession and redemption to produce pleasurable and fulfilling identities, those unable to fully participate in the consumption necessary to attain redemption are stigmatized through the use of a number of cultural tropes—with "immorality" being a popular one. One can see examples of this in the current "obesity epidemic" and the framing of its attendant effects. While corporate profits in the food and diet industry soar, consumers negotiate a morass of mixed messages.

Our analysis therefore also extends previous work on moral panics[16] to examine contemporary women and men in health and fitness texts by considering how, with the advent of consumer culture, the salvation once derived through the soul (and its confessions) has moved to the body and the flesh. The body, then, does not simply become a sign of morality (or immorality) by being matched by moral (or immoral) acts, but the body generates the sign of morality in consumer culture that becomes the moral act itself. While once the sins of the individual were thought to be written on the flesh, simply not having perfect flesh is now viewed as a sin in and of itself. During times of rapid social change, we show how themes such as war (chapter 3) and the resurgence of domesticity (chapter 4) offer clear reinvigorations of the links between fitness and gendered, racialized, and classed moralities (see especially chapters 3 and 6). It is not so much that we emphasize how individuals confess explicitly with words through the narratives provided within fitness magazines (as was the case with Carole Spitzack's findings in her work on women and "speaking transgressions" of the body),[17] but that who is included inside the frames of media analysis (e.g., moral, white, fit citizen dedicated to protectionism in times of war, redeemable, or fit mother) and who is left out (immoral, criminal, terrorist, of color, nonredeemable, bad mother) has much to do with our resulting perceptions of healthy, moral, or proper men, women, citizens, mothers, and families (see chapters 3–6).

Foucault argues that with the dispersion of power in the transition from premodern to contemporary society, power is not owned by one group used to oppress and dominate another, but rather, power is more dispersed and involves a willingness to internalize the gaze of a generalized other who may be watching. A near secular morality ensues through a series of internalizations of this general gaze (not of men or women, but of the possibility that others are watching). Some argue that "confessional bodies reveal their 'innermost selves' by employing particular 'technologies of the self' (e.g., self-help or fitness/health magazines) to assist their self-analysis and quest for self improvement (Giulianotti 2005). Furthermore, the parameters of the confessional are not constructed out of opinions but rather, a specific form of "truth" that is mutually created in social interaction among an expert and the one who speaks (with signifiers of the body). Here, the expert will be the health or fitness professional or the text infused with "science" or assumptions of linear progress, the imagery offers proof of success, while the confessee will be the viewing audience who reads the relationship between gender, bodily ideals, sin, and redemption.

Although there is a tendency to examine bodies and think of them as "natural," it is vital to recall that what you are viewing is not wholly natural but is also a social *effect* of cumulative purchases, internalized cultural norms, interactions with others, and social practices. We view the role of consumption as a central challenge to assumptions of the natural body, since self-identity, social practices, and social locations are so crucial in the consumption process. In this way, *Body Panic* participates in linking media and Cultural Studies that are so popularly associated with analyses of image and text (and that are sometimes accused of being too disconnected from social structures, social inequalities, and social institutions) with Sociology, a discipline that is more generally preoccupied with empiricism, social inequalities, and social structures. To this we will add an integrated analysis from Public Health and Medical Sociology—disciplines that are generally concerned with population-level health disparities and resolving these.

Readers will therefore note that within each chapter, we weave between an analysis of image and text to discuss issues of healthism, consumer culture, bodies, social inequalities, and social structures. Media is, of course, an important social structure in and of itself. In fact, we were presented with a surprising analytical opportunity with the literal closure of one particular women's sporting magazine (e.g., *Women's Sports & Fitness* in our sample). This magazine focused on the fight against structural inequality for women in sport, but when the magazine folded, it was replaced by a long-running magazine (*Self*). This move demonstrates a resounding emphasis on the individualized fit body and focus on consumption/fitness as the sole form of empowerment. Chapter 5 therefore takes the tension between second wave emphasis on structural inequality and third wave feminist emphasis on commodity feminism as its central task. Ironically, or perhaps not, at this very juncture between Sociology and Cultural Studies, it is here where the consumption literature extends contemporary positions on the body in fitness, crawling out of (and back into) an emphasis on oppression.

Consumption: From Bodily Oppression to Emancipatory Potential?

Aside from arguments of sin, redemption, morality, or self-surveillance, some see the role of consumption as providing "positive agency" (Gimlin 2002), and as offering pleasurable "identity functions" (Featherstone 1991). Others view consumer culture as a medium through which individuals find/use/deploy possibilities for resistance and social change. For example, Leslie Heywood and Shari Dworkin, in their book *Built to Win: The Female Athlete as Cultural Icon*, argue that an increase in the circulation of images of powerful, fit, athletic women served many purposes in the eyes of the youth and adults who examined them. Here, Heywood

Some researchers argue that there has been an increase in contemporary images of powerful fit and athletic women. (*Ms Fitness Magazine*, Summer 1999)

and Dworkin used focus group methods and asked young people in class-rooms to discuss their thoughts about a range of images of fit and athletic women. In front of other classmates, when young boys viewed images of strong women in sport and fitness, they discussed how they felt that athletic women could "protect them" in the event that they were physically threatened on the playground. This is a rather striking cultural reversal on the politics of male protectionism of women. Other girls in the class declared that they were more interested in trying to learn a new sport, and had not previously considered it possible for women to be active in male-dominated events.

Other studies outside of sport and fitness media also reveal the same types of progressive resistance in the sea of cultural representations. For example, a recent study examines how Barbie dolls—long assumed to lead girls to be cultural dupes for hyperfeminine actions (that would undermine their empowerment)—were actually hated by many girls for their "dominant" representations of the female form. Interestingly, such studies found that Barbie is often, well, pulled apart and tossed into a large box in the closet while girls go do something else (Quindlen 1999; Rand 1995). Surely, we are aware of rebellions, girl power, boy rage, and the ability of cultural subjects to act as they wish, no matter what messages "say." The polysemic[18] nature of texts mean that subjects can and do take alternative meanings out of texts.

Thus, critiques of the "dominated-body approach" focus on the cultural manufacturing of multiple meanings and identities, part of which can be empowering. The expressive body has the ability to participate in what Giddens terms "reflexive self-fashioning" (Giddens 1991). This means that through participation in consumer culture, an awareness is generated that a fluid identity can be self-consciously constructed. The individual becomes a conscious participant in the development of the self. Baudrillard notes, however, that individual desires are disguised expressions of social differences in a system of cultural meanings produced through commodities (Baudrillard 1975). The codes produced by cultural systems (e.g., fashion and fitness), he argues, are infinitely variable. The consumer can negotiate between a series of historically produced differences. For Baudrillard, the commodified body still acts as a marker of social distinction, but not a permanent one. Altering the physical body can operate to alter one's position in the social order. Signs and signifiers may float; however, they do so along currents of thought, at least somewhat.

Some theorists in media and culture have noted the import of signifiers moving more readily to some meanings than others. Scholars articulate the complexity of relations of power and privilege in consumer culture by examining the relationship between structure and culture. Gender-related scholarship on the body underscores the reworkings of the relationship between signifier and sign[19] that are possible and potentially emancipatory if included into media frames. For example, Leslie Heywood's book, *Bodymakers: A Cultural Anatomy of Female Bodybuilding*, identifies bodybuilding as feminist resistance to the risk of sexual assault; Martha McCaughey's *Real Knockouts: The Physical Feminism of Women's Self Defense* examines female martial artists' ability to self-defend against attack; and Nancy Theberge's *Higher Goals: Women's Ice Hockey and the Politics of Gender* examines how female ice hockey players in a male-dominated sport are shifting the terms of gender from lacking physicality to powerful aggression. All of these are examples of the fluidity of the sign, and it is likely that many more are possible after the passage of Title IX, the success of women in the Olympics, and other broad changes in gender

Evidence of the increasing objectification of the male body. Note that his gaze is downward and indirect, similar to how women's eyes have been posed in the past. (*Exercise & Health*, Fall 2001)

relations (Heywood 1998; McCaughy 1997; also see McDermott 1996; Theberge 2000).

Similarly, Pope, Philips, and Olivardia's *The Adonis Complex: The Secret Crisis of Male Body Obsession*, Judith Halberstam's *Female Masculinity*, Susan Bordo's *The Male Body*, Tim Edwards' *Men in the Mirror*, Leslie Heywood and Shari Dworkin's chapter in *Built to Win* on "Body Panic Parity," also underscore the ability of the male body to be objectified and for actors to galvanize signifiers of identity that need not form deterministic links between sex, gender, and sexuality. Hence, more bodies are opened up to objectification and its harmful effects than before, but consumers can enact resistance to the pressures of the marketplace, and market forces can be manipulated to facilitate progressive social change. In this view, the "floating signifier effect" enables consumers to re-appropriate symbols to be used in unanticipated and empowering ways.

The problem is, however, as gender, race, and sexuality scholars have pointed out, this re-appropriation is not equally accessible to all, and some meanings are more likely to be appropriated for some people than others.[20] Here is where culture and structure meet in important ways that have been overlooked in media analysis. In this view, though the signifier may float, it does not float as easily to some meanings as others depending on the visible body possessed and on the advertiser's array of meanings attached to image and text. We therefore spend considerable time on the relational aspects of gender analysis to make very clear that while there is some similarity and convergence between women's and men's consumer bodily practices and form, there are many ways in which whiteness, male-ness, and heterosexuality retain subjectivity. At the same time, women, femininity, men and women of color who are marginalized, and margin-alized sexualities may not experience equal opportunity benefits of these media framings (especially see chapters 2–5 for analyses of race and sexu-ality). Even where more empowering notions of gender are visible in the texts, chapter 5 highlights how consumer culture undercuts and depoliti-cizes resistant symbols, assimilating them into the lexicon of purchasable identities.

One version of an idealized female body at the turn of the millennium. (*Shape*, July 2004)

The idealized male body at the turn of the millennium. (*Men's Fitness,* November 2004)

The ways in which signifiers of "health" and "fitness" come together to mark moralities, privilege certain lifestyles, and exclude others in a given contemporary moment are even more meaningful given that the messages attached to images and ideals are often conflated with a state of health in the name of science. Ultimately, then, positions which assume that "positive self-identity" is the only proper analysis of consumption fail to consider social inequality and social locations (gender, race, class, sexuality), and therefore negate the effects of healthism as it is circulated through media. Focusing only on the empowering aspects of consumer culture literally erases the negative effects of healthism—that is, such analyses in media ignore the health implications of the demands of consumer culture and the ways in which ideals of liberation become overly conflated with consuming and bodily self-surveillance (Bordo 1997). Cheering the emancipatory potential of media also masks the structural production of health disparities and the ways in which neoliberalism relies on individual citizens to "accept their responsibility for securing their own well-being" (Rose 2001). It further reifies structures that generate privilege as those who benefit most from such systems are simultaneously legitimated and validated. Is the sale of gender difference (or similarity) really reflecting a state or image of health?

"Health" and "Fitness" As Near Science: Conflations of Health and Gendered Bodily Ideals

In *Body Panic*, we underscore how, through the practice of internalizing rituals that are prescribed as near science in health and fitness magazines, individuals confess their gendered failures not only to themselves but implicitly to the market when they purchase (and to audiences who will gaze at corporeal signifiers of success). Redemption is earned through continual engagement in the rituals designed to assuage one's constant failure. While a number of works explore the complicated relationship between ideologies of bodily lack and body image/self-esteem (Grogan 1999; Pope, Phillips, and Olivardia 2000), few have analyzed how public health and fitness discourse often conflate meeting gendered bodily ideals with a state of health (for exceptions, see Duncan 1994 and Monaghan 2001; also see Newman 2007). Since health and fitness discourses are perceived as operating within the realm of science, or as being unquestionably "healthy," such discourses are frequently overlooked as a site in which to critically examine how ideologies of masculinity, femininity, gender, and the body are constructed within such spheres (Fausto-Sterling 1985, 2000; Van den Wingaard 1997). While there have been several critiques of the assumptions surrounding fitness as "healthy" within journal articles on media, fitness, and bodies (Duncan 1994; Glassner 1990, 1992; Pope, Phillips, and Olivardia 2000; also see Grogan and Richards 2002), researchers tend to analyze only one magazine or type of exercise at a time, or carry out an analysis on men and women separately. Indeed, no book-length manuscript to date has tended to the topic empirically across multiple health and fitness magazines over an extended period of time to examine the ways in which imagery and text are deployed to signify a state of "health" for both women and men.

At times, we will undoubtedly shake hands with approaches that critique fitness imagery for conflating a message of feeling good with a discourse of looking good. That is, publicly defined signs of bodily failure are presented to audiences as private, individualized failures that require continual bodily self-surveillance. The concomitant practices necessary

NEW SCIENTIFIC
DISCOVERY!

Bill Davey
Musclemania Champion

SPECIAL 4-PAGE AD REPORT

The conflation of health
and gendered bodily ideas
is transmitted with signifiers of objective science.
(*Exercise for Men Only*,
October 1998)

to rectify this inevitable failure/lack are focused on historically variable
definitions of bodily appearance rather than health or instrumental bodily
functioning (Bartky 1988; Duncan 1994). Defining the body in terms of
appearance does, however, serve an important function. It allows the body
to become an object of consumption in addition to a site from which to
consume (Featherstone 1991; Featherstone and Turner 1995.

Throughout the text, it may be clear that we will partly reject postmod-
ernist claims that there is a rather free relationship between signifiers and
signs. We retain the strong need to struggle with the relationship between
social structures and culture or the fact that social institutions and social locations shape access to bodily subjectivities, health disparities, and
objectifying processes. In *Body Panic*, we examine how masculinity and
femininity are constituted relationally and are therefore prescribed different types of subjecthood and objecthood (chapters 2–3), how some bodies
are better able to reposition themselves to achieve this access than others
(chapters 3–5), how sexuality and race shape what kinds of subjects and

objects individuals can become (chapters 2–6), and how the market itself plays a key role in shifting the terrain of gendered possibilities around ideal bodies and health (chapters 4–6). A critical part of the analysis centers on how a discourse of health is used to validate relational gender and engagement in consumer culture, and how healthism legitimates neoliberalism and consumerism.

Throughout, we try to carefully underscore that the experience of the gendered body is played out against a backdrop of intersecting axes of privilege/oppression, including but not limited to race, class, and sexuality (Collins 1990). This means the experiences of male and female bodies are shaped by a host of relations of power and privilege that interact in a multiplicity of ways to structure the limits and opportunities of bodies. Hence, while this project focuses on gender, it should also be clear that race, class, and sexuality are considered imperative to the analysis. This will be examined throughout each chapter, where we include an analysis of cover models and also of those who demonstrate workouts (chapter 2). Furthermore, in our analysis of men's magazines (chapters 2 and 3 especially), we also could not ignore those magazines that had specifically deployed ideologies of fitness, morality, and protectionism through sports and the military, featuring only white bodies while referring to the ones "to hunt" as criminals or terrorists. Chapters 4 and 5 focus on women's magazines more centrally and underscore the ways in which women's bodies are disproportionately framed as white, middle-class women's bodies. Even though such women may remain the target demographic, we note how the ideologies used to sell products and practices even flow against the actual demographic needs of the readership at times according to their own fitness, work, and family patterns. At other times, omissions within the magazine by race were stunning, while ads were rife with people of color, creating the illusion that advertisers form the progressive potential of neoliberal ideals. Naturally, these aspects of the analysis bring in multiracial, third wave, and postmodern feminist challenges to the overarching emphasis on categorical notions of gender relations, pointing out that power analyses should rely on notions of intersecting social locations such as race, class, gender, sexuality, and nation (Collins 1990; Anzaldua 1987; Baca-Zinn and Dill 1994; Phelan 1994; Collins 1999; Stockdill 2002).

In terms of a brief methods overview, in order to accomplish its goals, this work draws upon empirical research carried out over a span of ten years of men's and women's health and fitness magazines. To this end, we conducted a content and textual analysis of men's and women's health and fitness magazines. When we began this study, we started with seven men's and seven women's magazines that make up the initial codes discussed in chapters 2 and 3. However, during the ten years we conducted our research, the magazines evolved and changed. We eliminated *Fitness Plus* from our sample because it evolved to resemble more of a bodybuilding magazine. In addition, both of the magazines that targeted a slightly older readership folded (*Prime* and *Living Fit*). *Living Fit* reappeared in 2004 and was re-included in our analysis. Finally, *Women's Sports & Fitness* was bought by Condé Nast during the study period and subscriptions were transferred to *Self* magazine. This change is covered and analyzed at length in chapter 5. See the appendix for a complete list of included magazines.

Using content and textual analysis as the method, we focus on the cultural assertions underlying the text of articles and imagery. In this way, our analysis is key to what is called "studying up" on contemporary cultural ideologies (Kane and Pearce 2002). This technique is often used for grounded theoretical approaches such as textual analysis in media studies in order to provide the empirical basis for critiques of preferred and/or hegemonic messages (Messner 1996). This technique was central to our being able to examine the ways in which women's and men's bodies are differentially and relationally constructed while paying close attention to intersectional analysis—the ways in which class, race, and sexuality are implicated at the same time.

The final sample included 11 different magazines, 122 covers, and 417 workouts. The covers were coded for the poses and body positionings of cover models, the perceived race of the model, and whether an activity was being demonstrated or was implied through the use of props. To code the workouts, we had two research assistants note the types of workout offered (e.g., cardiovascular, yoga "moves," weight work), where the workout was shown (indoors, outdoors), who was demonstrating the workouts (race and gender), any language that referenced gender, race, class, or sexuality. From this open coding scheme, we mapped the full range of themes that emerged, and subsequently the analysis was developed out of the range and frequency of text and imagery contained in the magazines. Certainly, studying mainstream texts in this way "studies up" on dominant racialized, classed, gendered, sexualized bodily ideals (Dworkin and Wachs 1998; Frankenberg 1993; Messner 1996).

It is important to note that "studying up" then becomes the basis for a new, innovative conceptual route to produce arguments about body panic.

As we will describe in chapter 3, previous historical moments focus on the moral panics of the behavior of the stigmatized, "studying down" on the oppressed. In a contemporary media environment, we instead used the method of studying up to identify the signifiers and images that constitute idealized discourses of "health." We argue that body panic works through discourses of healthism and the way in which media constructs the relationship between what is *included* and *excluded* in the media frame— through the preferred meanings and images that are marked with moral codes of citizenship, motherhood, manhood, womanhood, and more.

It is of course imperative when examining media imagery and representations to not only focus on the "preferred reading" in the text, but to simultaneously recognize the existence of "alternative texts" and the polysemic nature of representations. In short, audiences construct dominant, negotiated, and/or resistant meanings out of any particular message (Davis 1997; Duncan and Brummett 1993; Dworkin and Wachs 1998; Fiske 1994; Hall 1997). Audiences (you, me, and everyone in between) may not read texts or images in intended ways (e.g., a way that producers "intend" for us), and dominant and resistant readings (and social practices shown in imagery or text) can occur simultaneously. Our method of critical textual and image analysis offers one way in which to assess and understand how the material effects of mainstream media ideologies might operate (Dworkin and Wachs 1998), but we are not suggesting how individual actors might read these texts or act upon encoded messages.

We would like to note a few important points about the limitations of this work. First, our analysis of fit dominant bodily ideals does not disavow that there is a range of bodily ideals that are simultaneously circulating in consumer culture at any given time and that are viewed as acceptable in a historical moment. Given that our focus is on mainstream health and fitness magazines and not TV shows, movies, popular magazines, or newspapers, our statements are not generalizable to these other mediums. In addition, we do not know the extent to which readers are influenced by one form of media over another. In the best case, we would have also carried out an audience analysis so that we could examine the relationship between producer intentions (those who produce an image or piece of media content) and preferred readings (the meaning behind the intended message or image), or examine the ways in which different social groups interpret, use, challenge, or reproduce these messages in daily life.

Despite these limitations, there is much to be gained from the current analysis. We know of very few analyses that attempt to longitudinally and relationally examine the most popular and widely read women's and men's health and fitness magazines over an entire decade. Simultaneously, the field seems to be stuck in an analysis of objectification without using relational analyses of both women and men. When the literature does (rarely) rely on relational analysis, it is uncommon for works to combine multiracial feminism which offers the strength of intersectional analysis with analyses of healthism, consumer culture, and commodity feminism[21] as we do. Additionally, when works place emphasis on commodity feminism, such analyses are not often linked to multiracial feminist analysis that takes a matrix of domination[22] into account. In this way, our analysis will empirically unpack relations of power across multiple social locations and that are implicated in this particular set of bodily ideals, while recognizing the existence of other bodily ideals.

It is also important to note that while it is true that alternative discourses or ideologies are not totally excluded from imagery and text, and there are certainly alternative press and other media sources to offer a range of views, these do receive limited exposure. A few multinational corporations own and produce the vast majority of available media. While our analyses shake hands with concepts of polysemy or multiple messages, these are coupled with the influence of advertising, the need for profit, and the inner workings of media organizations. Hence, dominant text and image production may remain partly limited (Herman and Chomsky 1988; Jhally 1989; Theberge and Cronk 1986). Certainly the dominance of particular publishing firms, with Weider and Condé Nast representing two of the heavyweights, reflects limited control of dominant texts. Chapter 5 will tackle the assimilation of *Women's Sports & Fitness* into the Condé Nast empire and its usurpation by *Self*.

Because we were interested in conceptions of the mainstream fitness body, we selected only mainstream fitness magazines that focused on a broad array of fitness activities and did not include muscle and fitness magazines or magazines that centered on a single physical activity (e.g., *Runner's World, Bicycling*, etc.). Investigating how gendered bodies are "made" or "done" (West and Zimmerman 1987) in the context of mainstream health and fitness prescriptions, developed into this project. We found no coed mainstream health and fitness magazines, underscoring a near separate spheres mentality. This also suggests that health is distinctly and consistently gendered. Indeed, others have argued that not only is much cultural energy expended to market separately to men and women through product lines, but built into marketing assumptions are beliefs about gender difference which then help to construct differences between men and women.[23]

This was not all that we found in our results. Hence, we had to confront and challenge the previous literature and our own participation in a possible paradigm of difference. In other words, individual researchers are often trained or slanted toward looking for either similarities or differences around bodily domains such as size, shape, or workout content. At times, especially early in our research, even we failed to see the increasing number of similarities among women's and men's bodies. When we compared current coding results to a preliminary run, we found notable differences. We therefore changed course midway through our analysis and made sure that our longitudinal analysis was adequately split up across women's and men's magazines in order to capture change. Understanding the ways in which male and female bodies are treated similarly and differently in dominant discourse is equally important, especially with regard to edicts of consumption and healthism in the postindustrial market. Moreover, the paradoxical ways that difference and similarity merge across a matrix of domination (intersecting social locations of race, class, gender, sexuality) calls into question many cultural assumptions about bodies and their inherent limits and abilities. Such bold challenges underscore the need to more thoroughly consider a relational analysis of women's and men's bodies in contemporary health and fitness magazines. Such a relational approach allows us to not just simply claim that size matters, but when, how, for whom, in what contexts, and with what consequences.

2

What Kinds of Subjects
and Objects?
Gender, Consumer Culture,
and Convergence

[Women] are said to be accounted for by these theories–and yet
they barely make an appearance. On the other hand, if and when
they do appear . . . they surface only as objects of various different
agencies . . . which are seen to act upon them and force them into
a particular range of roles. The question of how individuals make
certain modes of behavior their own, how they learn to develop
one particular set of needs as opposed to certain others, is never
addressed. (Haug 1987, 24)

Women are not only objects of male desire: they themselves play
a part in their creation as such. To see femininity in this way is to
identify a subjective aspect within being-as-object, and thus effectively to recognize the inadequacy of the subject-object metaphor.
(Haug 1987, 131)

Consumer culture had discovered and begun to develop the un-
tapped resources of the male body." (Bordo 1999, 18)

How then is the idealized body constructed in consumer culture today? Examining mainstream health and fitness magazines provides
insight into dominant cultural constructions of "health" and by extension
allows researchers to examine what constitutes a privileged body. Given
the importance of sex assignment in Western culture, this body is always
already a gendered body. However, what the assignment of sex means for

bodies is changing and evolving in consumer culture. Instead of reiterating long held subject/object dichotomies that tend to analyze the situation from the position that men are given the status of subjects while women are objects, we rely on Frigga Haug's concept of the "subjective-aspects-within-being-as-object" (defined below) and apply it to the case of women's fitness media texts. For an analysis of men's fitness media texts, we introduce a concept we term the "objective-aspects-within-being-as-subject" and therefore extend Haug's work to consider the case of men, bodies, and consumer culture. Indeed, looking at the two terms side by side suggests greater possibility for overlap between subjective and objective status than has typically been offered in previous analyses of gender and the body.

Frigga Haug et al. (1987) coined and first used the phrase the "subjective-aspects-within-being-as-object" to refer to how women experience identity, subjecthood, and pleasure in the process of bodily objectification. In her book, *Female Sexualization: Questions for Feminism*, Haug described and analyzed cultural materials (newspaper articles, art, film) and women's own stories about what she calls "body projects"—for example, doing one's hair, shaving one's legs, choosing fashion trends, etc. Such an approach allowed Haug to structure an analysis of the relationship between subjectivity and objectivity in the process of female sexualization. A main part of her argument is that there is an extensive *process of subjectivity* (not necessarily harm and force) that goes unrecognized in the arguments on this topic. Previous arguments generally assumed that women were having something "done to them" by media images, texts, and larger cultural norms.[1] Haug's work demonstrates the agency of the subject in the creation of objecthood. This does not diminish previous analysis, but adds a critical dimension to understanding relations of power and privilege.

Adding subjectivity to an analysis of gender and the body was a much needed corrective to feminists who had long noted that in Western culture, there is an imperative toward the sexual objectification of women—and this was conceived of as wholly negative. To a large degree, according to this position, women's power and experience of self is based on the ability to meet current cultural ideals. Women and girls come to experience themselves as if someone were looking at them (as an object) and evaluate themselves based on appearance and their successful presentation of self as an object (Bartky 1990; Berger 1972; Young 1990). Some argue that this lack of subjecthood is not simply about the surface of the body but is linked to sexuality and the expression of desire. That is, the way in which subjecthood is constructed for young girls leads to a lack of female desire in heterosexuality, where girls and women are centrally concerned about making themselves into an attractive object of desire instead of "owning" or knowing desire for themselves (Tolman 1994). One might suspect that this more passive view of the body contrasts with what is found within sport coverage of female athletes, for example, that when female subjects are viewed as engaging in some type of action, the presentation of self is usually paramount to performance rather than some other standards.[2]

Despite sport as a realm of action, researchers frequently note that women's performances are "offset" by depictions of feminine aesthetics and beauty standards. By contrast, male subjecthood has often been linked directly to status, societal position, or power, while male appearance historically has been considered far less important (until recently). Certainly, the history of fashion and its current state demonstrate that men too have taken great care in the presentation of self. However, the links between attractiveness, status, and bodily ideals has had a long and complicated racialized, classed, gendered history. Indeed, for men, it is generally the characteristics of the powerful that come to be imbued with attractiveness.

The subject/object distinction around gender and the body needs to be understood in the context of Western philosophy more generally. The choice between subject and object reflects traditional Western cultural dualisms, or the tendency to present people, domains, and/or groups as categorical opposites. Feminist epistemology problematized traditional Western dualisms, such as nature/culture, male/female, and subject/object and how these dualisms have come into play in gender relations (Hekman 1990). This means that over time, femininity was associated with being an object and linked to emotion and nature. By contrast, masculinity was associated with subjecthood and was tied to Enlightenment principles such as knowledge and reason. Feminist theorists have long critiqued the exclusion of women's subjecthood, ways of knowing, and experiences from the production of knowledge and the limitations imposed on women as a result of these presumptions (Harding 1991, 1986; Harding and Hintikka 1983; Hartsock 1998; Hekman 1990). Certainly, it could be argued that women have effectively been denied a philosophical experience of subjecthood that does not center on the self as object.

It is certain that both men and women have been objectified; however, male power and privilege have been maintained by partly limiting women's source of power to their ability to be the "right" kind of object. Specific researchers argue that women's consent to being a valued object seals the deal, as Connell notes in his 1987 work *Gender and Power*. Connell defines "emphasized femininity" as the most valued form of femininity, and contrasts it to hegemonic masculinity, the most privileged form of masculinity. In these definitions, there is a difference between male privilege and female value, indicating a patriarchal gender order. The subject/object dichotomy further underscores the difference between these two terms.

Despite the above definitions, there are criticisms of these concepts. That is, postmodern, multiracial feminist, and critical masculinity theorists counter that there is no uniform object of woman (or man) around which feminine (or masculine) subject knowledge can be defined. Rather, the generation of the objectified woman is unique to a specific history, set of social locations, and set of societal circumstances. Women's complicity in the process of objecthood reflects the nature of power as one learns to experience subjecthood through the self-surveillance of objecthood (Bartky (1990). Feminist theorists have employed the work of Foucault to explicate this process of panoptic self-surveillance (ibid.). Though approaching ideals does allow negotiation of social status, ultimately the embedded structures of consumer culture create a situation of perpetual failure or lack. Multiracial feminism further demonstrates the intersectionality of different facets of identity (race, class, age, etc.). This results in women from different social locations having different abilities to meet dominant standards—women who hail from more privileged positions are more likely to meet ideals and to benefit from this process.

What Haug et al. contribute to the literature is an important understanding of how, in postmodern consumer culture, one can experience the "subjective-aspects-within-being-as-object," and that this experience is intimately tied to pleasure and the production of a unique self-identity —one that engenders meaningful engagement with consumer culture. In other words, objectifying oneself has subjective aspects to the experience that are both pleasurable to one's self-constitution as a desirable object or are meaningful in the production and negotiation of identities. This is the case no matter what combination of racialized, sexualized, classed, or gendered identities individuals enact (1987). Although a wide range of ways exists to enact femininity that varies tremendously depending on one's social location, dominant/privileged forms of objecthood and the ways one goes about meeting those dictums indubitably creates a subject-experience. The experience of those in the dominant categories must be understood as a privileged experience, even if there are disempowering

aspects to these experiences. Moreover, the bodies that result become jus-
tifications for broader social relations and positions. While a great deal
of literature has explored women's subjective experiences within being-as-
object, only recently have scholars begun to note the emergence of a parallel trend in consumer culture for men. Increasingly, men's experiences
of self and identity are coming to exhibit many of the characteristics of
women's experience of being objectified. However, the history of gender
relations leads to some key differences, and in this chapter and the next
we will flesh these out in detail.

While Haug does not offer a parallel analysis or terminology to characterize men's experiences, we argue that men experience (and are framed
within media as having) "objective-aspects-within-being-as-subject." Part
of the privilege of masculinity is the veneration of the way men simply
"are." In other words, the objective results of male experiences of subjecthood have become symbolic of power, and the experience of masculinity includes having a body that is at some level inherently "right." The
presumption that the male form is ideal and the female fails to measure
up relative to the male body has been well documented in the history
of Western culture (Laqueur 1990). Because masculinity has historically
been the privileged position, even subordinate men still maintain some
power and privilege over women, though the matrix of domination suggests this privilege is experienced vastly differently depending on other
facets of identity (Collins 1990). However, it is not the case that objectifying processes are excluded from men's daily living. Men from varying
classes, races, and sexualities certainly have experiences that diverge from
the white, upper-middle-class heterosexual male subject (though he too
is an object). With this new term we highlight how male subjecthood has
objective aspects to it and that men assess their subjecthood as an object,
relative to ideals.

As has been noted by Kimmel (2000), at the turn of the millennium,
men's and women's lives are becoming "more similar," at least for the most
advantaged. For the privileged, most professions are gender-neutral, and
women and men are routinely employed in the same professions, enjoy the same leisure activities, and engage in similar rituals of self-care.
Women's increased earning power can also mean that some couples and
single women are able to "buy off" the second shift of household labor
and childcare. The growing importance of women as consumers has been
linked to women's greater social power, especially in the world of sports
and fitness (Heywood and Dworkin 2003). These tendencies combine

with the objectifying propensities of consumer culture (for all bodies) to narrow the gap in how gender is defined, constructed in image, and practiced. This is revealed in the convergence of men's and women's bodily displays and practices in health and fitness magazines—the focus of this chapter.

Converging Bodies: Gender and Consumer Culture

Men's and women's bodily practices converge in several notable ways. First, fat is a powerfully feared cultural transgression for both women and men. Second, men and women are coming to be presented in a more similar manner, as objects (here, we analyze body positioning, smiles, head shots, and active/passive imagery). Third, what is marketed to male and female bodies is converging. Grooming practices and fashion expand, as it is framed as "imperative" for both women and men to be up to date in fashion. In addition, leisure practices are expanding as they converge for both women and men (manscaping, manicures, spa treatments, personal training, massages).

This ad demonstrates convergence in the presentation of men and women in contemporary consumer culture. (*Men's Health,* December 2003)

This ad demonstrates
the convergence of skin
care products by gender.
(*Exercise & Health*, Summer 1999)

In the first case, fat is now a powerfully feared cultural transgression. For both men and women, any visible body fat is presented as problematic. "Are you fat?" asks *Men's Health* (January/February 1999). The article includes a test to determine this with certainty, followed by ratings of different diet and exercise plans. Given this trend, it may not be surprising that 38 percent of dieters in the United States are now male within a diet industry that is now worth $58.7 billion (Financial Desk 2007). The obesity crisis has been much touted in the mass media (Campos 2004). Although we don't dispute the negative health consequences of being overweight, the link between (a relatively homogeneous) appearance and health is dubious at best. Moreover, there is an ongoing tendency to frame the overweight body as a threat to the self and to the general populace. Maintaining a fit body is no longer viewed as a personal choice, but as an obligation to the public good and a requirement for good citizenry (this point will be expanded upon in chapter 3). The once narcissistic body obsession has not only become a marker of individual health, but a form of social responsibility and civic participation. Over time, body weight has taken on the aura of a broader social problem related to public health (Sobal and Maurer 1999). This obscures the relationship between social privilege and the development and maintenance of a fit body, and reinforces the stigmatization of "othered" bodies.

Despite evidence that suggests a totally fat-free form can be unrealistic and unhealthy (Campos 2004), this form is idealized and venerated. Analyses of consumer culture suggest that this constructs a culture of "bodily lack" that requires constant maintenance (Featherstone 1991; Lasch 1979; Turner 1992). A key set of fundamental assumptions that shape the content and tone of the magazine center on the negative aspects of *any* body fat. Fat is unhealthy. Unaesthetic. Prevents you from being everything you can be. Leads to public ridicule, especially at the hands of the opposite sex. Is a sign of one's failure to demonstrate a proper "work ethic." The reification/deification of the fat-free form is visually reinforced almost continuously with the imagery in magazines. Idealized bodies with no body fat are featured on the covers and throughout the magazines.

It is not just imagery that offers this impression, but the tendency for magazines to blur the boundaries between the purpose of text, image, expert advice, and ads, increases over time in our ten-year sample. In fact, the difference between advertising and content imagery can become largely irrelevant, and indeed, one cannot meaningfully separate magazine content from ads in many places. This is most notable when examining the ubiquitous short "snippet" that promotes new products, practices, or services, and the photo essay, usually a magazine-prepared advertisement. The images merge seamlessly in the magazine from article to ad and back again. They reinforce messages of idealized physical forms and undermine text that might speak in a bold or trite way of self-acceptance (Eskes, Duncan, and Miller 1998). An analysis of the covers demonstrates that only a few models, whose photographed bodies have been trimmed and touched up, meet these ideals. Mainstream newspaper articles that interview athletes, fitness experts, or trainers, highlight that the athletes themselves are surprised at how their photographs have been altered in fitness imagery, underscoring that even professional athletes rarely measure up.

Advertisements also usually feature very slim or cut models, and similarly computer-altered, airbrushed, and trimmed photos of models. When taken together, they create the impression that the ideal body is *necessarily* fat-free. This is reinforced because more realistic but still presumably healthy bodies rarely appear. Heavier bodies appear only as "before" photos in "success stories." The paucity of a range of healthy fit images literally denies their existence, and refutes the possibility that a person can be larger and still be fit and healthy. The symbolic annihilation of the wide range of healthy bodies operates to conflate fat-free with "healthy" and undermines any textual references to the existence of this range (Eskes, Duncan, and Miller 1998; also see Duncan and Hasbrook 1988). The assumptions that emerge in the text further vilify fat while extolling the moral virtue of the fat-free form. (Our own students exalt the value of the fat-free form as inherently right and healthy; we frequently compare notes about how to discuss the lack of a continuum of body fat in imagery —much of which could be conceived of as quite far from "fat," but also rather healthy and plenty attractive.) The obliteration of this continuum leaves the impression that the range of fit bodies is far narrower than it is in reality.

The preponderance of articles on diets, health, nutrition, and workouts included a discussion of cutting body fat for both men and women. While men were encouraged to "eat to grow," cutting body fat was the second most common diet proscription for men, and was frequently referenced in conjunction with gains in muscle size. *EMO* encourages men to "Torch Your Bodyfat! New Supplements Do the Trick" (December 2000). *Exercise & Health* offers "25 Ways to Shed Fat" (Winter 2002). Because historically, reducing body fat had feminine connotations, it is necessary to masculinize men's fat reduction. Cutting fat is masculinized by linking it to the revelation of manly striations and cuts. Abdominals are specifically noted as visible signs of masculinity that can only be revealed when body fat is exorcised. While *all* men should spend their time attempting to reveal a minimum of six-pack abdominals, the "eight-pack" is appearing with increasing frequency. The diet industry is attempting to further masculinize weight loss; even the weight-loss giant Nutrisystem recently hired its first male spokesperson, former quarterback Dan Marino (Financial Desk 2007).

For women, decreasing fat (without mention of the striations or cuts underneath) was the most common diet recommendation, coupled with recipes and hints. For women, fitness and dieting are critical to attaining a slim, toned, and cellulite-free form. *Shape* provides "7 Sneaky Reasons Dining Out Is Making You Fat" (October 2004). *Fitness* (February 2001) promises to "Speed Up Your Metabolism in Just 10 Minutes." The magazines do not present any obvious benefits to a faster metabolism, except weight loss.

The majority of workouts further highlighted a fat-free form, even when many explicitly acknowledged in the text that one cannot spot reduce, or that toning will not be visible without removing fat, and that the only way to reduce fat is to consume less. Workouts for women focused on toning and tightening muscles that could only be revealed with a modified and rather Spartan diet. *Fitness* exhorts women to "Lose Your Ab Flab" (March 2006) with a workout that combines aerobics and pilates that "Not only will you get your heart pumping and burn 420 calories per hour (about 17 percent more than in a traditional mat class), but you'll experience total-body conditioning through balance challenges and see the ab-sculpting benefits." Workouts like "The No-Fat Back" (*Shape* 2001) promise a reduction in body fat with diet and exercise. Notice that despite textual references to the impossibility of spot reduction, the titles of workouts clearly suggest fat will be removed from a specific area of the body. For men, workouts also often emphasized lower fat intake to reveal cuts or to trim fat from the waist.

Success stories in women's magazines almost exclusively highlighted people who lost weight, with only a few that covered those who strove to gain weight or battled eating disorders. Weight loss was noted in pounds lost, inches lost, and accompanied by ab-baring before and after photos.[3] *Shape* (February 2001) features "Success Stories: A Special Guide—How 5 Women Got in Shape! You can too with our sure-fire plan." This piece features a diet, followed by success stories of five women who followed the diet. For each woman, inches and pounds lost are the first statistics provided with their pictures. The focus on these types of measures sends a clear message about the primary meaning of success in fitness. Though many articles on being satisfied with oneself at a larger size appear, the almost complete exclusion of alternative imagery contradicts the messages of acceptance (Spitzack 1990).

Control of the body remains a central organizing principle in postindustrial society. The need to control the unruly body emerges in the postindustrial world as a marker of the self. Linked to personal displays that demonstrate success or failure, the presentation of the body in the twenty-first century signifies a variety of meanings, not the least of which is one's moral worth. While the fat body remains stigmatized as lazy, undisciplined, or as a poor member of the social body, the fit body becomes a metaphor for success, morality, and good citizenship. Just as wealth marked morality for the Calvinists, the "fit" body marks a moral and disciplined self that demonstrates sufficient participation in the regimes of bodywork necessary to support consumer capitalism. As argued by Gimlin, "The body is fundamental to the self because it serves to indicate who an individual is internally, what habits the person has, and even what social value the individual merits" (2002, p. 3). Hence, the fit body simultaneously validates the individual and legitimates the value of such a body.

Further, the normalization of the completely fat-free form operates to stigmatize bodies left out of the frame.[4] Spitzack in 1990 and later on, Duncan, in 1994, employ Foucauldian thought to demonstrate how the confessional process centered on fitness and the body ultimately results in the disempowerment of the subject. While Duncan was studying the content of women's magazines and Spitzack studied women's narratives of "confessional excess" about their bodies, both of their arguments can be extended to men's experiences given trends of convergence.[5] Here, we mean that all readers lose the ability to define the image of a healthy body

This ad idealizes the fat-free form and offers a quick solution to readers. Both women and men have come to fear fat as the ultimate enemy. (*Men's Fitness,* July 2002)

as based on critical measures of health (cholesterol, pulse rate, blood pressure, cardiovascular fitness, pulmonary function, and so forth). Instead, an image of health becomes paramount and as Duncan suggests, "panoptic mechanisms" lead the reader to internalize self-surveillance of the surface of the body, conflating body image with morality, success, and good citizenship (Spitzack 1990). The fat-free fit form also serves as a marker of class status to some degree, as the bodywork required to maintain this form requires a significant amount of time and money.[6]

While body fat is one area where there is overlap across men's and women's magazines, there were other ways in which the presentation of male and female bodies converged. We examined the presentation of cover models to investigate this trend. First, consistent with feminist analyses of body positioning, gender, and power, we examine whether or not the model is featured in an active pose, a pose that implies fitness action, or is posed passively. An active pose means that the model is shown engaging in a health or fitness activity, such as lifting weights, riding a bike, or running. For action-implied shots, action is usually implied through the use of a prop, and often the model is posed to look as if he or she had just finished or was about to begin the activity that matched the prop. Passive shots feature a model simply posing for the camera. Often, the inactive model is posed against a blank background or a background involving water (ocean, lake, pool).[7] In 1997–98, our initial cover code of the activity level of the model appeared as shown in table 2.1.

The results of the initial sample are consistent with Duncan's (1993) analysis of sports media texts which revealed that mainstream media construct men as active and women as inactive. In this view, women are often shown as "being visually perfect" and "passive, immobile, and unchanging" (p. 357; Duncan and Brummett 1993). The initial sample reflects this tendency. Men are more often featured as active or with action implied. The presence of action implies subjecthood, that one is an active subject. In the initial sample, men are depicted actively engaging in sports or fitness with over 80 percent of the covers featuring them either directly engaged in action, or with action implied through the use of props. By contrast, women are far more often presented as objects, with just over 85 percent of covers featuring women engaging only in the act of posing, experiencing the subjective aspects of being as object. Further, the action-implied covers are almost exclusively from one publication, *Women's Sports & Fitness*. (This will be discussed in greater depth in chapter 5.) Though shown in revealing outfits, the men are far more often shown engaging in or with

TABLE 2.1
Cover Models and Activity Shown: Original Sample, 1997–1998

Cover Shots	Women's Magazines	Men's Magazines
Active	0 (0%)	4 (19.0%)
Action Implied	3 (14.3%)	12 (57.1%)
Inactive	18 (85.7%)	5 (23.8%)
Totals (N = 42)	21 (100%)	21 (99.9%)*

* Due to rounding

TABLE 2.2
Cover Models and Activity Shown: New Sample

Cover Shots	Women's Magazines	Men's Magazines
Active	0 (0%)	1 (1.7%)
Action Implied	0 (0%)	18 (30%)
Inactive	62 (100%)	41 (68.3%)
Totals (N = 122)	62 (100%)	60 (100%)

the accouterments of sports or working out, thus linking their physical form with successful performance.

Contrast these results to a second and final phase of coding that examines magazines from 1998 through 2006 (see table 2.2). Almost none of the covers could be described as active for either men or women. For men, only 30 percent of the covers in the new sample fall into the action-implied category, compared to 57 percent in the original sample. For men, in the original sample 76.1 percent of covers are either action or action-implied, whereas in the new sample, only 31.7 percent are. For women, all the covers are now simply posed.

For women, none of the covers in the new sample feature active or action-implied poses, most likely because of the demise of *Women's Sports & Fitness* discussed in chapter 5. Here, we simply want to note the growing convergence in the manner of presentation of male and female bodies. To further explore the presentations of men and women, we also analyzed the body and head positioning of the cover models.

Using Goffman (1979), Duncan (1990), and Henley (1977) as a theoretical guide for analyzing gendered power relations in media images, we coded covers according to models' facial expressions, gaze, and body positioning. These studies indicate that dominance and submission are transmitted through the body using nonverbal communication, reflective of one's status in society. Body language as expressed through body positioning, eye contact, head tilts, and facial expression (smiling, etc.) also provides culturally recognizable cues that media have used to produce and reflect gendered bodies. As Bourdieu (2001) argues, the enactments of gender come to operate as a form of capital that denotes the status of bodies, and makes gender difference appear to be "natural" rather than the result of cultural practices (Bourdieu 2001).

Duncan, in her examination of how sports photographers use corporeal cues to embody sexual difference, found that women were often portrayed with direct eye contact to the camera, accompanied by a sideways tilt of the head and/or slightly parted lips. Duncan labels these bodily cues as nonverbal heterosexual "come-ons" linked to those found in men's soft-core pornography (1990). Head-on poses are generally less submissive than head-tilted shots. The tilt usually involves the model looking up at the camera, giving the viewer a "come hither gaze." Similarly, body positioning that is straight toward the camera is less submissive than bodies that are tilted up toward the camera. Hip thrusts further indicate a provocative pose designed to please and entice the viewer. Finally, facial expressions indicate status. Inviting smiles versus serious expression indicate one's status. The models' poses for our original codes (1997–1998) are summarized in table 2.3.

TABLE 2.3
Body Language: Original Sample, 1997–1998

	Women's Magazines	Men's Magazines
Head Shots	0 (0%)	1 (4.8%)
Head-on	14 (66.7%)	18 (85.7%)
Tilted	7 (33.3%)	2 (9.5%)
Total	21 (100%)	21 (100%)
Body Tilt		
Untilted	8 (38.1%)	13 (61.9%)
Torso twisted	3 (14.3%)	5 (23.8%)
Hip thrust	6 (28.6%)	0 (0%)
Other	4 (19.0%)	3 (14.3%)
Total	21 (100%)	21 (100%)
Hands		
On prop	3 (14.3%)	14 (66.7%)
On hips	6 (28.6%)	2 (9.5%)
Hands in pants	2 (9.5%)	0 (0%)
Hands on head	5 (23.8%)	0 (0%)
At sides	1 (4.8%)	1 (4.8%)
Other	4 (19.0%)	4 (19.0%)
Total	21 (100%)	21 (100%)
Facial Expression	0 (0%)	1 (4.8%)
Full smile	17 (81.0%)	11 (52.4%)
Partial smile—mouth open	2 (9.5%)	1 (4.8%)
Partial smile—mouth closed	2 (9.5%)	2 (9.5%)
Serious	0 (0%)	6 (28.6%)
Total	21 (100%)	21 (100.1%)

TABLE 2.4
Body Language: New Sample, 1998–2006

	Women's Magazines	Men's Magazines
Head Shots		
Head On	25 (37.9%)	30 (50.0%)
Tilted	21 (31.8%)	22 (36.7%)
Other	20 (30.3%)	8 (13.3%)
Total	66 (100%)	60 (100%)
Body Tilt		
Untilted	14 (21.2%)	36 (60.0%)
Torso twisted	11 (16.7%)	16 (26.7%)
Hip thrust	35 (53.0%)	3 (5.0%)
Other	6 (9.1%)	5 (8.3%)
Total	66 (100%)	60 (100%)
Hands		
On prop	9 (13.6%)	23 (38.3%)
On body/head	45 (68.2%)	19 (31.7%)
At sides	8 (12.1%)	14 (23.3%)
Other	4 (6.1%)	4 (6.7%)
Total	66 (100%)	60 (100%)
Facial Expression		
Full smile	42 (63.6%)	22 (36.7%)
Partial smile—mouth open	10 (15.2%)	6 (10.0%)
Partial smile—mouth closed	12 (18.2%)	13 (21.7%)
Serious	2 (3.0%)	17 (28.3%)
Other	0 (0%)	2 (3.3%)
Total	66 (100%)	60 (100%)
Abs Exposure		
Exposed	50 (75.8%)	52 (86.7%)
Covered	16 (24.2%)	8 (13.3%)
Total	66 (100%)	60 (100%)

Note: Two women's covers featured two women—both were Ms. Fitness contestants and both featured National and International contest winners. Two men's magazines featured men without heads (only their bodies were shown).

In the original sample, men are more often presented in direct head-on shots, though the majority of both men's and women's heads were facing toward the camera. Men are also presented as serious in 28.6 percent of covers, while women were never shown with a serious facial expression. Out of the sample of men, 61.9 percent were positioned straight toward the camera, while only 38.1 percent of women were. Men never display a hip thrust. Hence, while there is a great deal of overlap in the presentation of cover models, men are more often presented as subjects. Table 2.3 shows the 1997–98 data, which is contrasted with the updated sample that tracks target magazines from 1998–2006 (see table 2.4).

While over 85 percent of the original men's sample featured shots that were taken head-on, only 50 percent of the second sample reveals the same tendency. For women, two-thirds of the original sample was shot head-on, while 37.9 percent of the new sample is shot this way. The shift to the "come hither look" for both men and women indicates a shift toward men as deploying self-presentation as object. As previously noted, the tilt usually indicates submission or enticement. This is further demonstrated in hand positioning. The hand on the self in the manner of most of these magazines connotes a "look at me" presentation, further enhancing the subjective aspects within being-as-object.

Trends toward bodily convergence by gender are evident in the models' facial expressions. Smiles have also been analyzed by Goffman (1979), Duncan (1990), and Henley (1977). The type of smile displayed reveals something about the status of the individual. An inviting smile is the most common facial expression in both codes. In the initial sample, 81.0 percent of women have full smiles, and the remaining 19 percent displayed partial smiles. In the full coding, 63.6 percent sport full smiles, 33.4 percent exhibit partial smiles, and 3.0 percent appear serious. Of the men's cover models in the original sample, 52.4 percent have a full smile, an additional 14.3 percent feature partial smiles, and 28.6 percent are serious. In the updated sample, 36.7 percent of men wear full smiles, but 21.7 percent present partial smiles, and almost the same percentage, 28.3 percent, have serious facial expressions. Though gender differences remain in terms of who can display a serious face and still be deemed desirable, Henley's work is particularly instructive, as she argues that women are often publicly responsible for a continuous display of pleasantness and amiability. We view the decrease in full smiles in favor of partial smiles for men and women as reflecting a shift. The partial smile also creates a more knowing look. We suggest the ironic presentation of the self as object is becoming more common. In other words, the model displays a realization of the self as object and the consciousness of display.

Researchers argue that women's smiles reify gender ideals of agreeableness or vulnerability, while men's smiles might be indicative of the fact that privileged and powerful men are allowed a wider range of emotional displays than subordinated men (Messner 1997). In our original sample, there are only three men of color featured on the men's covers, and it is striking that all of these men had partial or full smiles. This seems consistent with researchers who argue that smiles are often used to represent men of color so as to undercut prevalent (racist) associations of potential threat or danger (Cole and Andrews 1996; Hall 1997; Wachs and Dworkin 1997). In the original sample, boxer Oscar De La Hoya is shown boxing with his cocked fists aiming playfully at the reader. Boxing is a blood sport that has been widely contested as violent. Therefore, De La Hoya's smile might be employed to make him seem less threatening and aggressive. In the new sample, only two nonwhite men appear on the covers (a point we will return to later in this chapter). Both are smiling. One is an NBA all-star, the other, an unknown model. We will return to more comments on the racialized dimensions of the findings at the end of the chapter.

While the overlap was much greater than one would have expected given analyses by Duncan (1990) and Goffman (1979), the margins still reflect differences in social power by gender. In the full coding, 60.0 percent of men's poses are situated straight toward the viewer, while only 21.2 percent of women's are posed in this way. For men, this is almost identical to the initial coding at 61.9 percent, while for women, the initial coding features poses that are shot straight on 38.1 percent of the time. For women, over time, the hip thrust has become the most common pose. While in the initial sample, 28.6 percent of covers feature a hip thrust, 53.0 percent of the updated sample do. The hip thrust for women embodies the contradictions of women's experience today, on the one hand, the motion connotes power, while simultaneously invoking gendered norms of heterosexual desire and vulnerability (Segal 1994). It is at once strong and objectified. This move has feminine connotations, as no men in either coding phase were posed this way. However, men were frequently posed with the hand on the hip, the masculine variant of this pose.

Third, what is advertised to men and women shows considerable overlap. For example, compare *Men's Health* from May 2004 with *Shape* from May 2004. *Men's Health* is 218 pages total (including front and back covers) and has 111 full pages devoted to advertising (though some ads were several pages, and others only half a page). Thus, 50.9 percent of the issue is devoted solely to advertising. (Additional ads sometimes shared pages with content, but in the interest of clarity, we focused on full-page ads only.) Twenty ads are for cars or motorcycles (18.0 percent), ten are for food or meal replacements (9.1 percent), nineteen are for clothing or accessories (17.1 percent), six are for grooming products of various types (5.4 percent), and four are for medications or pain killers (3.6 percent). *Shape* is 324 pages, of which 156 pages are devoted entirely to advertising (48.1 percent). Nine ads are for automobiles (5.8 percent), twenty-six are for food or meal replacements (16.7 percent), thirteen are for clothing or accessories (8.3 percent), thirty-three are for grooming products (21.2 percent), thirteen are for medications or pain killers (8.3 percent).

Increasingly, men and women are encouraged to use a wide range of hair, skin, hygiene, and grooming products. While *Men's Health* features more advertisements for automobiles than *Shape* (18.0 percent compared to 5.8 percent) and *Shape* features more advertisements for food than *Men's Health* (16.7 percent to 9.1 percent) and grooming products (21.2 percent to 5.4 percent), there is a great deal of overlap in what is being advertised to male and female consumers. Body products, such as skin care and hair care products, are increasingly being offered to both male and female consumers.

In addition to the direct ads, regular columns often provide coverage of products. These products are presented with the same excited aplomb as significant information regarding health, making a "new way to make hair shine" or a "new fragrance" appear to be as significant as a new way to combat breast or prostate cancer. While this may sound like a strange characterization, it is easier to explain with examples. For example, *Fit* (December 2002) mixed information about strokes, jump ropes, aquaphor healing ointment, osteoporosis, pony tails, growing longer nails, and new

Compare this ad for men's fragrance with the one for women's makeup on p. 47. (*Men's Health*, October 1998)

Notice the similarities in the presentation of the subject as object in this image and the previous one. (*Self,* February 2003)

floral scents in snippets on different pages. *Men's Health* (October 1998) combined information on martial arts, Mr. Rogers, healthy meals, prostate cancer tests, pajamas, exercise bands, flashlights, sports drinks, digital voice recorders, airline tickets, how to shoot a basketball, microbrews, and more in just one "Malegrams" column. Mixing together different types of information, products, and expert advice creates the impression that all these topics should receive similar consideration.

The convergence of grooming products offered to both men and women is particularly noteworthy. Most of the men's magazines featured regular columns on grooming that cover such topics as alpha-hydroxy (*Prime,* Winter 1997), hair care products (*EMO,* December 2000), and potent scents (*Men's Fitness,* December 2001). Though men and women may use products that smell different, are packaged in different colored bottles, and are described with different adjectives, the range of products offered overlapped considerably. Men's grooming products are expected to be a $10 billion market by 2008, compared to the $15 billion expected for women's grooming products in the same year (Walton 2006). In 2006, the top-selling fragrance for 9 of 12 months was a man's fragrance (Financial

Desk 2007). Not surprisingly, men's products were masculinized by link-ing them to sports stars and celebrities. For example, in 2006, Yankees' shortstop Derek Jeter began marketing a line of men's grooming products and a signature fragrance with Avon (PR Newswire 2006). Clive Owen, the ruggedly handsome Academy Award–nominated actor, is on the Lancôme payroll.[8]

Additionally, leisure time activities were also de-gendered, having over-lapped across women's and men's magazines. A key example is the repack-aging of spa treatments and body services such as manicures and pedi-cures for male consumers. All of the magazines highlighted body treat-ments of various types for men. *EMO* included spa reports regularly, for example, in one issue they ranked body services such as the "Detoxifying Algae Wrap," "Holistic Back, Face and Scalp Session," and "Balneotherapy" (a combo tub soak, seaweed wrap, and massage) provided by Tethra Spa in Dublin, Ireland (*EMO*, January 2004). *Prime* compared two spas and offered tips on finding a spa near you (March 1998). One chain of spas reported that now, 15–20 percent of its clients are men, a new and grow-ing trend (Walton 2006). Manicures and pedicures are becoming regular recommendations for men in the magazines we studied and in popular culture in general.

Again, athletes and actors were used to market and masculinize such treatments.[9] Just as men were encouraged to try services traditionally marketed exclusively to women, women were encouraged to try activi-ties and experiences once thought of as more appropriate for men. For example, women were urged to try three North Spas that offer kyaking and other sport activities in addition to more traditional spa treatments (*Fitness*, June 1999). While privileged men have long been "pampered," modern conceptions of the hegemonic man have tended to exclude anything that carried the taint of femininity (Swiencicki 1998). The re-masculinization of these practices is discussed more fully in chapter 3. By the same token, more adventurous activities for women are also normal-ized as gender-appropriate for either men or women. In chapter 5, we will discuss how many of these activities are marketed to women under the auspices of feminism.

Vestiges of the Past Subject/Object Dichotomy or the Objective-Aspects-Within-Being-as-Subject?

Although there are key areas of overlap in the type of body constructed, there are some gender differences. Size (taken up more centrally in the next chapter) and functionality are two key differences. As men's and women's bodies and practices become more similar, it is more important to mark them as different and to re-affirm differences. Differences in size and the concomitant divergent practices provide a way to normalize and naturalize the idea that men and women are inherently different. While any excess fat was a transgression for both men and women, men were presumed to approach ideals when more muscular, while women tended to move toward their ideal by decreasing size. In addition, difference was reaffirmed in the language used to describe workouts and bodies. By simply using words with slightly different connotations, similar bodies and practices can be rendered differently. Firm versus hard and toned versus cut exemplify how the magazines use gendered adjectives to define appropriate goals as different, even as they actually converge. Further, the reaffirmation of the subject/object dichotomy was evident as men's workouts tend to be described as exercises, while women completed the amorphous "moves." In the next chapter, we will discuss how men may also perform "moves," but with military accouterments or might such as guns.

Functionality, or the type of things bodies ought to be doing, further differentiates men and women in fitness media texts (see table 2.5). Though men's and women's workouts are converging to some extent, vestiges of the links between sport for men and fitness for women remain (chapter 3 focuses on this distinction in-depth). Men's workouts were more often linked to athletes or sports performance than women's, and athletes graced the covers of men's magazines more often than women's.

TABLE 2.5
Cover Model Status

Status	Women's Magazines	Men's Magazines
Model	43 (65.2%)	49 (81.7%)
Actor	7 (10.6%)	6 (10.0%)
Athlete	0 (0%)	3 (5.0%)
Fitness Expert	3 (4.5%)	0 (0%)
Fitness Contest Winner	9 (13.6%)*	0 (0%)
Other	4 (6.1%)	2 (3.3%)
Total	66 (100%)	60 (100%)

*All were Ms. Fitness contest winners.

With the exception of *Women's Sports & Fitness*, no women's magazines included athletes on the cover in either our preliminary or final sample, while 5.0 percent of men's magazines displayed athletes. In addition, though only 2.5 percent of men's workouts were demonstrated by athletes, even fewer women's workouts (0.8 percent) were demonstrated by athletes. Athletes and images of men playing sports were frequently used in advertisements.

By contrast, fitness experts were more likely to appear on and in women's magazines, though most appeared in one publication. Women were featured engaging in fitness activities in imagery, rather than sports, and the value of fitness for childcare was highlighted. The relationship between fitness and femininity highlights the link between femininity and objective standards of beauty (Dowling 2000). Though consumer culture has made objective standards more relevant for men and women, men's physical displays are legitimated through the link to sports, professional, or life-saving performance ideals. However, we do note that functionality came into play for women, generally in feminine-defined tasks, especially childbearing and -rearing. We will return to this point in chapter 4.

The historical link between men and sport and women and fitness once reinforced differing social positions and roles by gender. Male physical superiority was reinforced by public displays of sport prowess (Hargreaves 1994, 2001; Lenskyj 1986; Cahn 1994). Racial, ethnic, and class relations among men were reinforced, challenged, and renegotiated in the world of sports. Even after women entered the arena, numerous strategies were employed to maintain the belief in male physical superiority. Along these lines, in the contemporary era, fitness contests for women emerged in the early 1990s, at the tail end of a waning popularity in women's bodybuilding (due to massive size increases among women) that led many within the sport of bodybuilding to wonder if it was too "masculinizing." Just as in the past, fitness classes offered a form of exercise that was viewed as more female-appropriate (Cahn 1994; Hargreaves 1994), fitness contests today offer an alternative that is viewed as more consistent with culturally valued views of femininity than bodybuilding. In this way, the boundaries of femininity are defined and reinforced as necessarily limiting women's size and strength relative to men's.

In the case of sexuality, heterosexuality is frequently invoked across both women's and men's magazines as a marker (although we will discuss the prevalence of "gay vague" in men's magazines below). For men, success with women is nearly omnipresent. By following the instructions laid out in these magazines, men are told they will be successful with women, simultaneously reifying sexual prowess as a key marker of masculinity and valorizing their important role in helping men access this marker. *Exercise & Health* promises "Super Sex: How to Get Her and Bed Her" (Summer 2000); the article offers a range of tips for "successful seduction." In fact, *Exercise & Health* contains a whole section entitled "Sex & Self." The Summer 2000 issue includes three articles on seduction, a photo essay featuring men and women cavorting in swimsuits, and the advice column "Ask Dr. Sex." *Exercise for Men Only* also features a regular column entitled "Sexual Health" with topics like "Libido-enhancing Botanicals" (*EMO*, June 2000).[10] The August 2001 issue of *Men's Health* features an article entitled "The Master Craftsman's Guide to Sex" that tells readers, "You already have the best tool for the job. Now you just need to hone your technique. Here, the proper method for whatever tonight's project might be."

For men, it is clear that sexuality, specifically the ability to please or control women through sexual performance, defines masculinity. As men in the most privileged category have lost much of their economic power over commensurate women, power is still maintained through different types of performances. As argued by Burstyn (1999), "as the identity-anchor of the provider role was weakened in the 1950s, 1960s, and 1970s, the importance of sexual performance per se . . . grew in significance in masculine self-definition. It was no longer good enough to be successful in financial terms; now a man had to be a tireless sexual achiever." Male anxiety over the erosion of patriarchal ideologies and gender norms can be assuaged with the reassurance that a real man can exert his power and authority through sexual prowess. It is consistently implied that sexual performance results in mastery and dominance of one's grateful partner. For example, *Exercise & Health* (Winter 2002) exhorts the reader to "Take Charge—How to Turn Her Into a Sex-Craving Machine." Next, we examine how other axes of identity shape the objective-aspects-within-being-as-subject and the subjective-aspects-within-being-as-object.

Race, Class, Sexuality, and Gender

Idealized gender intersects with other axes of identity. Given these intersections, it is imperative that ideals always be understood through what Patricia Hill Collins (1990) terms a "matrix of domination," or interlocking axes of oppression. One's identity categories shape the experiences to which one has access, and the meanings derived from individual bodies (Collins 1990). How bodies are read, what translates to valuable bodily capital, and what is normalized for bodies depends on the social location of each individual body.

In Western culture, the idealized versions of male and female bodies reflect a complicated array of historic and current relations of power and privilege. Race, class, sexuality, and gender intermix to construct an ideal that reflects and recreates colonial relations. No longer literally occupied, consumer culture and market forces leave many nations existing effectively as peripheral colonies, kept in line by global market forces, rather than directly by an occupying force. The privilege of white skin reflects this history and the continuing reality of relations today. The idealized bodies portrayed in men's and women's health and fitness magazines reflect privileged class status, the target demographic of the magazine. Certainly, in the United States this group is disproportionately white, though increasingly Hispanic and Asian American.[11] Given this, we expected to find whites overrepresented, with a growing number of images of Asian-American models and athletes, and some images of black and Latino athletes and models. Past research has focused on the display of the "other" in stereotypically exotic ways; hence we expected to find a myriad of images rife for analysis (Davis 1997). But instead the paucity of images left us explaining an absence.

The almost total exclusion of nonwhite individuals is quite an absence indeed. While multiethnic groups appeared in some advertisements, such as an ad that features a rainbow coalition of women united in their love of yogurt, or male buddies (one black, one white) playing a friendly game of basketball, cover models and images accompanying articles tended to be white. While a range of races were shown in ads, central players and images of individuals tended to be white. We examined the race of cover models and those demonstrating workouts in the magazines. Cover models and fitness models within men's and women's magazines were predominantly white. Similar to multiracial and feminist media analyses (Collins 1990; Davis 1997; Espiritu 1997a, 1997), we also found the tendency to only feature nonwhite "lighter" skinned models with straightened hair and European facial features regardless of gender. This cover code demonstrates that over 80 percent of women's magazines and almost 97 percent of men's featured white cover models (see table 2.6).[12]

TABLE 2.6
Cover Codes: Full Sample, 1998–2006

Race	Women's Magazines	Men's Magazines
White	54 (81.8%)	58 (96.7%)
Black/African American	3 (4.5%)	1 (1.7%)
Asian	0 (0%)	0 (0%)
Latino/Hispanic	4 (6.1%)	1 (1.7%)
Multiethnic	2 (3.0%)	0 (0%)
Other	3 (4.5%)	0 (0%)
Total	66 (100%)	60 (100%)

While the majority of cover models are simply models (66.2 percent for women and 81.7 percent for men), the few nonwhite cover models who appear are far more likely to be athletes. Dwain Wade of the NBA (*Men's Health*, April 2006) is one of the only two nonwhite men who appeared. The other unknown model appears to be Latino, but has what would euphemistically be described as "European features." Two of the three African-American women who are featured on women's covers are actresses —Vanessa Williams (*Ms. Fitness*, Winter 1998) and Traci Bingham (*Ms. Fitness*, Winter 2000)—the other is media conglomerateur Oprah Winfrey (*Living Fit*, January/February 1998). The two magazines on which these women appear have relatively lower subscription rates than other magazines in the sample during this time period.

In addition, an in-depth analysis of *Women's Sports & Fitness* was conducted over the entire run of the magazine, and is discussed in-depth in chapter 5. When examining the cover models of this one magazine across 25 years, it was disappointing and surprising to see how little changed over time when it came to race. The trend of only showing nonwhite people except in the case of a few high-profile individuals was apparent. Two covers a year were selected at random for analysis (see table 2.7).

It is also important to underscore that all three of the African-American cover models are athletes, two are world-class athletes, and the third is a relatively unknown snowboarder who competed locally and regionally.[13] The virtual exclusion of nonwhite women from every facet of the magazine except advertisements, with the exception of a few notables, speaks to continued underrepresentation.

We also coded the race of models demonstrating workouts for our randomly selected sample of men's and women's magazines. Again, almost all are white (see table 2.8).

TABLE 2.7
Women's Sports & Fitness *Cover Model Ethnicity*

	White	African American	Unknown/Other	Total
Self, 2000–2004	8	0	0	8
Women's Sports & Fitness, 1979–1989	22	0	0	22
Women's Sports & Fitness, 1990–1997	14	2 (Lisa Leslie, Snowboarder)	0	16
Women's Sports & Fitness, Condé Nast years: 1998–2000	4	1 (Marion Jones)	1	6
Women's Sports & Fitness, Total	40 (90.1%)	3 (6.8%)	1 (2.3%)	44

Note: Two models appeared on three covers. In one case, a wife-husband team is featured, with the woman featured more prominently. Two athletes are featured on one cover, and two models on another. Since the status of each was the same, each was counted as one for the cover code.

TABLE 2.8
Men's and Women's Health and Fitness Magazine Workouts:
Ethnicity of Person Demonstrating Workout

	White	Black	Latin	Asian	Other/Unknown	Total
Men's	176 (88.9%)	13 (6.6%)	1 (0.5%)	2 (1.0%)	6 (3.0%)	198
Women's	201 (80.7%)	19 (7.6%)	8 (4.0%)	4 (1.6%)	15 (6.0%)	249

Census data from 2005 indicate that 74.7 percent of the U.S. population is white, 12.1 percent is black or African American, 4.3 percent is Asian American, 0.8 percent is American Indian/Native American, 0.1 percent is Native Hawaiian or other Pacific Islander, 6 percent is other, and 1.9 percent is multiethnic. However, an additional 14.5 percent falls into the ethnic category of Hispanic/Latino but is subsumed under the other racial categories (meaning Hispanics are categorized racially as usually white or black) (www.census.gov).

Veneration of the image of whiteness has long served as a means to justify colonization and oppression (hooks 1992; Jhally and Lewis 1992; Omi and Winant 1986; Winant 1994). Since the advent of the Civil Rights and Women's movements of the 1960s, contestation of racist imagery and the exclusion of a wider range of images in the media have resulted in a greater awareness of the racially charged nature of imagery in the American consciousness (hooks 1992; Jhally and Lewis 1992). While we expected to find a range of images or a mixture of regressive and progressive imagery, the lack of imagery outside of advertisements was disturbing. The almost total omission of race, except as a consumer issue (makeup for every skin tone), leads one to believe that race has little bearing on health and fitness, or at least on the individual's ability to attain the ideal.

bell hooks underscores that the use of images of people of color tends to affirm the belief, often held by dominant groups, that society has put the problems of racism behind us (1992). While nonwhite individuals were not the centerpiece of covers, or articles, they appeared liberally in advertisements, usually appearing to enjoy cavorting with their white friends. When groups of men or women were featured, the rainbow coalition principle applied. A range of happy women of different ethnic backgrounds would bond over birth control, yogurt, or low-fat beverages. Multiethnic groups of men played sports, united by the effectiveness of their deodorant.

However, the lack of prominently placed nonwhite individuals on the covers and within the pages, especially in solo pictures or demonstrating workouts, would seem to suggest continued marginalization of racial and ethnic minorities in principal roles. Nonwhite individuals come to play a

This idealized rainbow coalition of the world is a common theme in advertisements. (*Men's Health*, October 1998)

different sort of role, that of featuring the progressiveness of the consumers of the products being marketed. The consumer can be associated with many different positive antiracist imaginings through which one can symbolically avoid complicity in a racist and classist social structure.

Given the critically important role that race and socioeconomic status play in the actual health of bodies, risk factors, medical propensities, and a myriad of other things that affect health, its obfuscation is problematic. By failing to provide meaningful information on health and "othered bodies," structural barriers to equitable health care, nutrition, and opportunities to exercise are rendered invisible, promoting healthism and neoliberal ideologies of meritocracy. Equally troubling is the failure to represent an array of ethnicities within the context of ideal bodies. By presenting a very limited image of the healthy ideal, numerous nonwhite bodies are left out of the frame. Dominant bodies are in the center of the frame, to be linked to the moral approbations afforded bodies that meet the ideal. By implication, then, white bodies are depicted as closer to the ideal, which is imbued with moral and civic value.

Ads such as this one exemplify the concept of "gay vague." While all of the articles on sex referenced female partners, the imagery such as this suggests otherwise. (*Exercise & Health,* Summer 1999)

CLOTHING FOR
EVERY LIFESTYLE

Y.M.L.A.® 110 EAST 9TH ST. B473 LOS ANGELES, CA. 90079 213 629-0778

Referencing the Village
People and the tag line
"Clothing for Every Life-
style" qualifies as "vague."
(*Exercise for Men Only*,
April 1998)

In terms of minority sexuality and men, men's magazines contained no
specific references to gay readers. However, many of the images presented
in the magazines could best be described as "gay vague."[14] "Gay vague"
refers to images presented in textually heterosexualized space, but with
images that create an ironic understanding for those "in the know" who
are internal to a marginalized community (or are aware of its existence).

As Oakenfull and Greenlee describe in their analysis of gay and lesbian imagery and content in magazines, "as with many subcultures, the
gay subculture has developed markers of gay identity such as clothes,
symbols, language and appearance that hold meaning to members of the
subculture while creating no meaning to those who have no knowledge
of the subculture" (Oakenfull et al. 2005, p. 427). As these authors go on
to describe, "the use of implicit gay and lesbian imagery allows advertisers to run less risk of backlash from heterosexual consumers than if they
were to target gay and lesbian consumers with explicit gay male or lesbian
content in their advertising" (ibid.). Brian Pronger describes something
similar within the institution of sport that he calls "gay irony." Gay irony

refers to the performance of masculinity as ironic given that it is coupled with the understanding that it is being parodied by those (e.g., gay men) who are internal to the locker room but who are outside of its markings in daily life (Pronger 1990). When read this way, the overwhelming insistence on the readers as successful with women becomes a case of protesting too much. At the same time, the implicit use of the markings allows gay and lesbian readers to feel like they are part of an inside joke that is being played on the less informed heterosexual reader (also see Penaloza 1996 on this point). While heterosexual readers probably take advice on relationships and the presentation of masculine self at face value, GLBT readers can use alternative reads to render some articles and images as having a hidden meaning, camp, or as erotic.

"Gay vague" has a long history in print advertising, as ambiguous yet homoerotic ads that appeal to a mass audience (Martin 1995). The growing consumer power of the gay and lesbian market makes them a demographic not to be alienated, and even to be actively courted (Ebencamp (2005). According to a Harris study, GLBT consumers have $600 million

Rainbow colors indicative of the gay community and "metrosexual" markers may code these fashions as "gay vague." (*Exercise & Health,* Fall 2001)

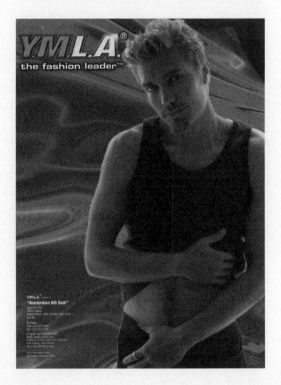

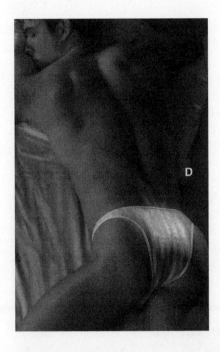

A beefcake shot that reveals the sexually available male object of desire
that could be classified as "gay vague."
(*Exercise for Men Only*, October 1998)

worth of buying power and are more likely to make purchases from companies who have actively reached out to the GLBT market.

Certainly, part of the ambiguity can be explained by the simultaneous cross-courting of a gay and heterosexual audience. The creation of
ads that can be interpreted one way by a gay audience and another by a
heterosexual audience is a strategy that allows companies to target both
audiences at once (Oakenfull et al. 2005). In addition, further ambiguity
is created by the shift of the presentation of male bodies as men adopt
the body habitus of the objective-aspects-within-being-as-subject. Given
that women have long been presented in this way, recent presentations of
men as objects carry feminine connotations. Conflations of gay and the
feminine are rampant in U.S. culture (Anderson 2005); hence, presentations of the male body as object are likely to carry with it the possibility
of feminine connotations.

Certainly, the magazines were well aware of a sizable GLBT readership.
The gay community acknowledges the appeal of men's health and fitness
magazines.[15] Ads for videos and websites suggest awareness by advertisers
that some readers are not heterosexual. We visited several of the websites
that advertised regularly in *EMO*, such as muscleweb.com, vistavideo.

com, and musclehunks.com. They ranged from what can euphemistically be called "beefcake" shots to pornography. *Fitness Plus* advertised videos that allowed one to "Workout with Hot College Guys" (January 1998), videos of "The Au Natural Football League," and a host of other naked sports competitions.

The ubiquity of the gratuitous gorgeous male is open to interpretation. One image in *EMO* (June 2000) features an ode to the "Human Form" that features an attractive man gazing saucily at the camera; his pants are unbuttoned and his hand is in the process of sliding into the front of his pants. Similarly, men were often posed together, engaging in activities that could indicate friendship, cruising, or couplehood, depending on how the image is "read." An example of ambiguity as to whether two men are friends or partners includes an article in *Men's Exercise* (June 2004) that features a "Partner Ab Workout." In this article, you may "have another person you must answer to on a day-in/day-out basis in the gym." The accompanying photo features two men posed at the beach. The

This ad reveals a common ambiguity in ads as to whether men are friends, cruising, or partners in several men's fitness magazines. This indicates how advertisers are "cross-coding" for "those in the know" while attempting to not be too direct—or risk alienating heterosexual readers. (*Exercise & Health*, June 2006)

ensuing workout features the two doing a "partner" workout. Another issue featured the "Two Men and a Towel Workout" (*Men's Exercise*, January 2000), which consists of a partner workout using only body weight and a towel. Two men box playfully in the first image, then demonstrate a series of partner moves. The term partner is left open to interpretation. In one of the photo demonstrations, one man performs push-ups, while the other kneels in front of him, providing resistance to the move. The shot is framed so the mouth of one man is inches from the other man's groin area. Ads in several magazines also offer similar ambiguities, including two men in a street scene that appears similar to what residents of West Hollywood, California or elsewhere would refer to as a cruising scene.

Finally, there was a trend to report on HIV/AIDS in men's magazines. New treatments and breakthroughs were the focus. For example, "Health Bulletin" featured in *Men's Health* (July/August 2001) has a section entitled "A Wall Against HIV." The article reports "There's a new line of defense in the treatment of AIDS. Researchers at MIT have designed a protein that prevents HIV from entering cells, even after the virus has sneaked into the body." While we are reticent to conflate sexuality with risk, as has been the argument in our other works, it would be naïve to ignore the devastating impact the disease has had on the gay community, or MSMs (men who have sex with men) in the United States. Hence, the regular reporting on this issue indicates acknowledgment of a readership to whom this information is particularly germane.

Neither the men's nor the women's magazines took an open stand on GLBT rights or issues. The silences observed in the men's were more stark in the women's given the lack of "gay vague." While men's magazines displayed "gay vague," women's magazines did not seem to. Given the history of associations between corporeality, masculinity, femininity, and sexuality, the prominence of sexuality in recent political debates over GLBT rights, and the real disparities in health (such as access to health benefits for domestic partners), the almost complete absence of any acknowledgment of a range of sexualities affirms heteronormativity. The readership was presumed to be heterosexual by default. Even *Women's Sports & Fitness*, which had featured a few pieces on "out" lesbian athletes over the course of the publication, was entirely mute during our study period, and featured only two prominent pieces in the extended sample coded for the entire run of the magazine (discussed at length in chapter 5). The primary message women received regarding sexuality was to love yourself in order to be a more confident (heterosexual) lover.

Conclusion

As the lives of men and women converge in consumer culture, we argue that key differences still remain that reflect the differences between the subjective-aspects-within-being-as-object and the objective-aspects-within-being-as-subject. The "objective-aspects-within-being-as-subject" refer to the ways that the experience of subjecthood is shaped and defined by external structures. For example, a particular type of muscular form will lead to a very different self-evaluation of one's body depending if one is male or female. The meanings associated with different manifestations of Giddens' reflexive project of the self (the idea that in consumer culture, self-identity becomes a project at which we all must work assiduously, and on which individuals must continuously reflect) does not seem to offer the wide range of opportunities for individual agency he supposed it would (Giddens 1991). Rather, evaluations of the results of the project of the self still vary tremendously depending on one's gender, race, class, sexuality, and background. Those who engage in projects that are inconsistent with ascribed characteristics are unlikely to find many dominant representations to emulate.

Health and fitness magazines venerate a specific set of intersections between class, race, sexuality, age, and gender. While race, class, and sexuality remain the unspoken assumptions that correlate with the ideal form, gender and the construction of idealized gender becomes the focal point around which these magazines naturalize ideals. For those in more privileged categories, work, leisure, and household responsibilities are less likely to be distinctly gendered as the second shift is displaced onto a service sector largely filled with third world nonwhite women (Hondagneu-Sotelo and Messner 2000). However, defining the natural boundaries of gender serves as a key means to re-articulate relations of power and privilege, precisely when the practices upon which these rest are in a state of flux.[16] By articulating what it means to be a man or woman physically, and by predicating this on "nature," relations of power are re-infused with meaning, experts are empowered as arbiters of these meanings, and social relations are justified.

The above process takes on a particular form in consumer culture. While the economically disenfranchised are subject to becoming "docile bodies" under the scrutiny of modern experts and subject to their "biopower," the privileged subject is enlisted to be his or her own judge. As we've noted, according to Foucault, the "technologies of the self" assist the confessional subject in his or her continual quest for self-improvement and assessment (Foucault 1980). The confessional subject comes to pattern middle-class behavior as the subject finds liberation through the suggested routes advocated by "experts"—in this case, the magazine and the arbiters of consumer culture (Giulianotti 2005). Having access to these practices then operates to legitimate the order by endowing the possessor with a valuable form of physical capital.

The subjective-aspects-within-being-as-object and the objective-aspects-within-being-as-subject come to be integral to the experiences of both men and women. While the objective-aspects-within-being-as-subject still undergird naturalized views of gender and continue to articulate male physical domination and ideologies of male physical superiority, increasingly, men are presented as objects. Through the presentation of the idealized objects, both men and women are sent clear messages about how each fails at achieving (gendered) ideals. Men and women fail at gender in both similar and oppositional ways. While size and some aspects of the presentation of self reaffirm physical difference, self-surveillance of body fat, the vicissitudes of age, and leisure possibilities converge in consumer culture.

It is imperative to note that while failure is inevitable for all, privileged bodies can redeem themselves with a series of ongoing successes. The failure to ever be thin or cut (depending on gender) enough can be assuaged by other successes. Using a great new scent, wearing the latest fashions, participating in the latest workout, updating one's hair, not having unsightly panty lines, losing weight or gaining muscle (depending on your gender), being hip and up to date, being more fit (even if one does not meet ideals) are all small successes that allow readers some self-satisfaction. It is perpetual failure, combined with perpetual success, that keeps individuals engaged in consumer culture. In short, consumer culture provides continual absolution to privileged bodies through these "small successes" and the self-satisfaction of participation in a set of identity-validating middle-class and upper-middle-class lifestyles. Docile bodies fare differently. Stigmatized as immoral, lazy, and poor citizens, docile bodies are presented as failing to follow the prescriptions attended to by the readers. The structural constraints are rendered invisible, as it is simply a question of "making time" or the right choices.

At a time when the long-term effects of poverty on health and wellbeing have been solidly documented, the singular focus on personal responsibility operates to promote healthism and particularly the neoliberal ideologies that underlie such ideas. In consumer culture, such ideologies are literally reified in the flesh as privileged bodies are able to use their existence as the justification for it in the first place. As noted by Baudrillard, the body has taken over the "moral and ideological function from the soul" (1998, p. 129). The relentless pursuit of bodily perfection seems to exemplify Baudrillard's somatization, the ultimate passivity of objecthood" (ibid.). While a host of very real threats to bodies exist, individual responsibility for appearance trumps social responsibility for access to social structures or a general quality of life. What seems most ironic is the preponderance of articles on issues that require a sense of public responsibility that are presented solely as problems of the individual consumer. This endemic problem of abdicating public responsibility for corporate purchases sets a dangerous precedent and ultimately is resulting in a less collective activism and a decline in resource availability, especially for the most needy (King 2006).

Neoliberal ideologies are further bolstered by the liberatory potential of consumer culture for the economically privileged. Because the corporeal can be read as a "sign" of success, it opens an avenue to success, one that might be more easily attainable than other promises made by the American Dream (Baudrillard 1998). Such an individualized focus might be deemed apolitical by some, but bodily performativity of many sorts (and sports) can also be termed an "ironic" third wave feminist strategy that can result in more successful maneuvering through social institutions in a postmodern world (Heywood and Drake 1997). Bodywork can create a space for personal liberation even if the activities associated with it lead to negative social and/or individual effects (Gimlin 2002). At the same time, individualized bodywork certainly has its attendant effects on social structures. For some, options expand in consumer culture. However, while some privileged female consumers may see an expanding array of options, men come to experience the subjective aspects of being-as-object codified in the dual problems of size and male body panic, the subject of the next chapter.

3

Size Matters

*Male Body Panic and the Third Wave
"Crisis of Masculinity"*

Within the last two decades, a plethora of scholarly work has explored the interrelationship between images of female bodies, gendered power relations, and consumption (Bartky 1988; Bordo 1993; Brumberg 1997; Grogan 1999; Heywood 1998; Duncan 1994). As noted in the last chapter, it has been assumed that gendered power relations necessarily over-determined men as powerful, privileged, and active subjects (Messner 1989), and as such, male bodies were not viewed as capable of being objectified (Bordo 1999). Indeed, because the male body has long been the presumed norm against which female bodies are found lacking (ibid.; Synnott 1993), it has been largely assumed that male bodies do not "lack." Thus, while specific attention has focused on an "ideology of lack" surrounding women's bodies and the need to consume products and services in order to "correct" that lack, it is only very recently that scholarly attention has turned toward the complex ways that the (hegemonic) male body has also been subjected to intensive scrutiny and objectification.

The previous chapter shed light on the ways in which the subject/object dichotomy has not fully elucidated the complexities that circulate around gender and the body to reflect contemporary changes in gender relations in the postindustrial consumer era. We therefore spent some time challenging the traditional emphasis on a subject/object dichotomy (and an active/passive one) by underscoring evidence of a convergence of bodily practices, imagery (poses), and fitness prescriptions among women and men in fitness texts. We introduced Frigga Haug's concept of subjective-aspects-within-being-as-object and noted how Haug's framework allows space for a rebuttal to traditional analyses of women and the body, such that women are not solely objectified but rather, find useful, identity-validating, and pleasurable aspects of being an object (and are framed as such).

We then extended Haug's concept to include men by introducing our own new concept termed "objective-aspects-within-being-as-subject." This concept captures the ways in which traditional notions of male subjectivity have been partly objectified. Such a concept involves recognition that men are not simply subjects, but experience objectifying processes within processes of subjectivity, particularly given that men as a category are not unified (with differences by race, class, sexuality). The analysis in the previous chapter of fitness media texts over time underscored that the framing of both men and women in fitness texts involved an intersection of consumption, gender, and objectification that has evolved in both convergent and divergent ways (and continues to evolve). As was noted, this is consistent with other researchers who have made similar claims about the newly objectified status of men (Miller 2001; Dowsett 1994; Bordo 1999; also see chapter 5, "Body Panic Parity," of Heywood and Dworkin 2003).

In this chapter, we extend the challenges to the subject/object dichotomy offered in the last chapter to argue that men in fitness are not only constituted as having objective aspects within being-as-subject, but that men's objectified status still offers powerful forms of subjecthood in fitness media that are linked to the display and actualization of hegemonic masculinity. As we will show, this is represented in fitness media texts as large physical size, institutionalized links to sport and the military, and the constitution of hegemonic masculinity as different from and superior to subordinated masculinities and to femininities. This chapter therefore explores in detail the construction of the idealized male body through health and fitness texts and how a third wave crisis of masculinity (masculinism, fears of social feminism, and backlash to feminism) is paradoxically constructed and partly resolved through body panic.

Scholars argue that "male body panic," or male preoccupation with physical appearance, has become more prevalent with the advent of consumer culture in the postindustrial era. Just as scholars underscore the negative impacts of consumer culture and corporeal demands on women, men's experiences must increasingly be recognized as having serious social and personal consequences (Pope, Phillips, and Olivardia 2000). The importance of bodily display as a means to establish and negotiate social status, and the ways that body image reinforces or challenges relations of privilege and oppression (whether by sexuality, race, or other social locations), must be investigated, particularly given that all bodies are said to be subject to forms of "body panic." As we will show, health and fitness discourse, and healthism in particular, play a vital, albeit complex role in paradoxically constituting and solving contemporary "male body panic" (Gillett and White 1992; Heywood 1998; Kimmel 1990; Pope, Phillips, and Olivardia 2000).

Body Panic—The Role of Consumer Culture in Diffuse Moral Panics at the Turn of the Millennium

Stanley Cohen introduced the notion of "moral panics" to account for a recurring social pattern that emerges and recedes based on sociopolitical contexts: a group is marked as deviant or dangerous, media overstate the risks associated with this group, and a public outcry ensues to maximize control of these individuals, against whom policy is eventually enacted (Cohen 2002). Once the panic recedes, the focus shifts to the next constructed threat, and the process resurfaces with new contours for the next (usually marginalized) social group. Jeffrey Weeks applies the concept of a moral panic to the AIDS epidemic, demonstrating a link between embodiment and morality, and the ways in which conflations of identity status (e.g., race, class) and behavior create moral hierarchies among different bodies (Weeks 1985). Such analyses not only press us to think further about the ways in which bodies are subject to and constituted by moral orders, but they also underscore the ways in which the social behaviors and identities of *dominant and marginalized* bodies need to be carefully disentangled in times of rapid cultural change or instability (or, as we will note, war).

Furthering an analysis of the links between social identities, morality, embodiment, and masculinity, our own earlier work (Dworkin and Wachs 1998; Wachs and Dworkin 1997) agreed with Weeks's basic claims about embodiment and morality, but subsequently extended his analysis to consider the ways in which intersecting social locations (e.g., race, sexuality, masculinity) reflect and challenge deviant markings and placements into hierarchical moralities. In our previously published media analyses of the differential moral frames that three major newspapers (*Washington Post, New York Times, Los Angeles Times*) provided in their media coverage of the HIV-positive announcements that male athletes Greg Louganis, Magic Johnson, and Tommy Morrison made to the public, we demonstrated the ways in which media conflated sexual act, risk, and sexual identity.

In that work, we analyzed how newspapers conflated sexual act, risk, and identity, which worked to disseminate erroneous health information about HIV/AIDS risks and constructed different moral orders depending on the specific interaction between social identities and masculinities (e.g., marginalized/subordinated and dominant) that each athlete offered (according to their race, class, sexuality, gender). Men whose bodies were subject to a discourse of "otherness" (e.g., such as Louganis, a self-identified gay man) were not "redeemed" in media coverage when Louganis made a public confession about HIV status, and his body was the subject of panic (e.g., through his blood in the pool) and deviant markings on the basis of his sexual identity. The press assumed that he was promiscuous when he had in fact been in a monogamous relationship with someone to whom he was faithful but who was unfaithful to him. Providing much contrast, men in dominant categories (e.g., in the analysis, self-identified heterosexually active men such as Johnson and Morrison) were successfully redeemed in media coverage and avoided the stigma of contagion, even when literally contagious. This was so despite the fact that this media case study was rife with discourses around sexuality and HIV, and it is noteworthy that racist or classist discourses of sexual excess could have easily been more directly invoked.

However, instead of blaming the heterosexually active men or their behavior (e.g., Morrison and Johnson), as was done in the coverage of Louganis, or blaming the social organization of masculinity within sport (that normalizes "scoring" and multiple sexual partners as central to the constitution of masculine identity), blame for Morrison's and Johnson's behavior was displaced onto the women with whom they had sex. These women were blamed in media coverage for being "groupies" and having "uncontrollable" desires for male athletic objects of desire. Heterosexually active male athletes were discussed in terms that described them to be doing "what any normal man would do" in responding to the women's "requests." Our analysis certainly underscored the need for gender and the body scholars to not only push beyond monolithic notions of hegemonic masculinity to include various subordinated masculinities, but to thoroughly interrogate men's intersecting social locations while carrying out relational analyses of gender (e.g., both women and men). Indeed, the moral order reflected social stratification in order to reify notions of good and bad behavior, identities, and practices in unfortunately predictable ways.

Not all would agree with our claims that this is an example of moral panic.[1] For example, in their analysis of the relationship between moral panics and contemporary media practices, McRobbie and Thornton

(1995) reference Simon Watney's book titled *Policing Desire* and state that he "rightly points out that gradual and staged creation of a 'folk devil' as described by moral panic theorists applies neither to gay men and lesbians nor people who are HIV positive. Instead, there is a whole world of monstrous representations" (p. 563). Given that our analysis showed clear differentiation between which bodies are able to be redeemed and which were not, we certainly hold to the original claims in our analysis. Hence, our previous media analyses move us to consider the ways in which media rely on the relationship between dominant and marginalized social categories to produce signifiers of morality and reproduce moral panics. Specifically, we have to consider how moral panics operate to (re)produce relations of privilege (heterosexual men) and oppression (gay men, women). Body panic in the current analysis, by contrast, is not part of a mass social movement, but is disseminated through diffuse relations of power found in media representations. It urges one to consider how relations of privilege and oppression are not only represented in media but are literally embedded in the flesh through repeated practices, thereby marking the social stature of individuals and serving as a justification for social positions.

In the current analysis, then, instead of relying on an analysis of the ways in which the "subordinated" are framed within moral panics, we "study up" on dominant ideals in order to extend an analysis of social hierarchies, moral panics, sport, and bodies. For this project, we examine the ways in which body panic is produced as a form of diffuse moral panic through the relationship between what is included and excluded within media frames. While previous work on moral panics in media have emphasized how representations demonize "the other" through directly representing them inside the media frame, we will argue that contemporary media creates a more diffuse "folk devil"[2] through the creation of the "folk angel"[3] that links morality and privilege—and, by extension—ties immorality with those left outside the frame. In this way, we underscore how body panic must not be seen solely as individualized anxieties but must also be understood as part of the broader structure of more diffuse power relations found in postindustrial consumer culture.

While both our previous and current work consider the racialized, gendered, and classed dimensions of moral panic, here, we will consider how, with the advent of consumer culture, the salvation once sought to be derived through the soul has moved to the body (Baudrillard 1998). The body, then, does not simply become a sign of morality (or immorality) by being matched by moral (or immoral) acts, but the media works to mark bodies with signs of morality that become markers for the moral act itself. In a strange reversal of Oscar Wilde's novel, *Picture of Dorian Gray*, the surface of the body becomes the locus of sin itself, with sin coming to signify particular values that are associated with bodily imperfections. Wilde's book critiqued Victorian presumptions that degeneracy was written on the body, and that bodies not marked by degeneracy were necessarily more moral than stigmatized ones. Dorian Gray in Wilde's book maintains an outward appearance of immaculate perfection, while his portrait shows the immorality/degeneracy to which he is becoming a more frequent participant. Wilde's book underscores that the sins of the individual were thought to be written on the flesh. In contemporary terms, however, simply not having perfect flesh is currently viewed as a sin in and of itself (and, as will be discussed in this chapter, as antithetical to the interests of U.S. nationalism in the war against terror). Indeed, moral hierarchies intersect with consumer culture in unique ways, given that there are those who are (included) within and (left) outside of the moral frame in fitness media texts, helping to define, shape, and "solve" contemporary social dimensions of body panic.

Some argue that the moral panic of the new millennium focuses on the obese and the out of shape body.[4] While the World Health Organization (WHO) states that rates of being overweight or obese are reaching "epidemic proportions," and there is a large range of bodies in between slender and overweight, body fat itself has come to symbolize the out of control, unproductive, and morally inferior worker/citizen (as was seen in chapter 2). Each person is now called upon in consumer culture to work assiduously to minimize the ever-increasing set of flaws to which his or her body is subject. Other scholars have noted how body panic is part of a re-emergence of expressions of crises in masculinity. While previous analyses of crises of masculinity centered only on the institutional and structural realm (e.g., the development of sports and the boy scouts), we center here on the embodied, cultural, and symbolic realm of what we term a "third wave crisis of masculinity" that is both similar to and also somewhat unlike previous "crises of masculinity" at the turn of the twentieth century (the wave crisis) and in the 1960s–70s (second wave crisis).

As the contemporary male body becomes a negotiable profit-generating commodity (with a shift from instrumental use to appearance), men are increasingly sold bodily problematizations which are largely assuaged through continual purchases (Bordo 1999; also see Dotson 1999; Armitage

2005). American men spent over $2 billion in 1999 on commercial gym memberships, another $2 billion on gym equipment for the home, and these numbers have risen in great magnitude since that time. The paid circulation of the most popular magazine in our sample, *Men's Health*, climbed more than sevenfold in seven years—from 250,000 to 1.8 million in 2005. The circulation of *Men's Health* currently exceeds that of *GQ* and *Esquire* combined. According to the latest Audit Bureau of Circulations figures, overall circulation grew in the 2005–2006 for masculinist magazines like *Maxim* and *Men's Journal*. According to the same source, sales also increased for fitness and fashion magazines such as Condé Nast's *GQ*, and data from Rodale Press indicated that *Men's Health* was up 5 percent partway through 2006.

The features editor of *Men's Health* recently pinpointed the "why" of this trend in an interview available on the web, in which he is quoted as saying: "Some people might say that we're doing well because men are more vain now, but I think they're just more aware of everything that comes with health—the idea that it is more than skin deep." And while health reasons may be part of the "cause," much vanity and bodily anxiety is certainly reflected in broader purchasing trends. Estimates from 1997 indicated that men spent $3.5 billion on hair color, skin moisturizers, teeth whiteners, and other toiletries (Pope, Phillips, and Olivardia 2000). Between 2002 and 2006, there was a 3 percent increase in cosmetic surgery among men, continuing the trend of cosmetic surgery for men that exploded in the late 1990s and the early part of the new millennium (PR Newswire 2007). Cosmetics and skin care, once the domain of women, have seen a sharp increase in male usage as most major companies expand to offer grooming and skin care lines for men (Morago 2007). Companies rolled out 800 new men-only products in 2006 according to the consulting firm Datamonitor, up from 459 only five years earlier (*Business Week*, September 4, 2006, p. 48). Such trends suggest that claims by scholars and consumers that men were "missed" in the consumer revolution are no longer accurate, if indeed these ever were on the mark.

Some scholars in the disciplines of psychology and sociology argue that men have displayed greater satisfaction with their bodies and less of a desire to change even though they recognize that they often do not meet ideals (Grogan 1999). Still others argue that men are nearly as dissatisfied with their bodies as women, binge eat as much as women, and are highly preoccupied with products and practices that help to construct today's hegemonic ideal of increased musculature and decreased body fat (Pope,

Phillips, and Olivardia 2000). And, while some claim that gay men are as dissatisfied with their bodies as heterosexual women (Grogan 1999), others argue that gay and straight men are equally dissatisfied (Pope, Phillips, and Olivardia 2000). We suspect that the myriad of competing information reflects a time of transition—that men overall are in the process of becoming less satisfied with their bodies.

The argument here will center on the fact that while there are a number of forces that lead to a convergence of bodies and practices among women and men—and men may in fact be framed as having objective aspects within being-as-subject within fitness texts—it is also true that men's objectified status still offers powerful forms of subjecthood that are linked to the display and actualization of hegemonic masculinity. This chapter explores in detail the construction of the idealized male body and analyzes this body in light of current "third wave" crises of masculinity. This work demonstrates the typical responses characterized by masculinism as including large body size, links to all male domains such as the military, sport, and other male-dominated occupations in the state, fears of social

Clearly, size is paramount to masculinity. *Men's Fitness,* November 2004)

Jim Cordova
Team MuscleTech Athlete

SPECIAL 4-PAGE AD REPORT

Men's fitness magazines are focused on size, as evidenced in ads such as this one which promise big gains. (*Men's Health*, April 2006)

feminization, and antifeminism. When one explores the construction of the ideal man today, certainly, size matters.

We conducted content and textual analysis of all available articles from our sample of health and fitness magazines for men. We coded all available articles for thematic emphasis and examined the five (of six) modal themes here: size, power and strength, natural elements, the links made between men's fitness, the military, sports, fears of social feminization, and antifeminism. By examining these themes, we do not mean to suggest that audiences do not offer multiple readings of images or texts, as we suggest throughout the book. Rather, we underscore that while magazines do present a range of alternative viewpoints, they commonly offer "preferred" readings (see chapter 1). The preferred or dominant reading refers to an interpretation in line with what producers of the text desire. We do not argue that "preferred readings" and meanings necessarily reinforce "dominant ideologies" or practices, as many scholars have previously argued, but rather, that dominant ideologies are built into the preferred reading and serve to displace blame for the negative aspects of consumer culture onto gender relations (and failed unhealthy choices), rather than the structures of postindustrial society or consumer culture itself.

What Makes a Healthy (Hegemonic) Man—Size Matters

The fundamental belief in dichotomous difference is bolstered by the core assumption that men are big and women are small.[5] Men's and women's health magazines provide step-by-step instructions for meeting these ideals while simultaneously (re)creating them. As numerous scholars of gender and the body have stated, ideal (Western, contemporary) men are primarily big and, secondarily, cut (Gillett and White 1992; Dotson 1999; Olivardia, Pope, Borowiecki, and Cohane 2004). The fundamental assumption that underlies most recommendations to men is that healthy and fit are defined by the image of musculature, muscle size, greater muscle density, and less body fat. All of the covers of the men's magazines featured well-defined, muscular, and almost always shirtless upper bodies. Most male models were not only toned, but large, and often vascular (displaying enlarged veins). Bulging pectoral muscles, biceps, shoulders, and well "cut" "six- or eight-pack" abdomens adorned almost all of the men's health and fitness covers. The fundamental assumption that underlies men's fitness is that men should strive to increase their muscle mass and decrease their body fat. As noted in the previous chapter, meeting this ideal takes on the importance of a moral injunction—workouts, advice, and images combine to send a clear message that size does matter and makes the man.

The focus on size comes across in the workouts, as almost all articles explicitly set an increase in muscle size or density as a goal (87.8 percent, N = 174). Only 12.2 percent of men's articles (N = 24) focused on cardio, flexibility, or other forms of alternative workouts. For example, one article was entitled, "More Muscles Guaranteed! 10 Secrets for Adding Quality Pounds Fast" (*Men's Fitness*, November 2004), another is entitled, "Add Size and Power to Our Arms" (*Men's Exercise*, September 1998), and *Exercise for Men Only* (*EMO*) (July 2004) exhorts readers to "Super-Size Your Chest!" At the same time, *Men's Health* (May 2004) calls for men to "Get Sets, Grow!" while an April 2006 issue of the magazine features "Twenty-Four Muscle Rippers!" on its cover. One *EMO* cover featured "Get Big Fast!"(May 2006), *Men's Exercise* cheered for men to seek "Superman

Shoulders in 4 Simple Moves!" on its April 2003 cover, and *Men's Fitness* offered "136 New Ways to Build BadAss Muscle" (May 2006).

While the men's magazine *EMO* offers a "Dumbbells-Only Back and Trap Workout" (June 2000) and asks, "What's the point in having huge 'guns' for arms and 'cannonballs' for delts if your back's as thin as a string of spaghetti?" women's magazines frequently offered workouts like *Self*'s "The 3-in-1 workout" that promises "you'll fix trouble spots, lose inches and drop pounds" (February 2003). Further, men's magazines contained far more ads, articles, and snippets (short bits of information that are part ad, part information whose purpose is to promote new products, practices, or services) on supplements designed to add size or muscle mass. While women's nutritional aids almost exclusively focused on weight loss, men's magazines admonished individuals to cut fat while increasing size. For example, *Men's Exercise* offers the regular feature Nutrition News, which promotes beef liver extract as "one of the most dynamic muscle-building supplements around" (July 2001). By contrast, the women's

These advertisements provide visual cues to appropriately feminine and masculine goals. Even in the case of a muscular woman and a muscular man, her captions are about leanness and a low number of calories and he is her "mean" male counterpart who needs no mention of being low cal. (*Men's Exercise*, January 2000)

Side by side, this image
highlights prescribed gender differences. Notice
that the direct association
between men and sport
and indirect association between women and fitness is
put forward. (*Men's Fitness*,
December 2001)

magazines center on the time-honored theme of women controlling their
diet for weight loss, but supplements are almost never mentioned. *Fit* features "Losing the Last 10 Lbs: Confessions of an Aerobics Instructor" that
provides hints on how to manage your diet in order to lose weight (December 2002).

Size reduction is the focus of the majority of women's workouts, fitness
advice, and nutrition advice. Only 10.5 percent (N = 23) of women's workouts instruct women to gain strength. Most of the workout articles focus on "toning" (52.1 percent, N = 114) and injury prevention (17 percent,
N = 37). Our sample of women's magazines had seven times the number
of weight loss articles as men's magazines (7.3 percent, N = 16). In addition, the preponderance of articles that discuss fitness, focus on losing
weight as a key component. "We Lost a Ton!" (*Fitness*, October 1999) profiles 18 women who lost 2,000 pounds among them. *Fitness* sums up the
goal with the piece "Body 2000" (October 1999): "C'mon, admit it. You'd
love to kick off the millennium with a tighter tummy, trimmer legs and
a jiggle-free behind. There's still time! Our three-month plan tackles the

whole package with step-by-step cardio, weight and stretching routines that will give you a new body to go with the New Year." Women are fairly consistently sold the promise of a "new you," centered on improving their appearance.

Of course, bodily ideals have changed over time, and some claim these ideas are broadened to include a wider range of femininities. While women's new fit bodies are celebrated as normalizing a wider range of beauty ideals for women, research suggests the parameters of femininity still contain significant size requirements (Heywood and Dworkin 2003; Duncan 1994; Duncan and Brummett 1993). The minimal attention given to strength gains for women makes it clear that this is not an appropriate goal (we have both often wondered why, if women's lower bodies are so problematic, magazines do not suggest that women lift a lot of weights in the upper body to make the lower body appear smaller). The women's workouts (10.5 percent of articles) that focus on gains in strength as the primary goal do not highlight gains in size that generally accompany almost all of the men's workouts with the same goal. If we are to accept that

Left: Women are more often prescribed fitness activities, such as these exercise ball moves, than are men. (*Shape*, September 2006). *Right*: Women are more often prescribed fitness activities, such as graceful dance "moves," than are men. (*Shape*, September 2006)

Left: Men are much more often prescribed upper body weight work than are women. (*Exercise for Men Only*, May 2006). *Right*: One can see the contrast between men's and women's fitness routines and prescribed physical forms by examining fitness images and texts relationally. (*Exercise for Men Only*, February 2002)

men are naturally bigger and stronger than women, it seems surprising that gaining size wouldn't be recommended for women. One could easily rationalize size gains with feminized ideologies, such as: gaining strength assists in performing "appropriately feminine" tasks such as carrying youngsters or groceries (although, as we will see in chapter 4, babies are the preferred and recommended "barbells" for new mothers).

When taken together, these magazines make it clear that masculinity is displayed through strength and size. It is not simply size requirements that constitute masculinity and femininity, but the fact that gender and corporeality are strategically produced in certain parts of the body. Particular body parts especially signify masculinity (upper body) over and above others.

Table 3.1 appears to, upon first glance, reinforce some aspects of bodily overlap between women and men, as substantial commonality is seen in all categories, and especially in the "combination" of upper and lower body workouts category, the largest category for both women's and men's

TABLE 3.1
Not Just Size Matters, but Where Matters

	Upper Body Only	Lower Body Only	Abdominals Only	Combo of Upper/Lower and/or Abs	Other	Total
Male	61 (30.8%)	17 (8.6%)	32 (16.2%)	84 (42.4%)	4 (2.0%)	198
Female	25 (11.4%)	36 (16.4%)	16 (7.3%)	126 (57.5%)	16 (7.3%)	219

workouts. Combination workouts that included both the upper and lower body clearly did provide more overlap in workouts for women and men. However, in this category, in men's magazines, combination workouts were far more likely to include the upper body and abdominals, or only one or two lower body exercises combined with several upper body exercises. For example, *Men's Exercise* (July 2001) promises "Tremendous Traps!" through "6 State of the Art Shrugs." This piece is billed as "The best way to cap off your physique with mountainous muscles." An earlier issue (*Men's Exercise*, September 1998) features "Call to Arms" that claims: "As I've grown older, I now understand that the biceps make up

In our analysis, men's fitness magazines contained three times the number of upper body workouts than women's fitness magazines. The historical association between muscularity in the upper body and masculinity is made here. Note that men's lower bodies are not often shown or emphasized, while women's lower bodies are often presented as a "problem" area. (*Men's Exercise*, June 2006)

only one-third of the total arm size, even if they are the most impressive to look at. To better fill out your shirtsleeves, you've got to concentrate on the triceps just as much. Likewise, a mammoth upper arm coupled with a stick-like forearm looks positively ridiculous, so you've got to work them, too." The wisdom of age is marshaled in an effort to fill out one's shirtsleeves.

For women, the "problem areas" of hips, thighs, and rear end were ubiquitous. For women, combination workouts included mostly lower body workouts with abdominals with a few upper body toning moves. *Shape* (October 2004) advises readers to "Improve Your Rear View" with a workout that offers "3 moves to chisel your butt and thighs." And two years later, the same publication features a workout that promises to "Re-size Your Thighs: 3 Moves to Slim Down Fast." *Fitness* (June 1999) advertised a workout entitled "Lower-Body Blast," which claims: "Besides giving you a fat-blasting aerobic boost, it also offers a spot-on lower-body workout-a shortcut to slimmer hips, sexier legs and a firmer, shapelier butt."

The upper body/lower body divide is not new. Women in Western culture have long been stigmatized as physical, tied to the body, and rendered less rational and physically capable due to their reproductive organs (lower body). By contrast, men have been venerated by the linking of the male to the cerebral, logical, and rational (upper body) (Grosz 1994; Laqueur 1990; Sennett 1994). In addition, research has demonstrated that while on average men have slightly stronger upper bodies, women have slightly stronger lower bodies (Fausto-Sterling 1985). Hence, the cautions aimed at women's lower bodies and the restrictions on their size indicate the potential for cultural devaluations of women's strength. At the same time, the continued association of masculinity with upper bodies, and the presumption that upper body strength is more central, further highlights the privileging of the male form as ideal, with the female form as consistently not measuring up (Dowling 2001). While many argue that idealized gender differences reflect innate natural differences between men and women, the wide range of bodies and practices employed over time and across space suggests culture plays a significant role in defining idealized bodies and the way individuals go about attaining one (Bordo 1993).

Men's magazines contained three times the number of upper body workouts as women's. They were rife with calls to get "Bigger, Better, Biceps Fast!" (*Men's Exercise*, November 1997), "Shock Your Biceps into Growing!" (*Men's Fitness*, July 2002), "Add 2 Inches to Your Arms!" (*Men's*

Fitness, May 2006), "Build Sleeve Busting Biceps!" (*Men's Exercise,* June 2006), "Chisel a V-Tapered Back" (*EMO,* February 1997), "Cannonball Delts! Build Massive Shoulders in No Time Flat! (*Men's Exercise,* February 2003), "Mountainous Traps in Just 6 Sets (*EMO,* October 1998), "Keeping Your Shoulders Healthy and Wealthy with Size" (*Men's Exercise,* April 2003), and "EMO's Superior Guide to a V-Tapered Back" (August 1997). As in our examples from women's magazines above, clearly, reducing size was the goal. While men as actual readers are far from cultural dupes who will merely passively absorb the messages in any kind of uniform manner, it is interesting (and surprising to us) that these titles are quite consistent with actual surveys of men's bodily dissatisfaction which show particular contempt for the lack of muscularity in their upper bodies, historically constitutive of ideal masculinity (Olivardia et al. 2004; also see Grogan 1998; Bordo 1999).

Another key demarcation of corporeal perfection was the six- or eight-pack of ab muscles. For men, the importance of lean, ripped or striated, and cut abdominal muscles was clear due to their ubiquity in image and

Six- and eight-pack abs are one of the hallmarks of corporeal male perfection in men's health and fitness magazines. This ad states that "a tight, lean mid-section can be yours with the help of the right fat-loss supplement . . . Hydroxy-cut!" (*Exercise & Health,* Fall 2001)

text. Almost all of men's magazines featured one or two abdominal workouts. Overall, approximately one in six (17 percent) workouts were specifically for abdominals, such as "Diamond Hard Abs in Just 10 Minutes a Day" (*Men's Exercise*, November 1997), "Incredible Abs! The Inversion Boots Workout" (*Men's Exercise*, December 2004), "Lose Your Gut for Good!" (*Exercise and Health*, Winter 1998), "Ab Exercise! Lose Your Love Handles!" (*EMO*, May 2006), "The Easy Way to Hard Abs" (*Men's Health*, February 2006), and "Complete Super Definition Ab Training (*EMO*, February 1998). By contrast, women had the goal of "flat" and "toned" abs. Self (February 2003, cover) promises "Sexy Arms, Slim Hutt, Flat Abs in *Less* Time."

The cumulative social practices necessary to obtain the right abdomen or any other body part are clearly intensive and require continual scrutiny. In this way, the panoptic gaze discussed by Bartky (1988) and Duncan (1994) as applied to women is clearly applicable to men. Men are counseled to push well beyond average to get closer to a more elite athletic level and are told that "transforming the stomach from flabby to firm is part of any smart man's fitness plan. With a sensible diet and regular abdominal exercising, it's a reachable goal. Taking the next step, from firm to sculpted, is another matter entirely. That takes a spartan diet, of the almost fat-free variety, and adhering to a much tougher fitness regimen" (*Exercise & Health*, Winter 1998). Special tips to move men toward the pinnacle washboard status included: "Prolonging the pause" at the top of abdominal crunches (*Exercise & Health*, Winter 1998), "punching combinations," plyometrics (for "explosive execution" (*Men's Health*, April 2006), use of a "body wedge" for increased elevation (*Men's Exercise*, June 2006), use of an "ab pavelizer II" (EMO, July 2002), working the abs from multiple angles (*EMO*, May 2006), martial arts for "shredded abs," and high-intensity, high-repetition training plans (*EMO*, February 1997) and more. Men are also prescribed meticulous eating and exercise plans that included limiting calories, eating fat-free foods, increasing protein intake, using meal replacement to get more protein, eating 5–6 times a day, eating a high-fiber diet with plenty of vegetables, and of course, carrying out all of the recommended exercises in the articles.

Unlike women's magazines, which tended not to directly humiliate women by calling their "flawed" or "problematic" body parts disparaging names, at times men's exercises are presented in a manner similar to that used by a football coach or military commander, yelling denigrating remarks at his athletes to encourage them to try harder. Men's ab exercises are named "inner tube deflator," "spare tire changer," "beer belly buster," and "love handle handler." The text is full of comments that make it clear that once the body "plateaus" and you are no longer getting results, it is always necessary to "ramp up" the body maintenance stakes with new products and to an even more disciplined stance that truly requires almost unrelenting diet and exercise plans. "Once you comfortably reach one step, you've got to move up to the next if you want to keep the gains coming," reports *EMO* (December 2001). Genetics are framed as something that should not get in the way (e.g., genetics is "no excuse"), as diet, exercise, and the right attitude should overcome all other influences. Failure to acquire the perfect abdominal muscles is framed as a symbol of a lack of discipline and a lack of moral fortitude, as evidenced by the way in which men who "fail" at this task are said to be "making excuses" or not showing "commitment" or "lacking self-control." Some articles even caution men to stay at it and not to "fall off the bandwagon," as if not working out is analogous to being a person with a substance abuse problem.

An emphasis on the constant activity and purchases necessary to achieve the ideal body is similar to previous scholars' findings on women's health and fitness magazines, where analyses have centered on how women face "disciplinary self-surveillance" that they then internalize, becoming the individualized moral guardians of their own bodily presentation. This point will also be linked in this chapter to the moral fate of the nation and the links between military, civilian populations, and "terrorist" or "enemy" that is constructed during times of war. (We also return to it in the next chapter where pregnant women are called upon to get their bodies back after giving birth in order to participate in "family values.") Magazines encourage such individualized internalizations without offering critical considerations of where cultural norms came from to begin with, either in historical or contemporary terms (this, of course, does not bode well for training or purchasing behaviors, nor does it bode well for negating the need to expand the male body in the effort to expand democracy, nor for creating a body that elicits the desire of others).[6]

Interestingly, the lower male body remained somewhat haunted by the specter of the feminine (e.g., working on giving yourself a nice ass is a practice designated mostly for women) and was therefore framed more often than the upper body with military undertones or as functional for participation in male-dominated occupations. Only 8.6 percent of men's articles referred to the lower body, such as "Powerful Legs From a Paratrooper" (*EMO*, August 1997) and "Mr. America's Thigh Workout" (*Fitness*

Plus, March 1997). There were also "Legs of Iron" (*EMO*, January 2003), and "Skinny Legs? Beef 'Em Up Today! (*Men's Exercise*, December 2004), and "Are You a Hardass? You are if your glutes are powerful! Here's how to make them just that" (*Exercise & Health*, Summer 2000). We argue that though size and power are both used frequently and interchangeably to describe the male body, size is less clearly a goal for men's lower bodies, since the upper body is the preferred signifier of masculinity for the male body. No matter what body part is being worked, however, power is consistently a proposed property for the ideal male body, presented both as a natural element that is simply a part of manhood while also being simultaneously acquired. As we will see next, the hardened and larger masculine body becomes inextricably intertwined with fantasies of national power during wartime, and does so in a context where clear themes are re-emerging around contemporary fears of the social feminization of men.

Power, Strength, and Natural Elements

Power and/or strength are presented as fundamental goals and attributes of the male body. Examples include "Push-Ups for Power-Packed Pecs" (*EMO*, February 1997), "Power Up! Barbell Blast for Super Biceps and Perfect Pecs" (*Exercise & Health*, Spring 2006), "10 Steps to Super Strength" (*Men's Exercise*, June 2000), and "3 Ways to Power Up Your Grip!" (*Men's Fitness*, November 1997). Through engagement in health and fitness practices; the body can become like a natural element, and this is shown in many articles: "Hard Muscle: Your Start-up Plan" (*Men's Health*, January/February 2000), "Hard Abs" (*Men's Health* July/August 1999), "Rock Solid Shoulders" (*Men's Health*, April 2006), "Granite Abs" (*Men's Exercise*, September 1997), and "Stomach of Steel" (*Exercise & Health*, Spring 2006). Such muscularity within health and fitness discourse was usually described as a hard man-made or natural element like "steel," "iron," "diamond," "granite," or "rock hard." Phallic references aside, others have noted how the rock hard body provides an aura of invincibility in uncertain times.

The emphasis on natural elements and suggestions of linear process of building the body through hard work links the relationship of the body to advanced technologies and the latest products that science can produce to control the fate of the human body. As was noted in chapter 1, recent cultural trends, such as increases in the size of boys' toys, male bodybuilders, male playgirl centerfolds, and male athletes, suggest a reaffirmation of a dominant muscular male identity as men struggle to redefine themselves in an era of shifting gender relations. At the same time, the common fragility of the human body is a trait that is antithetical to Western ideals and is mostly kept out of the public eye, particularly around images of masculinity.

For example, while the NFL injury rate remains at 100 percent, the average TV viewer only sees a flash of a stretcher whip across the screen when an athlete is injured, and a new, healthy, active player takes his place in a few moments. There is very little imagery concerning the long-term effects of spinal, nerve, muscular, tendon, or other injuries that most professional male athletes carry over the remaining course of their lives. Images on the nightly news show the violence in the war in Iraq, and the ensuing deaths of American soliders are counted meticulously (over 4,079 in May 2008), but few stories center on the much more common physical vulnerabilities of the injured that stand at 40 times the number of deaths when this book was going to press (as reported on www.icasualties.org).

Consumer culture morphs fragility into a moral imperative toward strength, or more specifically, the appearance of strength. The same can be said for other supermasculine figures outside of the military or team sports, such as male bodybuilders. But the analysis can't easily stay only at the frames of vulnerability and invulnerability. While size and strength are fundamental to making oneself into a faux invulnerable object—as in the words of Wacquant, "what we may call the irony of masculinity: that its dutiful pursuit leads to results nearly opposite to those it promises but with the paradoxical effect of fuelling the continued search for its elusive accomplishment" (Wacquant 1995, quote on p. 171). Size and strength are also fundamental to the creation of making oneself into a bodily object upon which others might pin their desire; historically, such links are especially important during times of war. Our analysis reveals that fitness texts did not avoid direct associations between the fit body, the military body, and the needs of the state, and we turn to an analysis of this topic next.

Idealized Masculinity and National Power

As other scholars have noted, "the concern for physical fitness, at its core, set about redeeming manhood, re-energizing masculinity, and restoring force, dynamism, and control to males in a culture full of doubts and contradictions about men's futures" (Griswold 1998). An emphasis on physical fitness has been circulated widely in public during previous times of war as well. During such times, it was (and is) not unusual to call on the populace to internalize the state's needs to expand and "strengthen" democracy by pressing for it in other regions and to prioritize the need for physical prowess, ensuring that it is built into the bodily habitus of individual civilian men.[7]

President Bush viewed the immense tragedy of September 11 as a turning point for America, and the reason to usher in the now well-known "War on Terrorism." The U.S. strategy to embrace the "expansion" of "freedom" through the "spread" of democracy was put forth as the Bush administration's "central effort." In such a war, the efforts were not going to stop, according to Bush, "until every terrorist group of global reach has been found, stopped, and defeated" (Bush 2001). Within health and fitness magazines, the fate of the nation clearly rested on the biceps of white middle-class American males in male-dominated occupations such as firefighting, the military, and law enforcement. One article reports on an "Air Force Blast: 20 Minutes to Powerful Pecs and Tris" and argues:

> Considering the current state of world affairs, it's safe to say that the preparedness of the United States Armed Forces has never been more critical. And a major aspect of this readiness is physical conditioning. With this in mind, the military has developed mission readiness physical criteria to ensure that its members are ready to roll. And if you think this means simply running a couple laps around the track and completing some push-ups and situps, guess again. (*EMO*, July 2003)

The reader is ultimately urged to serve the needs of the state—and the self—through the hardened, protective masculine form, or to simply aspire to achieve the morality and protectionism of its signifier. Consistent with Bush's new "culture of responsibility" (Bush 2001) and his call to the American populace to help fight the war on terror, the desire for military and bodily expansion meet at the very juncture where the goals of the state and the goals of a profitable multinational corporation overlap (consumption and building the body).

In January 2003, *EMO* reported, "In the post-9/11 world, the role of law enforcement in our lives has changed drastically." The article then offers a brief profile of police Officer Christian Dryer's workout. He states,

" 'We take a vow to serve and protect . . . and we live by that creed. Body-building helps me do my duty and definitely makes me a better officer of the law.' No argument here" (*EMO*, January 2003). Photographs of Christian posing with a number of different guns are followed by a detailed description of a workout for the arms. Similarly, calls for civilians to be "Ready for Action! US Marine Corps Rifle Physical Training" (*EMO*, February 2003) shows a shirtless man in camouflage pants standing outdoors —he holds a gun throughout the workout while demonstrating thigh, back, shoulder, tricep, and abdomen exercises. The gun is said to weigh 9 pounds, and readers are asked to substitute a barbell for the gun to "perform these drills."

Most of the magazines either reflect on the way in which military training will help the average man make his body and routine more like a disciplined military man or demonstrate a workout by a man dressed in military, firefighter, or police officer garb (either from an actual military program, or just a model in uniform) in order to show men how to muscle up properly. One article titled "Boot Camping! Exercises to Toughen Up" states that "nobody shapes up their charges like the Army," and men are told that "while you won't be forced to perform the regimen with a drill sergeant barking orders, it would be a good idea to make this routine a once-weekly session" (*Exercise & Health*, Spring 2006). Similarly, "Full Body Muscle: Train Your Way to Mega Mass" (*EMO*, May 2006) features Troy Saunders, who is said to be the "strongest man in the Air Force" and has won many military power lifting contests. In the article, he is shown bare chested, with a shaved head, gargantuan muscles, and he sports camouflage pants while standing out in the wilderness among the leaves. He teaches the reader (in a gym) how to do bench presses, seated rows, one arm dumbbell presses, squats, and curls.

"Power & Strength" is another article from *EMO* that pays tribute to the armed forces (December 2000). Featuring a Nordic man in camouflage army pants, dog tags, and boots, he poses with a sword near a fence, and performs a number of classic exercises like push-ups and pull-ups. Police officers, firefighters, and military personnel were all featured along with workouts that carried the legitimacy of masculine force. Men in this issue are urged to "Get Fit with the Armed Forces." The word "guns" is placed right next to the "guns" of the cover model, who has hoisted a very large gun over his shoulders. The ubiquity of the "guns" is a double entendre that further emphasizes the connection between military and bodily might.

Other state sectors also call for an inculcation of fitness in order to be the best man on the job and to remain at the top of the moral order. An article titled "Police Power—Law Enforcement Exercise" (*Men's Exercise*, September 1998) shows "The Strong Arm of the Law" (one of several times this phrase is used across men's magazines) and features an officer demonstrating a workout. The article features a white male police detective from New Jersey who is pictured in uniform on one page, shirtless and muscular on the next. He calls for his fellow officers to pass up the doughnuts during work and to lift weights outside of the office. He competes in bodybuilding contests outside of work and assists other officers in proper police training techniques. Not unlike other bodybuilders, he refers to himself as "once skinny" and claims that his peak condition makes him feel confident, might save his or other lives on the job, and helps him to perform his work duties better. Such findings remind us of the scholarly examination of the "extent to which the built body promises safety, security, and freedom while contributing to the militarization of civil society" (Saltman 2005).

This ad simultaneously encourages fitness for men by linking it to a life-saving career and professional athletics (ad shows a firefighter and a pro athlete), and masculinizes sports fashion through these same associations. (*Men's Health*, January/February 2005)

This military recruitment ad makes the sport-military link explicit through the use of a military gas mask shown through a professional football player's helmet. (*Men's Health*, December 2003)

The rock hard male body not only renders the individual body (potentially) more invulnerable, but also represents the invulnerability of the nation. Consistent with the notions of empire and power that ushered in modern Western sports during the Victorian era, dominance on the sporting field is synonymous with military and national success.[8] Just as the Duke of Wellington expressed Victorian beliefs when he observed that "the battle of Waterloo was won on the playing field of Eaton," current links between Olympic medal counts or Super Bowl wins and national military superiority reflect the potent link between the male body and military might. Hence, men are expected to visibly display not only their own success, but the success of their nation through the body.

A wealth of research has examined how sport was used in colonial periods to demonstrate the superiority of the colonizers, and the importance of sport to American society during the Cold War (Dowling 2001). Simultaneously, representations of the powerful male body offer the opportunity to deploy links between bodily capital and a habitus that will help to "get the job done" in an increasingly unstable occupational structure.

By extension, it is the flesh of individual male bodies and not the occupational structure or its harmful effects that will lead to "failure." And, as is often the case for soldiers, bodybuilders, and professional sportsmen, there exists the paradox that "the goal of the image of security comes before the safety, health, and security of the [actual] body" (Saltman 2005).

During a time in which military might is clearly a function of national spending priorities and a complex array of race/class/gender/national relations of power, the chiseled/disciplined body becomes symbolic of invulnerability precisely when the body of the soldier is rendered more irrelevant by technology. Scholars such as Ensemble and others have underscored how the "new soldier does not have to be a combat troop 'fighting eyeball to eyeball' in order to be key, even heroic, in a military effort" (Ensemble 2005) given the key roles that logistics, technologies, and intelligence now play compared to times past. While articles in fitness magazines emphasize the need for physical might, daily news stories in national newspapers underscore how troops in Iraq typically travel in armored Humvees or are themselves armored at the neck, chest, and elsewhere. In such a war, it is no longer clear who the "enemy" is; instead, the image of the omnipresent lurking terrorist is potentially everywhere.

The constant threat of terrorist attack creates more amorphous demands on the fitness of citizens called to protect their nation. Fitness magazines put forward ideologies that "indicate an assortment of practices consisting of the conversion of civilian bodies to military use and the inculcation into such bodies of military principles" (Armitage 2005). The consumer marketplace translates these demands to injunctions on individuals to construct bodies that signify power and invulnerability, even when participation in the consumer marketplace can be quite irrelevant. Articles mock the men who choose not to engage, and treat those who do like comrades in arms in a struggle that carries the weight of the nation upon well-defined deltoids. This institutionalizes a form of power relations at the fundamental level of the flesh, and negates alternatives and critiques as seemingly "unnatural." Actual victory is rendered irrelevant in the daily life of those immersed in domestic consumer culture provided one can create the appearance of a victorious body. And while such images and tropes present themselves to the reader as part of men's personal liberation, "health," moral strength, and civil responsibility, it is a process that can also be considered "at odds with democratization" (Saltman 2005).

The specificity of these signifiers (power, invulnerability) and the text used to describe them (size, strength, protection) also help to constitute a contemporary moral order that is definitively gendered. This is elucidated by considering who/what is included "inside" the sport/military frames of fitness media texts and who/what is "left out."[9] In terms of gender relations, the expanding male body and the need to make it grow for purposes of the strong state takes on its specificity of meaning in a context where (white middle-class) women are more integrated into male domains than ever before. Additionally, a specific form of racialized masculinism emerges—a more muscular nationalism is put forward that includes conceptions of subordinated masculinities—here, feminized or emasculated terrorist others who one must defend against and overpower.[10]

Despite the increasing integration of women into sports, the military, and other male-dominated occupations, women remained largely invisible in the magazines (except as prospective sexual partners, or to blame for feminizing men, as we will soon discuss). Additionally, there were no military tropes in women's fitness magazines (despite the increasing number of women serving in the armed forces), and sport remained a signifier linked largely to men while women were largely framed in the realm of fitness (as is discussed below). Instead of examining any number of social forces to explain men's increasing uncertainties in postmodern society, fitness texts commonly centered explicitly on gender relations as the cause of men's problems, reinvigorating classic fears of social feminization centered around women's annexation of male domains, and the failure to properly "masculinize" boys through socialization practices.

Fears of Physical and Social Feminization

We have already partly discussed the role of size in the relational construction of gender. Certainly, part of what underlies the role of size in masculinity is the contradistinction it makes to the ideal feminine form. When women's and men's bodies and activities have the opportunity to become more similar, fears of physical and social feminization become more prevalent. First, the sport and fitness movement has closed the gap between ideal male and female forms during a time period in which many social and cultural gender distinctions have been challenged. Increasingly, women are entering formerly male-defined spheres such as male-dominated occupations, the military, politics, and professional sports (Messner 1992; Crosset 1990; and Kimmel 1990). Second, as was discussed in chapter 2, the objectification of the body to which women have long been subjected becomes a key part of the male experience in postmodern consumer culture.

Third, while these tendencies mean a broadening of certain aspects of what constitutes masculinity, a simultaneous trend is exhibited in which there is a stigma attached to those practices most associated with femininity or the female body. In the case of fitness, working on the lower body, cardiovascular exercise, and stretching all carry the stigma of the feminine; hence, these activities are downplayed and when carried out, the stigma must be partly removed to encourage male engagement. The stigma of the feminine is removed from men's working out and engaging in consumer culture in a number of ways, for example, by linking practices to unquestionably powerful male pursuits such as sports performance, the military, or male-identified jobs. Finally, complex social relations based on race, class, nation, militarism, the needs of the state, and gender are turned into a simplistic gender war discourse that pits individual men against women. In fitness discourse, men are framed as struggling to retain their manhood and are prescribed firmer distinctions between manhood and womanhood (men are linked to sport and the military, women to fitness and service to the home) coupled with disdain for those social trends that are viewed as responsible for improvements in women's status or the creation of shared spaces.

Masculinity and Sport, Femininity and Fitness?

Fitness emerged as a more feminizing alternative to the male domain of sport at the turn of the twentieth century, and therefore it may not be surprising that it continues to require masculine markings within fitness texts by linking it to sports performance, generally in a hegemonic male sport (Crosset 1990; Kimmel 1990; Gruneau 1983). Consistent with historical links between sport, activity, and masculinity, articles were centered on increasing strength to improve a skill for some other sport, such as "Weight Training for Skiing Power" (*Men's Exercise*, January 1998), "Kicking for Martial Arts Power" (*EMO*, August 1997), or "Basketball Basics: Eight Simple Drills Will Have You Smokin' the Court" (*Men's Fitness*, March 2000). Workouts were billed as helping to improve traditional sports skills for basketball, football, or general sports performance. For example, magazines featured "Build Baseball Biceps" (*EMO*, May 2006) to argue that muscularity was not simply for the purposes of aesthetics but also for sports functioning such as throwing a baseball. Another article titled "Sport-Specific Fitness Drills" (*Exercise & Health*, Spring 1997) notes that "if it's your dream to whack a baseball out of the park, hit a golf ball incredibly long and with deadly accuracy, or slam-dunk a basketball after leaping for the rebound, one of the best places to start is the weight room."

Moreover, sports performance was akin to knowledge about fitness and weight training, and athletes' workouts were often structured with articles about a particular athlete. For example, "Jason Sehorn: Athlete Profile" (*Men's Exercise*, November 1997) profiles a football player and includes his workout. Another issue features James Bentley, a college freshman who seeks to play on a professional soccer team or in the World Cup tournament (*Men's Exercise*, January 2001). He is quoted as being "extremely aggressive and competitive" and a "furious worker who never surrenders." The article discusses how he "pumps iron furiously" and that this dramatically improves his sports performance. Similarly, *Men's Fitness* (September 2005) contained an article titled "Barbell Brawl" which teaches

New, improved MESO-TECH® has arrived to help you finally build the muscle you've always dreamed of.

Supplementing your diet with new, improved MESO-TECH® could be the best musclebuilding decision you ever make!

Masculinity is often constituted by size and sports performance while women are often represented via the ideals of emphasized femininity. (*Exercise & Health*, 2001)

This ad for a creatine body supplement demonstrates the link between masculinity, muscularity, the idealized male body, and sports. (*Exercise for Men Only*, April 2003)

men, through the principles of boxing,[11] how to fight by featuring the Ultimate Fighting Championship (UFC), a new reality TV show. The article begins by telling men to "stop wimping out. Building muscle means beating your body into submission—till it gives up and grows." Through the "warriors of the Ultimate Fighting Championship" men are shown punching and kicking one another in a ring without headgear protection, and where bleeding, breaking one another's arms, and mangling or choking one another are fair game. The article also features an instrumental use for muscle—instructions were provided for how to beat up another man if rowdiness occurs in a bar scene.

Aerobic or cardiovascular activities often were marked as male or linked to unquestionably male contexts. For example, the stigma of aerobic activity was often removed by linking it to membership in the military, police, or firefighting. Despite a seemingly widespread understanding in the fitness community that cardiovascular work helps to reduce body fat to reveal the muscles underneath, only 8 percent of the articles prescribed cardiovascular aerobic activity for men's fitness routines (though a very small sampling of articles mentioned that one should warm up with 15 minutes of cardiovascular exercise before beginning the "real" workout). One of the only articles that had the word fitness in its title in men's fitness magazines argued that the "Five Pillars of Fitness" are strength, speed, endurance, power, and agility, and featured stars from basketball, baseball, soccer, football, and hockey to demonstrate the pillars (*Men's Health*, April 2006), all of which can be characterized as sports that represent hegemonic masculinity.

The invocation of sport must be understood as an invocation of the masculine (but is still surprising considering the strong entrance of women in sport since Title IX passed), given the role certain sports have played in defining and valorizing specific forms of masculinity (Bush 2001).

By contrast, fitness activities have been long associated with femininity and achieving the ideal female form (Hargreaves 1994, 2001; Lenskyj 1986; Cahn 1994). Hence, few of the men's workouts were aerobic. When aerobic activity was featured, the taint of femininity had to be removed. Aerobics were framed as merely an afterthought that needed a reminder: "To Burn Fat, Don't Forget Aerobics!" (*Men's Exercise*, March 1998), or are marked as masculine and somehow different than women's aerobics—"Men's Aerobics for Fat Burning" (*EMO*, December 1997). At times, aerobics is linked to physical power, such as "Aerobic Fitness: Burn Fat and build explosiveness with power running" (*EMO*, December 2001). In other cases, the activity is linked to the omnipresent masculine careers and contexts. "Boot Camp Aerobics" (*EMO*, August 1997) invokes the military to demonstrate the masculinity of the context. Finally, cardiovascular exercise is masculinized by tying it to sexual performance. *Men's Fitness* (December 2001) encourages participation in cardiovascular exercise by enticing the reader to "Burn Fat, Have Great Sex." Contrary to popular advice that cardiovascular fitness is very healthy for the heart, it seemed that classic masculine and feminine separate spheres ideologies infiltrated "objective" fitness discourse.[12] For instance, "The 10 Rules of Weight Training" for men recommends:

> Keep weight training and aerobic fitness separate. Do you do resistance training with light weights and high reps as a form of cardiovascular exercise? If so, you'll certainly build muscular endurance and burn lots of calories, but in a way you're giving yourself the worst of both worlds. (*Men's Fitness*, September 1997)

However, sex was referred to as a cardiovascular activity and as having healthy benefits for the heart. Articles were even titled "Sex Protects the Heart" (*Men's Fitness*, March 2001) and the text notes that "early to bed, often to rise is the new prescription for the healthy heart." One could argue that the feminizing taint of cardiovascular activity is removed from the unquestionably masculine activity of sex.

The need for separate spheres mentality even permeated the text of actual letters from men, some of whom wrote letters to seek advice on the taint that aerobics would cause to pursuits of gaining size. One letter from a reader in *Men's Fitness* (2001) asked, "I work out about 12 hours a week, half aerobic, half weight resistance. How much aerobic activity can I do before I risk breaking down the muscles I'm trying to build?" The assumption here is that building muscle and size, not necessarily "health" and/or "fitness," is the goal that underlies men's fitness choices. By contrast, we discussed how health and fitness magazines cautioned women from using too much weight, especially in the upper body, recommending that women use the same light weight across sets to avoid increasing size, and women were frequently prescribed lower body "moves" coupled with long cardiovascular workouts in order to maintain a compact size (we will return to this point in the next chapter). The limited frame for desirable bodies constructs idealized masculinity and femininity, and the limited frame for idealized masculinity and femininity constructs "healthy," desirable bodies.

Despite the proliferation of separate spheres that might imply the safety of difference in these separations, magazines centrally emphasized men's fears of becoming feminized. Here, fears emerged from claims that gender could be socially constructed as opposed to biological. (The concept of a range of masculinities and femininities isn't even on the radar screen.) These claims were very common in articles, particularly those with the largest readerships such as *Men's Health* and *Men's Fitness*. For instance, one article (*Men's Health*, February 2000) titled "One Sex Fits All?" specifically counters any assertions that gender could be culturally produced and touts that "the parenting police tell us boys and girls are the same. We say: not in our sandbox. Men are aggressive and hierarchical, women nurturing and cooperative. That's how nature, which knew exactly what it was doing, wanted it." Another article frames men as having a mental health problem if they do not express interest in violence in sport, an interest that is assumed to be a natural part of manhood. For example, in "Ask Men's Health," in response to a reader's question about seasonal affective disorder, an expert on men's health responds that men's depression is identified with, among other things, "you lose interest in hockey brawls" (*Men's Health*, January/February 2000).

Prescription drugs are even blamed for trying to take away boys' presumed natural rowdiness, which will make them more like girls. For example, "A Man's Life" (*Men's Health*, June 2000) expresses deep concern that boys in U.S. culture are being socialized and drugged into "acting like girls." Symptoms of boys who have been feminized include: the ability to sit still and focus. The article expresses anger at what is considered to be a backlash against "normal" masculinity: "Their claim: Only by raising boys to be more like girls can we help them to become better, more acceptable boys." The magazine asserts that boys are at risk from the over-prescription of drugs like Ritalin, and are being punished for acting in normally masculine ways. The magazines paradoxically make clear through image, text, and prescribed workouts that consumer culture expects men to make them into successful objects—once reserved only for women—and then blames socialization processes and not consumer culture itself for its "feminizing" trends.

The fear that boys won't become men if they are "overly" exposed to "non"-masculinizing influences has been a popular historical debate during periods termed "crises of masculinity" where broader societal concerns emerge over what kind of men boys should grow up to be. However, while focusing on the kind of men boys should become, the answer is usually masked by assumptions of categorical difference, natural male superiority, and vitriolic assertions that boys won't grow into men at all. The implication is that men will be like women, and therefore not men. In addition to masculinism and fears of social feminization representing historical crises of masculinity, improvements in women's status in the articles were met with another common historical trend: overt antifeminism.

Backlash to Feminism and Antifeminism

As noted in chapter 1 in the discussion of Gayle Rubin's work on the sex/gender system, different activities are often prescribed for women and men and different valuations of these activities can serve to structure the specifics of a gender and sexuality order. Where challenges to difference are made through codes of similarity, backlash can result. Antifeminism is one of the modes of backlash when challenges are made to gender relations throughout the course of history.[13] Antifeminism was coded in the magazines most often on the topics of sport, crying, or on several cultural phenomena that made men's and women's behaviors look similar. Such similarity was framed as distinctly negative and as women's—and feminism's—fault. For example, in "Read 'Em and Weep," an author detailed how feminists are ruining fiction for young men. The article objected to stories about boys who are "different" and books about boys with the courage to try ballet. A "real boys reading list" accompanies the article in order to assure that boys are socialized properly into manhood (*Men's Health,* March 2000). The article cites specific objections to stories which featured female characters (in particular, having the *Little Engine That Could* be a female character was denounced) or "feel-good" messages that seemed to villainize women for "making" men emotionally "soft."

In another article titled "Why Can't I Cry?" the author takes note of the contemporary shifts in men's recent public allowances to cry. For example, the author notes that "Now things have changed, and not for the better. Michael Jordan wept profusely when he won his first NBA championship. Allen Iverson buried his head in his towel and wept during the waning minutes of a quarterfinal round loss to the Indiana Pacers a few years ago. That's right: He wept after the quarterfinals. George Steinbrenner now weeps openly about everything." The article also underscores popular fascination with the topic by describing that "*The New York Times* ran a lengthy article investigating the explosion of public weeping by athletes, citing everyone from teary-eyed Wimbledon champion Roger Federer to choked-up slugger Mike Schmidt. Not to mention Bill Clinton. . . . The implied message was clear: It was ok for rough and tumble athletes and the most powerful man to shed tears . . . so it was ok for everybody else" (*Men's Health,* August 2004). The article draws on the chairman of a counseling center in the Cal State system as an expert to explain that "feminists find this sort of statement infuriating, but there exists both a physiological and a cultural reason why women cry more frequently and copiously than men." At the end of the article, the author states that to help his own plight of not being able to cry, he wishes to "get myself reborn into an ethnic group that actually has emotions." In this way, dominant men remain different from and superior to both women and subordinated masculinities.

Numerous articles expressed disdain for women's "inferior" physical abilities, anger at women's perceived "advantages" in acquiring healthcare funding (for issues like breast cancer) at the expense of men's health (for issues like prostate cancer), and many articles addressed socialization trends that treated boys and girls similarly. For example, a *Men's Fitness* article in 2001 notes, in an "active man's guide to damn near everything" that "We can't dress ourselves, but at least we can throw." The article notes that "*You throw like a girl*! is no longer just a chauvinist taunt—it now has some science behind it. A study by the U.S. National Institute of Health and Human Development tested how accurately people could toss objects into a bucket placed nine or eighteen feet away. On average, men hit the target 32 percent more often than women did. See, we knew all those years of Nerfhoops would pay off." No mention is made of whether the two samples of women and men were comparable according to sporting experience or participation.

Other antifeminist stances take place around the topics of sexual assault and violence. For example, one article centers on "male-friendly" colleges that were described to increase the attractiveness of college attendance for men, with male-unfriendly colleges being defined as those that "prosecute sexual assault." Another article, "One Sex Fits All" (*Men's Health*, February 2000), argues that if you "fight biology you get zapped," noting that a mother who would not let her son play with toy guns found sticks shaped like pistols and "shot the hell out of his mom when she came to pick him up." In the same article, the author also explains that sport is naturally suited for boys and not girls, and that parents should not socialize sons and daughters into thinking that they can both play sports adequately. He argued that "these days, boys and girls are supposed to be the same, and you're not permitted to treat them differently." The author states: "This, anyway, is the party line of the PC loudmouths, which, increasingly, the larger culture has pliantly picked up. In the wake of the recent triumph of the U.S. women's team in World Cup soccer, a major corporation tried to cash in on this sentiment with a refrigerator commercial showing a couple viewing their unborn child via sonogram. When he learns that he will soon be a dad to a little girl, the man's attitude is, 'Makes no difference; we'll play sports together just the same was if she were my son.' My thought when I watched this commercial was that although this guy may love his new fridge, he'll end up one disappointed father."

Previous work underscores how discourses of sport and natural gender difference are strategically pursued by men during times of shifting gender relations. For example, in Messner's analysis of retired professional male athletes in his work titled *Power at Play: Sports and the Problem of Masculinity* (1992), he turns to an in-depth interview with a white working-class male whose workplace has promoted a woman to a position of authority. Messner asks how the man feels about this and he replies: "A woman can do the same job as I can do—maybe even be my boss. But I'll be damned if she can go out on the football field and take a hit from Ronnie Lott." Messner argues that sport serves an important purpose in the lives of men during times of rapidly changing gender relations since hegemonic male sports (football, basketball, baseball) "gives testimony to the undeniable 'fact' that here is one place where men are clearly superior to women" (1992). At the same time, he underscores that it is also true that most men could not take a hit from Ronnie Lott either. Differences among men are often ignored when the strategic (re)construction of gender relations takes place in the face of having to contend with evidence of contestation in the gender order. In a time of complex and rapid global changes whereby both men and women experience increasing uncertainty, a nostalgic desire for a previous mythic institutional and ideological gender order emerges.

In the past, such crises were usually resolved in the institutional realm, but in a third wave crisis of masculinity within postindustrial consumer culture, the crises and its resolution rest on the symbolic level and at the level of the flesh of the individual American male body. This is paradoxical, as consumer culture assists hegemonic men in making them into successful objects, a task once reserved for womanhood and subordinated masculinities, and then necessarily reiterates the masculinity of the task in both image and text through institutional links.

Conclusion: Consumer Culture, Male Body Panic, and the Third Wave Crisis of Masculinity

The sport and fitness movement, the success of the second wave feminist movement, an increase of women in male realms, an increasing role of fathers in family life, and broader emotional displays for the most privileged men have closed the gap between ideal male and female behaviors. Simultaneously, as was discussed in chapter 2, the objectification of the body to which women have long been subjected has become a central part of the male experience in postmodern consumer culture. As possibilities for similarity emerge, some argue that increases in men's body size can be described as a "masculinist" response to changes in men's and women's roles and positions in society where incontrovertible evidence of men's physical superiority is reiterated. Our analysis has underscored the importance not only of examining the size of the male body within media texts such as magazines, but also of examining the text of articles that describe what male and female bodies are, can do, and should do.

Our analysis is analogous to what Kimmel chronicles concerning how men respond to "crises in masculinity" that occur when there are rapid shifts in gender roles. These three responses include profeminism (those efforts that support gender equality), masculinism (those efforts that reinforce separate spheres and value all-male realms as different from and superior to women), and antifeminism (hostility toward women's advances) (Kimmel 2000). The first crisis in masculinity was said to occur at the turn of the nineteenth century with changes in work and family life and the rise of first wave feminism that culminated in women's right to vote. Examples of a masculinist response to a historical crisis in masculinity during the nineteenth century are the development of all-male organizations such as the boy scouts and the institution of sport. Such responses were believed to be necessary given that they provided men with separate all-male environments which (a) affirmed men as different from and superior to women; (b) allowed for masculinist rituals and male bonding; and (c) constructed physical and psychological "manliness" as a response to women's increasing access to institutions that lead to fears that boys and men would be feminized by women (ibid.). We found several of these trends in our contemporary analysis of men's health and fitness texts.

The "second" crisis of masculinity in the 1960s and 1970s occurred when gains made by (largely white) women during the second wave feminist movement again challenged gender roles and male hegemony. In response to this crisis, some scholars have emphasized how the formation of various masculinist and antifeminist men's movements such as the Promise Keepers, the Million Man March, and the mythopoetic men's movement emerged (Messner 1997). The second wave women's movement which provided increasing opportunities for women's entrance into male-dominated realms is often touted in the public forum as "ruining" and feminizing men, and much antifeminist public discourse emerged (e.g., "feminazis"). While previous analyses have emphasized the responses offered by men in terms of social movements and institutional responses, our own analysis at the level of consumer cultural trends finds similarities at the level of image and text.

In a third wave crisis of masculinity, despite evidence of a cultural convergence between women's and men's imagery/posings and prescribed

practices that we examined in chapter 2, it is clear that these symbols remain bounded and contextualized by institutional and structural forces in
the culture at large. For example, men's bodies in fitness magazines were
clearly linked to displays of hegemonic masculinity through signifiers of
size/power, sport, and military, while women's bodies were clearly more
limited to fitness, toning and reduced size, and service to the home (as
we will see in the next chapter). The consumption of valued products and
practices to construct a large body in a third wave crisis do paradoxically
shift gender relations by increasingly marking men's success as making
oneself into the right kind of object. Cultural trends such as these have
also extended physical definitions of heterosexuality for dominant men
to include the "metrosexual" (mentioned in chapter 2—a self-identified
heterosexual man who takes on the signifiers and markings of gay male
culture) with qualities that were previously considered feminized characteristics (e.g., grooming, hair styling, shopping). Such codes also allow for
the facilitation of desire from gay men and women to be hoisted upon
heterosexual male bodies, destabilizing the 100 percent heterosexual gaze
that is assumed in many cultural corners and is explicitly unmarked in
the magazines.[14]

But a third wave crisis of masculinity cannot stop at an analysis of gender relations (as the other two waves of analysis should not have) and our
analysis should not only extend an examination of contemporary versions
of this crisis to the realms of the body and consumption. It is true that
the dictums of consumer culture, bodies as national figurations, changing gender relations, and fears of social feminization combine to generate the cultural conditions conducive to male body panic. The specificity of the signifiers (size, protection) that emerge to respond to changes
in broader society help to constitute a contemporary moral order based
not only on gender, but on race, class, and nation as well. That is, actual
men in hegemonic sports and the military are disproportionately subordinated masculinities (men of color, working-class men) while models in
the magazines depicted as moral and responsible for protection are overwhelmingly white and middle class (see chapter 2).

The demographics of the magazine readers are largely middle class,
while the "enemies" (e.g., "criminals," "terrorists") who men must build
themselves up to protect against are disproportionately of lower socioeconomic status or are perceived as a feminized Middle Eastern other
who is left out of the muscular frame.[15] Domestic increases in spending on prison systems and policing surges in a context of vast inequities

between rich and poor (Reiman 2000), while fears of becoming a "victim" to criminals or terrorists feed the perceived need for (imagery and discourses of) corporeal protection. Thus, it is vital to remember that "the norm against which male bodies were defined" (in previous times of war, and we would add in times when there are perceptions of increasing crime) "was set by the suitability of the body for combat. At the outbreak of war, the classification of the body created a single powerful construction of physical, and by implication, moral fitness. Bodies are always immersed in cultural and normative presuppositions in wartime, not only within but also outside the military environment" (Chanter 1999, as cited in Penniston-Bird 2005).

At the same time that signifiers of fitness include those of the moral citizen or man, circulating representations of the powerful male body also offer the opportunity to deploy ideas about bodily capital that are definitively linked to a habitus that will help to "get the job done" in an increasingly unstable occupational structure. The importance of bodily display as a means to establish and negotiate social status is made clear, but asking men to internalize individualized solutions to structural problems is problematic, as it is likely that muscles, strong abs, and a new tie or shirt cannot resolve ongoing global complexities. Just as corporations profit from offering the most privileged women "Just Do It" (e.g., Nike) slogans which tout empowerment to women by selling liberal feminist ideologies of freedom through an individualized, fit bodily politics (Cole and Hribar 1995; Dworkin and Messner 1999), men too are falsely sold masculinist promises that fit bodies will likely not bring. Furthermore, as is consistent with much of American ideology, while bigger is thought to be better (Ritzer 2004; also see Baudrillard 1998; Baumann 1999), the costs of such expansion for men (or this form of spreading American "democracy") are never discussed in terms of health.

Baudrillard, Bauman, and others critique consumer culture as unquestioningly privileging the idea of economic growth (Baudrillard 1998; also see Baumann 1999). They argue that growth itself is predicated on inequality, and that affluence and poverty are both dispassionately produced by economic structures. Neoliberal market imperatives toward growth such as these are literally embodied in men's ever-expanding bodies while making it men's responsibility to impart "health" through masculinism. As Baudrillard notes in his work, *The Consumer Society*, the fundamental growth imperative of consumer markets must be understood as inherently problematic since growth creates the ills that then require further market expansion to alleviate. In the same way, male body panic creates an ever-expanding set of dictums, often designed to undo the effects of other practices.

We argue that male body panic is not simply a pathology of individual men as other scholars have claimed, nor is it a reasonable response to a perceived or actual obesity crisis, nor is it a realistic fear of the loss of social status that accompanies a failing body. Body panic relies on healthism —the idea that the individual is responsible for the health of the self and the nation—to simultaneously displace critiques of the social structure onto individual bodily failures and onto gender relations, while stigmatizing those who fail to participate and succeed in the existing system. Body panic marshals resources to a morally valued but socially depoliticized subject in their continual quest for bodily perfection. Those who are privileged enough to be able to participate are able to wield a valuable form of capital[16] and enjoy the pleasures of producing valued identities, thus making the project appealing, yet they experience a real cost to failure, further inducing body panic. Indeed, some argue that broader economic concerns such as the dismantling of social safety nets, social security, public schools and universities, welfare, social services, and health care "intensifies and accelerates" bodily anxieties and undermines collective action that can tend to the cause of the insecurities (Saltman 2005).

Although magazines suggest that successful bodily capital will translate into success in the workplace and in life, what is the actual transferability of bodily capital to the workplace or elsewhere? While this question needs empirical testing, there are researchers who have been interested in the question of whether bodily capital easily transfers to other realms, such as the occupational structure.[17] We suspect, given our read of other work and our understanding of social justice principles, that those who have the most institutional privilege are most likely to be able to garner the benefits from successfully acquiring signifiers of the fit body. This is because social and bodily capital may intersect among the most privileged men in unique ways that can maximize its benefits in several realms. We also suspect that subordinated masculinities (men of color, working-class men) would be most likely to pay the costs of garnering individualized bodily capital, as the occupational structure that requires such signifiers comes with its own set of occupational insecurities and job/health hazards (e.g., NFL, boxing).[18]

Thus, some argue that the cultural capital that individuals acquire through the body can be selectively deployed by more privileged individuals for their benefit, as a type of "mobile resource" (Skeggs 2004), or it can be overwritten onto the bodies of the marginalized and used as evidence of their sense of "lack," immorality, or being an "other." Overall, consumer culture reflects, produces, and changes the symbolic economy through the creation of values that are "deemed to inhere in certain types of bodies, but that nonetheless can sometimes be selectively adopted by others as additional resources or forms of capital within particular contexts"(ibid.). We recognize that even though we deploy an analysis of body panic as a contemporary form of more diffuse moral panics, individuals may reproduce, resist, or challenge the preferred meanings contained in media representations. How dominant and marginalized categories (and intersections of the two) read and interpret the "folk devils" and "folk angels" within media frames could be determined even more effectively through an audience analysis instead of our reliance on imagery and textual analysis.

At the same time, we have examined how, within the cultural realm, inclusion in the fit frame involves the reflection and production of "natural" notions of manhood. This is the case, even as these are also clearly constructed, from the careful prescription of the placement of muscle to its size, all predicated on and depicting a moral and symbolic order that is corporeal and is simultaneously gendered, classed, racialized. These bodies are also contextualized and shaped for productive purposes and instrumental need in the overlap between consumerist desires for profit, identity-producing validation, and the needs of the neoliberal state. In the next chapter, we again examine the racialized, classed, and gendered corporeal form within consumerist fit culture. This time, we expand the analysis of morality and health to include fit mothers and the pregnant female form in a relatively new fitness magazine for women, *Shape Fit Pregnancy.*

4

"Getting Your Body Back"

Postindustrial Fit Motherhood and the Merger of the Second (Household Labor/Child Care) and Third (Fitness) Shifts

Researchers have noted how feminine ideals have shifted from social behaviors such as privatized domesticity to contemporary gendered norms that include dual-career couples, more involved fathers, and a merging of public and private roles for all (Gillis 1996; Skolnick 1994; Stacey 1996). For both women and men, many argue that valuations have now moved toward appearances within consumption-based postindustrial society (Featherstone and Turner 1995; Goffman 1979, 1976; Lowe 1995). As has been described in this text and elsewhere, obtaining a valued appearance requires the consumption of a host of goods and services that assist individuals in adhering to an ever-changing set of gendered ideals (Featherstone 1991a).

Fitness has certainly played a key role in the production of the gendered body. Adding the pregnant form to an analysis of fitness and gendered bodily norms offers a unique opportunity to extend established arguments on feminism, bodies, and sexuality. Specifically, a new area of feminist analysis opens up when considering the corporeal tensions faced by the contemporary pregnant woman: exactly at the moment when a woman's body is accomplishing a highly valued route to femininity, she is least likely to be viewed as aesthetically ideal.

Given more widespread acceptance of women's sport and fitness activities, the way that feminism has stretched bodily norms to include unprecedented levels of physical strength, and the fact that "nobody" escapes bodily objectification in postindustrial consumer culture (Bordo 1999; Pope, Phillips, and Olivardia 2000), it is particularly timely that a new fitness magazine emerged in 1997 titled *Shape Fit Pregnancy*. The magazine is devoted to pregnant women's "pre- and post-partum fitness needs."

This chapter examines how *Shape Fit Pregnancy* frames and resolves the cultural tensions between classic definitions of motherhood as nurturance and contemporary ideals that prescribe toned, taut, fit femininity for women.

Fitness, Feminism, Pregnancy, and the Body

The female body is often framed as failing in myriad ways so as to encourage adherence to an always shifting, idealized "feminine" form (Bordo 1993; Synnott 1993). This is of course lucrative for multinational corporations, since profit is sustained from continually developing new ideologies of "bodily lack" for both men and women. As we've been describing throughout *Body Panic*, flesh or fat on the body has been framed as a signifier of excessiveness and being out of control, but it is also a particularly strong devaluation of the feminine, and is viewed as failed individual morality needing earthly discipline. This is especially the case within Western culture given Christian asceticism, and a Cartesian mind/body dualism, but is increasingly true within cultures influenced by the West (Bordo 1993; Grogan 1999).

Adding pregnancy to the analysis of the gendered body reveals the unique plights associated with femininity and the maternal body. Mothers' bodies in particular were presented as needing technocratic medicalized procedures in the twentieth century given the rise of Fordist assembly-line logic and industrial production (Davis-Floyd 1993; Martin 1992). This logic then shifted in postindustrial consumer culture to an emphasis on resolving the Madonna/whore dichotomy through the making of the sexualized "hot mama." Such tensions have been explored in research that uncovers how breastfeeding was framed as central to maternal responsibilities in the 1960s while the shapeliness of the breast was viewed as at risk. From the 1980s to the present, breast-feeding is still viewed as a maternal duty but is also frequently sold under the rubric that it "burns extra calories" and facilitates rapid weight loss (Blum 1999). In contemporary Western cultures, then, selling the sexualized possibilities of the maternal body allowed for pregnant women—for better or for worse—to participate in the cult of objectification and bodily surveillance from which they had been previously "excluded." Inclusion has meant that the maternal body has been caught between popular cultural health messages (e.g., doing what is best for the baby) and imperatives for women to have slim and sexy bodies (note that the name of the magazine is *Shape Fit Pregnancy*, and does not include the term health).

Some researchers have argued that media imagery and texts define pregnant women's bodies as particularly unruly and in need of fitness discipline (Bordo 1993). While many women internalize such messages, other researchers have noted how women may reject such ideals since pregnancy offers a unique opportunity for women to find freedom from norms of physical containment. That is, similar to bodybuilding, pregnancy can potentially offer women a transgressive opportunity to take up more physical space than is normally allowed under patriarchal definitions of womanhood (Bailey 2001; Heywood 1998). Finally, some research underscores how women feel relieved when released from the demands of feminine bodily requirements during pregnancy given a more "functional" emphasis on the body Bailey 2001).

Given that the pregnant body is particularly resistant to containment, it may not be surprising that research reveals that many women feel overwhelmingly unattractive during pregnancy. This is because the already difficult to achieve tight, toned body that exemplifies emphasized femininity is even more unattainable at this time (Hofmeyr, Marcus, and Butchart 1990). Instead of viewing this process as something that is "natural" for mothers and as therefore being exempt from the dictates of the consumer market, intensification of consumer prescriptions and self-surveillance can result. The market is certainly there to step in during such times of need because, as Spitzack notes, women are culturally required to confess bodily transgressions since "encouragement for female confessional is proportional to women's resistance towards traditional depictions of femininity. Arguably, confessions are demanded of women with greatest urgency precisely when women are most actively involved in a questioning of, and potential resistance to, dominant representations" (Spitzack 1990, p. 62). In other words, instead of the potential for the market to capitalize from women's rejections of having to adhere to emphasized femininity during pregnancy, larger cultural imperatives that define women's bodies as deserving of size control are intensified. Spitzack links this process explicitly to the confessional process and argues:

> A recounting of wrongs, in other words, assumes knowledge of correct or morally acceptable thoughts and behaviors. Moral imperatives ground the confession, and in fact, it signifies an internationalization of "truth"

as represented in scripture. As in panoptic power, the confession forces one to see the "truth" about oneself through continuous self-inspection, accepting with humility and graciousness absolution from those who legislate the "truth." (1990, p. 59)

Feminist researchers have underscored how women do not frequently critique larger cultural norms as problematic; rather, many self-blame and internalize a sense of private bodily failure, embarking on fitness routines, plastic surgery, and dieting practices to rectify anxieties about bodily lack (Bartky 1988; Duncan 1994).

Feminist researchers have also critically analyzed how multinational fitness campaigns have successfully sold anxieties about "bodily lack" to women through the commodification of ideologies of feminist empowerment (e.g., choice, control, winning, "having it all") in a larger climate of declining social activism and dissipating social movements (Cole and Hribar 1995; Dworkin and Messner 1999). The implications for women are complex, since ideologies of fit empowerment can paradoxically intensify women's own bodily self-surveillance. However, increased agency can also result for some women; for instance, researchers have highlighted how feminism and sport intersect to stretch physical ideals well beyond docility to include physical empowerment, independence, muscularity, and athletic competence (Heywood and Dworkin 2003; Theberge 2000). It is clear that the tension between the physical experiences of pregnancy and the dictates of gendered bodily norms allows for corporations to capitalize on intensified feelings of anxiety about the body to sell the "benefits" of fitness to pregnant women.

Our main research question in this chapter concerns how and to what extent fitness texts deploy discourses of self-surveillance and feminism to resolve societal tensions surrounding pregnant form. How is feminist discourse used, if at all, when viewing the pregnant form as a highly valued route to femininity (motherhood/birth) while being simultaneously far removed from dominant aesthetic ideals of femininity (toned, taut)? First, we underscore a key feminist tension surrounding pregnant women's bodies within health and fitness discourse: that the pregnant form is presented as maternally successful yet aesthetically problematic, in need of "getting your body back." Next, we show how contemporary mothers are defined as responsible for *both* a second shift of household labor and childcare *and* a new "third shift" of fitness practices.

Recent work suggests that heterosexually married (often middle-class) women now need even more endurance—not only to sustain a first shift (paid labor) and a second shift (childcare and household responsibilities), but also to carry out a "third shift"—fitness regimens that allow for adherence to the latest bodily requirements (Dworkin and Messner 1999; Dworkin 2001). The third shift is daunting not only in terms of time and energy, but due to the unique way in which contemporary ideals of compact emphasized femininity clash with the pregnant form. Finally, we examine the way in which fitness discourse paradoxically draws on "empowerment" discourse derived from feminist gains of access to the public sphere while (re)inscribing women to the privatized realm of bodily, consumptive, and fit family values.

We use textual analysis to uncover how fitness discourse and practices constitute fit womanhood for pregnant women and new mothers in issues of *Shape Fit Pregnancy* from 1997 to 2006. It is vital to keep in mind that in a postindustrial economy, media serve primarily as a vehicle to produce audience-viewing time for advertisers (Jhally 1989). Certainly, not all lifestyles and bodies are featured indiscriminately; rather, relations of power work to define content in articles and ads to capture the attention of a specific target demographic. In order to ascertain who made up this demographic, we conducted a phone interview with the sales staff at *Shape Fit Pregnancy* in the summer of 2001. At that time, the annual readership for the publication was 1.8 million women, with a median age of 28. Sixty-three percent were employed, 72 percent had attended or completed college, and the median household income of the membership base was $58,706 (compared to $41,990 nationally, according to U.S. Census data).

We called back in the spring of 2003 and found that the median age stayed the same, while readership had risen only slightly, to 1.9 million women. Median income had dropped to $50,168, and 64 percent of readers at that time had attended or completed college. We made a final follow-up phone call in the spring of 2006 and found that the median age remained the same, readership had risen to 2.2 million, 55 percent were employed, 81 percent had attended or completed college, and the median household income rose somewhat from the prior year, to $53,590. In this way, the readership could certainly be described as middle class, and is described by the magazine producers as "young, intelligent, affluent, and professional." Staff stated that the magazine did not collect information about racial or ethnic status in their membership base. In the final phone call, the sales agent noted that "8 percent of the readership is now male."

Debuting in the late 1990s at a peak in women's sports and fitness, *Shape Fit Pregnancy* is owned by Weider Corporation, one of the largest publishers of health and fitness magazines. Weider also publishes numerous other health and fitness magazines such as *Shape, Fitness, Muscle & Fitness, Men's Health,* and *Men's Fitness.* Due to the intensification of conglomeration, we have noted that relatively few corporations own, produce, and distribute most of what is read in newspapers and magazines (Herman and Chomsky 1988). While we acknowledge that media texts can be read by individuals in resistant and polysemic ways (Fiske 1994), it is also true that the maneuverings of multinationals limit the number of texts and the ideologies that are presented to a mass audience. While multiple and competing ideologies continually contest the terms at play, we focus here on the "preferred meanings" in the text of fitness articles.[1] In fact, publishers of magazines tend to rotate a small package of preferred meanings in the featured articles each month.

Using textual analysis, then, we focus on the cultural assumptions underlying the text of articles in *Shape Fit Pregnancy* that make workouts their central focus. Our exploration of the underlying assumptions contained in the logic of media texts is key to what is called "studying up" on contemporary cultural ideologies (Kane and Pearce 2002). As we've noted, this technique is often used for grounded theoretical approaches such as textual analysis in media studies in order to provide the empirical basis for critiques of preferred and/or hegemonic messages (Messner 1996). We examined all available issues from April 1997 to the present. The final sample included 25 magazines and 67 fitness articles. We had two research assistants distinguish the type of workout offered (e.g., cardiovascular, yoga, "moves," weight work), where the workout was shown (indoors, outdoors), the perceived race of the model, and any language that referenced gender (for example, "women are not just baby machines" or "dads should give new moms a break"). From this open coding scheme, we mapped the full range of themes that emerged, and subsequently developed three main categories of analysis that were cited most frequently in the text of the articles. The modal themes that constituted the preferred meanings were: (1) start training for labor; (2) getting your body back; (3) the required intersection of a second shift of household labor/childcare with a third shift of fitness. These modal themes form the basis for the analysis.

The New Pregnant Woman: Start Training for Labor

While the pregnant female form was once prescribed rest and restricted from physical activity, contemporary fitness discourse advocates training for the physical demands of labor. *Shape Fit Pregnancy* embraces and even requires fitness for a smooth pregnancy and delivery. Cardiovascular work, light weight work, yoga, and upper and lower body "moves" are all prescribed as appropriate and necessary to ease pain and stay in shape during and after pregnancy. While pregnant women are cautioned about using heavy weights, they are told that there are "no reasons to stop pumping iron" during or after pregnancy (Spring 1997). Many of the weight workouts involved upper and lower body "moves" or body resistance (34 percent) and light weights (19 percent)—those that are considered central to helping women to conform to the dictums of emphasized femininity. Cardiovascular work was commonly prescribed (15 percent) as a workout in the articles, along with walking and hiking (10 percent), using babies as weight barbells or as weight resistance for pilates (12 percent), yoga (7 percent), and stretching (8 percent).

The majority of the models shown carrying out the workouts were white (81 percent), while 10 percent were black or African American, 3 percent were Asian or Asian American, and 5 percent were biracial. Paid labor was not mentioned in 95 percent of the articles despite the fact that 55–63 percent of the readership was employed according to demographic data on the readership for the years of the magazine that made up our sample. Workouts were often but not solely prescribed for appearance-oriented or aesthetic goals. Fitness was often touted for how it can be used to instrumentally accomplish tasks—the tasks of pregnancy and delivery itself.

Instead of emphasizing the health benefits of fitness for the mother or for a healthy child, many of the prenatal fitness articles hone in on how fitness activities train women to get in shape for delivery, making it easier, quicker, less painful, and requiring less time to "bounce back." Few workout articles focus solely on scientific health benefits of fitness for pregnancy. An exception was an article which relied on the *American Journal of Public Health*, where medical experts offered that "women who did moderate to high amounts of exercise while pregnant had almost half the risk of pre-term delivery compared with non-exercisers; they also had a significantly lower risk of delivering after their due date" (Winter 1999). According to new research, the article claims, "staying active during pregnancy isn't just safe, it bestows important benefits." The listed benefits include: fewer varicose veins, less shortness of breath, lower risk of Cesarean, improved stamina and pain endurance, less leg swelling, cramps, backache, and shorter labor.

Prenatal fitness prescriptions do focus on relieving physical tension, lessening back strain and pain, and strengthening the abdominal muscles used during delivery. For instance, in an article titled "Focus on Delivery," prenatal exercises such as modified sit-ups are offered to "help expectant mothers to better carry their babies and strengthen the muscles that will be stressed during delivery" (Spring 1997). In another issue, women are warned that if "you haven't prepared your muscles, labor can take an uncomfortable toll on your body" (Summer 1999). Some articles note that the training is preparation for labor specifically during the "pushing phase" (December/January 2005). While the abdominals are cited as the key to pushing the baby through the birth canal, this is not always presented in the context of helping delivery, fostering better health, or embracing women's strength. At times, the prescriptions are blanketed in a discourse of maternal care, for instance, women are asked to answer the question of whether they are "taking good care" of their abdominal muscles, for these are the ones that "literally hug your baby" (Spring 2000).

Unlike previous public and medicalized discourse that highlighted the way in which fitness might ruin femininity, motherhood, and the reproductive organs, athletic analogies are now strategically deployed by media to normalize fitness as necessary for the "big event" of delivery. Fitness is touted to "help to make the big day easier" and it is reported that "if you were planning to run a 10K, you'd probably prepare for it by gradually increasing your mileage. So too, should you train for labor" (Summer 1999). A 2001 article agrees that "strong muscles help to endure the marathon of labor" (December/January 2001) while another argues that "just like any other athlete preparing for an event, exercise that you do while pregnant should mimic the circumstances you'll eventually experience" (December/January 2001). The training is mostly physical, but also involves some mental preparation. For instance, "Do It Right" highlights how women need to "train mentally and physically" to be prepared "for the day you'll deliver" (Spring 1997). Women are reminded that delivery is like a race, for as they "head into the final stretch," it is important to "remember to keep eating right and exercising" so that "you're in the best possible shape for labor and delivery" (June/July 2002).

Historically, sport and fitness have been analyzed as bodywork that is both industrious and involves regimes of internalized self-surveillance (Bartky 1988; Rigauer 1981). For women, fitness discourse now prescribes fit femininity as being highly compatible with motherhood, deploying athletic analogies to make "winning" deliveries possible. While there may be empowering aspects of being in shape or taking care of oneself upon entering the delivery room, placing the emphasis on women's control of her body negates the numerous medical processes outside of women's control that are often involved during birth (Davis-Floyd 1993). Paradoxically, then, feminist discourse is being deployed to train women for labor precisely when women are increasingly subject to high-tech medicalized gadgetry that often renders the birth process more passive (ibid.). It may also be paradoxical that the very act (athletics) that once defined women as unfit for public life now demands adherence to the capitalist work ethic for successful motherhood. At the same time, it is clear that the pregnant body needs training not only for the actual process of giving birth, but also for containing the unruly pregnant form. For example, articles explain that "no matter how big your belly gets, nicely toned arms and legs will help you feel beautiful" (June/July 2005). Once a woman gives birth, many of the magazine themes switch directly from training for labor to women's familial and feminine duty that includes "getting their body back."

"Getting Your Body Back": Bouncing Back as Dutiful Femininity

Ideals of contemporary motherhood now prescribe a new set of tasks beyond the first shift of work and the second shift of household labor and childcare. There is now a required third shift of bodywork (Dworkin and Messner 1999). After birth, there are clear warnings that "letting the body go" constitutes failed womanhood and motherhood. Featured article titles in *Shape Fit Pregnancy* indicate this rather explicitly in their titles, and include "Secrets to Bouncing Back," "Getting Your Body Back," "Bouncing Back After Baby," and "Bounce Back Better Than Ever."

Getting one's body back is normalized not only in the titles of articles, but also the text, where the prescribed exercises make clear that the goal is to erase the physical evidence of motherhood so as to "resemble" the "prepregnancy self" (Fall 1997). For instance, "sexy" or "beautiful" "mamas" are aided with "keeping your midsection in prime form during and after pregnancy" (May 2000). Another article titled "Exercises for Strong, Lovely Limbs" reminds women to "look forward to the days where they can see their legs again" (October 2000). "Strollercizing" the waist away is suggested (Winter 1999), along with moves, light weight work, and several cardiovascular exercises. Celebrity "secrets for dropping the baby fat fast" are shared through custom-designed workouts from star trainers (June/July 2004). Regaining control of the unruly pregnant form is normalized in pursuit of an openly stated central goal: to return to one's former size. It is noteworthy that 81 percent of the featured models in the workouts are white, underscoring not only the racialized, classed nature of the target demographic, but also the way in which ideals of maternal beauty are racialized and classed.

In one article, a white woman is pictured with short brown hair, sitting on a step in (what is presumably) her house. She is clothed in a long

Left: This ad is for "back-to-normal" undergarments which help women to "get their body back" after pregnancy and birth. (*Shape Fit Pregnancy,* Summer 1997). *Right*: As this ad reveals, women are not only responsible for "Getting one's body back" following delivery, but are expected to maintain it as much as possible throughout. Adhering to emphasized femininity and remaining as "sexy" as possible without showing many signs of pregnancy is desirable. (*Shape Fit Pregnancy*, August/September 2002)

Discourses of "taking care of the self" during pregnancy are merged with keeping sexy for a male partner. (*Shape Fit Pregnancy,* August/September 2002).

white sweater, and has a baby on her lap. Her eyes are glancing upward at a child, perhaps two years old, who is standing above her on a step, tiny hands draped over her mother's shoulders. The mother's lean, tanned, long, toned legs stretch out past her sweater, and she has no pants on. One can only speculate as to whether the partly undressed mother is preparing for a gaze that belongs to her husband or if it is simply sublimated into the gaze found in the culture at large. Ads throughout the magazine seem to imply the former. In this article, gently sandwiched between two sets of little hands, amidst smiles and warmth, there is a bright, soft white light that illuminates the three bodies. The article is titled "A Family Affair: An All-Over Strengthening and Shaping Program That New Moms Can Do With Their Babies" (Winter 1997). The text opens with the naming of the problem: "Now that your baby has arrived, you may be wondering which you'll regain sooner: your pre-pregnancy shape or a sense of control in your life. Thankfully, an exercise program could be the solution to both" (Winter 1997).

Articles define the postpartum body as chaotic, disorderly, and stressful: "Your Baby's Perfect, Your Body's Beat, You're Blissful, You're Blue" and "You're Probably Most Distressed to Discover Your Own Body Out of Shape" (February/March 2000). New mothers are said to be "primed for anxiety" (Fall 1997), and bodily "discoveries" are framed as sinful, out of control, shameful, or as evidence of a lax body that must be quickly corrected. Women are described through their confessionals of bodily excess[2] through feelings of being "caught off guard" while asserting that "I hadn't expected to feel out of control, nor had I known that pregnancy and childbirth would be a completely body-changing experience" (Spring 1998).

Despite the clear mandate for bodily surveillance of the pregnant form that is implied by the need to fix such "discoveries," the text paradoxically deploys cultural tropes of empowerment from feminism. Specifically, "taking control" of the body through exercise is undergirded by a discourse of liberal feminist empowerment and choice (Cole and Hribar 1995). New mothers are framed as strong, empowered women who can easily handle any leftover gender inequality that exists. One issue features an article which explains that there are men who will use "the old mindset" and tell women to "sit down" when pregnant. Such a mindset is said to be problematic in contemporary society since women can "break free" through

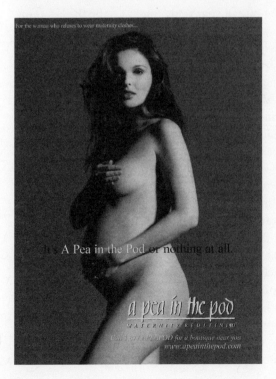

For the woman who refuses to wear maternity clothes...

A Pea in the Pod or nothing at all.

a pea in the pod
MATERNITY REDEFINED

www.apeainthepod.com

While the content of the magazine focused on empowerment, feminism, and smashing leftover gender inequality, the ads imply that an empowered woman "refuses to wear maternity clothes" (caption of the ad) while revealing a near-perfect naked form. (*Shape Fit Pregnancy*, April/May 2000) exercise (December 2001). Exercise is framed as evidence of a liberated woman and shows that a woman is "not just a baby machine" and that you "are doing something for yourself" (Spring 1997). The "revolution" for this target demographic is clearly framed solely as a gendered one, and "breaking free" from oppression only requires individualized Nike-style decisions to "just do" exercise while caring for one's baby.

Fitness is not simply framed as an empowering haven for the self, but as an entire regime of gendered bodily practices that is required by a postindustrial speed-up. Time is of the essence, as it is clear that bouncing back should be tended to immediately—even the day after giving birth. New moms are warned that fitness "should be at the top of your postpartum list," while others emphasize that being a new mother should not stop fitness at any time: "you can even just do abdominal contractions or Kegels while you're feeding the baby" (Winter 1998). Notes one article: "No-one expects you to look like a super model right after giving birth," "but you can regain strength, tone, and flexibility" and "begin doing mild exercise the day after you've had your baby" (April/May 2000). Articles note that "You've got enough to worry about with a brand new baby" and it is understood that "taking care of your body might just be the last thing on your mind," but "here's an easy way to get back in shape" with an "at-home routine" that will "help you get back into prepregnancy shape fast!" (December/January 2005).

Despite a few sparse suggestions that women "shouldn't even think about stepping on a scale after delivery," due to water gain (August/September 2002), or that women should cut themselves some "slack" since the goal is to "relax and enjoy your baby and your body" (Summer 1997), excuses for not exercising are defined as lapses in fitness that require fixing. Lapses in the highly valued third shift of fitness are even blamed on the second shift of household labor. For example, one new mother's confessional states that: "amid frequent feedings, diaper changes, endless loads of laundry and caring for children, something in my life had to give. Regular exercise was the first to go" (Summer 1999). This is consistent with Spitzack's analysis that "women are represented as deviant and as persons who are held accountable for their wrongs, who must display their imperfections . . . expected to testify openly to deficiencies or 'sins'" (Spitzack 1990, p. 61).

Fitness becomes something a new mother should do as a gift to herself, while the surveillance and constant maintenance (and privilege) required to sustain it are subsumed under the realm of feminist liberation. Here, fitness texts have been critiqued for dangerously merging "self-scrutinizing subjectivity" with a "state of liberation" (Bordo 1997, p. 39). Asked to simultaneously prepare the body for a smooth birth in order to be a good mother, but to show no physical signifiers of this process, a new shift of bodywork emerges. In this way the "confession reestablishes the order of the dominant by extracting from women nonreciprocal and self-referential disclosures which, in the same move, reprimand women for stepping outside the parameters of femininity and endorse prevailing images of women" (Spitzack 1990). At the same time that *Shape Fit Pregnancy* espoused feminist empowerment for a process of surveillance and victory through "getting your body back," it also presented the third shift of fitness as wholly necessary given women's responsibilities for household labor and childcare. As will be shown below, the magazine strategically draws on feminist stances to help women "get their body back" but paradoxically reinscribes women to the domestic and privatized realm of bodily and household maintenance in order to do so.

Merger of the Second and Third Shifts

Medical experts used to deem that women's destiny was to serve others, and that sport and fitness would deplete "nerve-essence," contribute to inferior offspring, and promote excessive muscular development (Lenskyj 1986). Given that exercise was thought to hurt women, doctors during the late 1880s paradoxically attempted to popularize the claim that housework was exercise that was beneficial to femininity, as it was consistent with responsibilities in the domestic realm. On this last point, our analysis uncovers the same tendency over 100 years later, except the discourse is put forward not by medical doctors but through health and fitness discourse.

Readers of *Shape Fit Pregnancy* are reassured that fitness and baby care are highly compatible. An article titled "Ooh Baby!" features an image of a smiling white woman with her baby. The text notes that "some people really like getting lost in the whole aura of mothering . . . the fuzzy feelings of taking care of the baby around the clock" (Fall 1997). Even though women are described as being exhausted from continual baby care, as not having any time for themselves, or as being "barely able to find time to brush [their] hair" (Fall 1997), a resurgence of maternal values prevails when it is explained that "there's only one really important thing to focus on, and that's your baby" (Winter 1998). Workouts inside (90 percent) or outside the home (10 percent) are featured as being done "without missing a single baby moment" (August/September 2000). New mothers are encouraged to exercise when babies are sleeping: "switch on the monitor" and "try doing some alternative intervals of, say, ab work, pelvic-floor exercises, push-ups, and jump rope" (August/September 2000). While the articles say that mothers are consumed with how to combine fitness and childcare, fathers are only mentioned in 5 percent of the articles and their role is described as either "helping" mom with childcare while she goes out to the gym, or as the household quarterback who plays with the kids and family outdoors (as discussed below).

At the same time that 55–63 percent of *Shape Fit*'s readership were employed over the years of publication, there is a very strong and notable silence on the juggling between child care and paid labor in the text. Instead, the magazine emphasizes how a third shift of fitness is necessary to allow for the successful completion of the second shift of household labor and childcare. For example, women are informed that they will "be amazed at how often you need upper body strength just to get through the day" (August/September 2000). Another article, "Leg Work: Exercises for Strong, Lovely Limbs," agrees. It explains that the suggested exercises will "get you into the habit of using your legs instead of your back to pick things up" and that "this is important since you'll soon lift your baby dozens of times a day, hoist a car seat and stroller in and out of your car, and carry a diaper bag stocked with more essentials than you ever knew existed" (October/November 2000). The second shift is constituted as something to train for and it is suggested that women should "pump up your lifting muscles so you can feed and hold that new baby" (February/March 2001). Exercises are offered that will "help you get in better shape for all the bending and lifting you'll need to do as a new mom" (May 2000). Newer issues openly state that the time struggle is not one between work and family for women and men but a struggle for women only to juggle the demands of the second and third shifts: "You may be eager to get back in shape after the birth of your baby, but it can be tough to find time to exercise when you're juggling feedings, diaper changes, and piles of laundry—all on minimal sleep" (February/March 2006).

At the same time that mothers are constituted as needing fitness to carry out the second shift, household responsibilities and childcare are framed as something that should be strategically used to get fit. For instance, one article tells women that "as a new mother, fitness is where you find it," and that women should "get baby into the act" by "looking at your daily environment as a gym and find ways to incorporate exercise into daily routines" (Summer 1997). Suggestions for new mothers are to "do some squats while you're making the bed or picking up a basket of laundry, or put baby into an infant carrier or sling and do some pliés or toe raises." It is suggested to carry out "chores with a vengeance, with baby in bouncy seat and music playing, clean, clean, clean." Graceful dance and aerobics moves, aligned with white, middle-class, and heterosexual definitions of femininity are frequently emphasized as the appropriate fitness analogies, and not aggressive, contact, or other sports deemed to be more masculine.

Numerous articles not only argue that "fitness is where you find it" but that women should view their own babies as barbells. For instance, the February/March 2000 issue of *Shape Fit Pregnancy* contains an article called "So Happy Together" that offers a "new mom workout that allows you to build strength and play with your baby." Articles feature "bonding time" through "kiss the baby push-ups" where the mother places the baby on the floor underneath her body, does push-ups over the baby, and lowers herself to kiss the baby before pushing back up. In another form of "baby crunches" for abdominal work, the baby is draped over the shins of the mother as she lies on her back and does sit-ups while holding the baby with one hand. An article called "Back in Action" describes a "baby bench press," "baby overhead press," and "reverse baby curl." "Baby bench press" is described as follows:

Lie on your back, knees bent and feet flat on the floor. Contract abs, bringing your spine to a neutral position; squeeze shoulder blades together. Hold baby under your arms, your palms on her chest and your fingers wrapped around her torso. With baby lying on your chest . . . gently raise her up in the air, straightening you arms without locking your elbows. Pause (say "peekaboo"), then lower her to starting position. Do 10 reps. (Winter 1998)

Newer issues of the magazine begin to include the baby as resistance not only for weight training workouts but also for pilates routines and hiking workouts. For example, one article titled "Pilates Playtime" notes that "in each of the moves your baby is strategically placed to help you maintain proper form, focus, and add resistance" (February/March 2006). Another article titled "Walk It Off!" notes that women should "grab their baby, head outside, and get back into shape!" (June/July 2005).

The texts seamlessly combine fitness, childcare, baby play time, and household chores. Another article features a photo of an African-American woman holding onto her baby's crib, doing side crunches and "baby lifts" while keeping her eyes on her child. "Crib lift games" are also featured where women are taught how to lift the baby out of the crib and to put the child back down repeatedly as a workout. Upper body games are complemented with lower body ones, termed body dips and mock deadlifts that use the child as a weight. A series of "real-life scenarios" are provided that emphasize women's responsibility for both the second and third shifts through exercises which teach new mothers how to lift babies off the floor, "as well as get a great leg workout picking up toys" (Winter 1998).

A 1998 issue takes exercise outdoors with a "rock and roll" strollerciz-ing lunge walk, rife with peekaboo leg stretches and "moment of peace" leg squats for the thighs. All rely on the woman keeping one arm on the stroller at all times (Spring 1998). Another article that includes baby as a barbell in a pilates routine mentions that this workout "strengthens the entire body" but also offers an "opportunity to stimulate your baby through movement, touch, eye contact, and facial expressions, all of which can enhance cognitive development and motor skills" (February/March 2006). The cited expert for this particular article is the author of a book on pilates; once her quote is completed, the authors of the article add that women should not "forget to smile, laugh, play and talk to their little buddy during the routine," and the subtitle of the article notes that these moves will "help you to get your body back and bond with your baby at the same time."

Consumption, fitness, and domestic imperatives merge more often in the later issues of the magazine, with articles that tell women to take a trip to the mall to squeeze in a workout or specifically prescribe certain kinds of baby packs, strollers, or the "right gear" during workouts. One article features a mother who carries out lower body lunges outside of stores at the mall while she is shopping with her baby. She is shown standing to do push-ups against a hallway wall and also does squats while holding the baby stroller, which is stationary since the brake is on for her mall work-out (February/March 2003). While the text of the magazines does not fea-ture much mention of paid employment, the ads in the magazine do take note of this and further reinforce the conflation of fitness, consumption, and the maternal. Ads generally accomplish this intersection with images

Ads in *Shape Fit Pregnancy* make it clear that pregnancy, which is often viewed as departing from idealized physical femininity, need not ruin it, if one only stays fit and makes the right purchases. This ad shows a woman maintaining her office style, flawlessly. (*Shape Fit Pregnancy*, April/May 2000)

of fitness apparel for "sexy mamas," baby joggers, and stylish work apparel so that women "do not lose their office style" while pregnant.

While combining the second (household labor and childcare) and third (fitness, consumption) shifts may be one way to work fitness into a busy schedule, such messages are not necessarily representations that reflect health, nor do these reflect the experiences of the specific demographics of the readership. It is vital to recall the way in which women have been viewed as the moral guardians of the home as they facilitate the leisure time of men and children while forgoing their own. Fathers in *Shape Fit Pregnancy* are rarely mentioned until the 2005 issues and are not depicted as facing struggles between a second shift of household labor and childcare or a third shift of fitness, nor are they framed as having work/family struggles.

One of the few articles that shows men working out with their kids highlights the morality of fitness in the family. This article, titled "Play

Time," says that "a family that works out together, stays together," explaining that young children should also be indoctrinated into "developing consistent exercise habits" (June/July 2000). This is considered "focused family time" and includes the father through a "huddle and hike" passing of the baby from mother to father. Common themes presented in the articles agree that "a family that works out together stays healthy together." This particular article describes one mother as honorable for the way that she "gets creative" and sees her "everyday situation as a workout," including using the baby as a "free weight of sorts" and "chasing soap bubbles with the kids" (June/July 2002).

One of the only articles that shows dad working out with the child on his own without the mother does not show an actual person doing a real workout. Instead, the article is a series of cartoons that show dad in a variety of situations, such as: going on hikes with the baby, fathers dealing with postpartum blues, babies needing time and love from fathers, and where to get advice on how to be a good dad. This article, titled "A New Dad's Field Guide," focuses on fatherly anxieties about what to do with their new fatherly role. It constructs masculinity not in relation to needing an improved body but as related to sports participation and work status. The article notes to fathers that this is a "manual for earning your merit badge in surviving pregnancy and fatherhood" and that "just as you can learn to be a better baseball player or businessman, you can learn to be a better dad" (June/July 2005). There are almost no articles that include creative fathering as a difficult juggle between work, family, and fitness except those tidbits that ask fathers to take the child once in awhile to give mom a "break." Indeed, there are no articles that include single mothers, and it is always assumed that mothers are partnered with a man.

Conclusion: Fitness and Moral Motherhood

During the nineteenth century, it was not only paid labor but also the domains of higher education, leisure, and sport that were considered detrimental and stigmatized for women. Such realms were seen as potentially damaging not only to cultural constructions of femininity but to women's reproductive system (Hargreaves 1994; Lenskyj 1986). The moral imperative of motherhood thus required that women refrain from any "vigorous" physical activities. While moderate exercise was seen by some as helpful to reinvigorate lost energies, overdeveloped arms and legs were said to take away the vital force of the reproductive system (Cahn 1994). Fears of women's physical masculinization also emerged in these realms, and are easily understood when considering the historical role sport has played in constituting and reproducing dominant forms of masculinity (Kimmel 1990; Messner 2002).

In contemporary fitness discourse, sports analogies are used to train women before, during, and after labor, while "getting your body back" with the baby normalizes women's bodily self-surveillance and responsibility for two shifts. Contemporary fit motherhood draws on sports analogies for "winning deliveries" but then mitigates the long feared loss of feminine and reproductive capacities with reinscriptions of female domesticity. The feared masculinization of women's bodies that has long come with certain sport and fitness activities (especially weight lifting) is safely minimized not only through domesticity but by suggesting that babies are the preferred feminized barbells. Additionally, as has been noted by Shannon Jette's recent work on the media frames used to depict pregnancy in *Oxygen* magazine, "by drawing on medical discourse that constructs the pregnant body as 'at risk' and in need of exercise in order to have a smooth pregnancy and healthy child, the magazine plays a central role in disseminating notions of a 'fit' pregnancy. The emphasis on the risks of not being physically active when pregnant construct the mother-to-be who is not able to exercise—perhaps due to a medical condition or lack of time or financial resources—as an 'unfit' mother" (Jette 2006, quote on p. 341). Consumer culture merges healthism (responsibility for mom's own health and that of her baby lies with the individual woman) the moral, good mother, and the "yummy mommy" to simultaneously promote self-surveillance, product purchases, happy babies, fit bodies, and magazine purchases (ibid., p. 346). In this way, the magazine promotes a conflation "between the ideals of commodity culture and public health" while promoting the slim, attractive ideal (Petersen and Lupton 1996, p. 80).

Our analysis also reveals how a racialized, classed, gendered, sexualized matrix of domination (Collins 1990) is uncovered in the preferred meanings of the text. Sixty-two percent of the readership had full-time jobs, yet little mention is made of getting back to work. Eighty-one percent of models are white, and fathers are only featured in 5 percent of articles. Single mothers and lesbian mothers are never shown or discussed. The underlying preferred meanings in the text and imagery privilege whiteness, heterosexuality, stay-at-home motherhood, continual baby and self-care, and a largely indoor third shift of bodywork for women that helps them remain attractive to male partners. Racialized and classed frames operate to reinforce idealized definitions of womanhood and motherhood. By framing pregnancy as shameful for women's bodies and recommending individualized fitness as the feminist solution, the majority of fitness messages do not speak to poor women, working-class women, Third World women (Hargreaves 1994), or even the more general struggles of diminishing wages and health care for the middle class. Our results are similar to work within family literatures that uncover how ideologies operate to privilege a racialized, classed, gendered heterosexual haven in a heartless world (Stacey 1996).

It is vital to consider not simply what is included "inside" media frames, but also to consider the silences in the texts (Lutzen 1995; Messner and Solomon 1993). By strategically drawing on the more empowering "gains" of feminist liberation, fitness media frames silently erase the fact that the full-time readership is likely struggling with work-family conflict, men's role in household labor, and the external realities of job competition in an increasingly unstable global market. Media frames are also silent about the retraction in funding for and support of women's sport, health care, and reproductive rights. We began this chapter by noting that feminine ideals have shifted from social behaviors such as privatized domesticity to contemporary gendered norms such as dual-career couples, more involved fathers, and a merging of public and private roles. Paradoxically, media reconstituted women's empowerment as healthism and aestheticism through privatized domesticity that merges the second and third shifts while negating work frames for women and family frames for men.

These findings are consistent with other researchers who argue that signifiers of feminism are often co-opted, deployed for purposes outside of social justice intentions, and the process moves "from an objective with feminist potential to a market-oriented objective."[3] Such trends are also consistent with the ways in which the neoliberal era creatively deploys other signifiers of empowerment from other social movements (Civil Rights, the Gay and Lesbian Movement) for the purposes of profit.[4] Here too, under the prevailing discourse of healthism, "the maintenance of good health is the responsibility of the individual and poor health is itself a distasteful state."[5] Personal transformation becomes the way in which "every individual is now observing, imposing, and enforcing the regulations of public health, particularly through the techniques of self-surveillance and bodily control" (Lupton 1995, p. 76). It is not so much that the articles emphasize health, but the appearance of health (and appropriate behaviors), conflating what some researchers call "looking good" with health and "feeling good" (Duncan 1994).

Further conflating a body that looks good with proper domestic roles in the household clearly underscores that confessional bodies are those that are financially able to employ technologies of the self to aid in self-analysis and improvement. Such bodies are also able to engage in the process of confession and redemption. While middle-class bodies are able to use fitness magazines in the process of confession and redemption to produce pleasurable and fulfilling identities, those unable to fully participate in the consumption necessary to attain redemption are stigmatized through the implicit cultural tropes of failure, lacking family values, unfit motherhood, and immorality.

Liberal feminism has long been undergirded by the assumption that access to institutions is a key route to women's empowerment. It has been central in (disproportionately) aiding (white middle-class) women's entrance into education, work, sport, politics, and more (Lorber 1994). Feminist researchers have noted how corporations have successfully commodified the empowerment messages of feminism and sold these back to the target demographic (e.g., "just do it" commodity feminism) who benefited the most from these gains (Heywood and Dworkin 2003; Cole and Hribar 1995). In our analysis, women's relationship to feminism is not simply framed as a set of empowering purchases, but rather as bodily fitness practices that contain a familial morality through winning deliveries, a body lost, won back through disciplinary self-surveillance, and regained (perhaps for the husband) through the right products and practices. Ultimately, families that stay together are framed as having enough strength to carry the laundry and do kiss the baby push-ups.

One must be cautious of acritical cheers for "choice," "control," "strength," and "having it all," whether this is prescribed to women in the public or private realm. Asking women to structure their relationship to feminism through "empowering" bodily practices may seem as if it encourages free choice, far from disciplinary and medicalized practices to which women are so frequently subject (Blum 1999; Martin 1992). However, such dictates may ultimately aid the most privileged women in turning inward toward consumerism, domesticity, and increased bodily self-surveillance. A more feminist version of media frames need not only deploy feminist discourse when fitness means better mothering or the nuclear family form. Multiple family forms are feminist and need not be ignored along with other issues faced by the readership such as wage gaps, occupational sex segregation, inequitable divisions of household labor, buying off the second shift, the dearth of work-family policies, access to solid health care, and the lack of childcare in workplaces.

Drawing on feminist discourse to produce fit mothers in the private sphere is ironically quite removed from the way in which liberal feminism fought for women's access to the public sphere in the first place. This may underscore the way in which feminism is indeed an unfinished revolution—a lesson learned from a careful analysis of *Shape Fit Pregnancy*: that women need to "get something back" beyond their bodies. As will be seen, it is in the uncomfortable juncture between second- and third wave feminism that underscores questions about how commodity feminism transforms feminism into a marketing tool rather than an identity grounded in praxis (Goldman, Heath, and Smith 1991). The next chapter explores these issues in depth by examining the structural and cultural transitions the magazine *Women's Sports & Fitness* went through during its 25-year existence.

5

From *Women's Sports & Fitness* to *Self*

Third Wave Feminism and the Consumption Conundrum

While working together on this book project, each of us had collected piles of fitness magazines. Stacked in several corners of our respective apartments, sometimes these mounds stood tall . . . straight up in the air, majestic . . . at other times, willowy, leaning towers of Pisa. Sometimes the piles were flat, spread out, completely covering hardwood floors or carpets as we debated cover images and stood over them with an air of authority. In the early phases of this project, after we carried out an initial coding, we met to discuss preliminary summaries and findings. We then discovered that both of us had independently decided to subscribe to *Women's Sports & Fitness*. That wasn't entirely a surprise given that each of us couldn't ignore that this particular magazine was clearly different from the other magazines (both men's and women's) in important ways.

How was *Women's Sports & Fitness* "different"? First, we discussed the covers—these didn't look like the other magazines. The cover of one of the first issues we coded quite unique. It depicted a woman hiking across a green, rugged hill, snow-capped peaks rising majestically in the background. Shot from a distance, she was smiling, not at the camera, and her gaze seemed to follow her unmistakable anticipation of the trail stretching out in front of her (October 1997). Wearing hiking boots, a large pack, a long-sleeved shirt, and shorts, she seemed totally unaware of the camera. The content of this publication appeared to be different, too. There were profiles of women athletes, articles that focused on sports performance, discussions about long-term participation in sports, a get-out-and-do-it attitude that didn't apologize for a resoundingly feminist stance. And, there was the coverage of key debates in the field of sport, such as demands for equity in sport for women, the demise of the AIAW,[1] and the enforcement of Title IX.

We discussed the content and noticed that, unlike other magazines that defined "problem areas" in terms of large thighs or butts, this magazine spoke of problem areas in terms of improving sports performance, media coverage of women's athletics, and inequitable access to sport. "Trying something new" in other magazines meant trying a new diet, workout ball, spa treatment, or exercise gear, but here it meant a new sport or activity. Less than one year after our initial subscription purchase, *Women's Sports & Fitness* was acquired by Condé Nast, the publisher of magazines such as *Vogue, Allure,* and *Self.* After the merger/acquisition, changes in covers and content began immediately. In brief, what arrived in our respective mailboxes began to look a lot like all of the other health and fitness magazines on the shelf—a repetitive player in an increasingly homogeneous, oversaturated market.

But still, there were some vestiges of what had drawn us to the magazine. We realized that there were female athletes on the new covers, and at least they posed with the tools of their trade. But now, the accomplishments of female athletes were paired with the workouts of fit actresses. Now, when the text made claims of "getting out there and doing it," it started to mean fitness or beauty-oriented activities in dazzling new athletic wear. Calls for institutional and cultural change seemed to disappear, while individuals were prescribed self-improvement (physical or self-image). While not initially obvious, the magazine did seem to be caught in a larger set of changes and tensions—the same tensions faced by feminism in a postmodern consumer market. Through an analysis of covers, content, and workouts we explore the shift from calls for institutional, cultural, and individual change to primarily individual change. We argue that such transitions reflect the ascendency of neoliberalism and commodity feminism, the "aesthetically depoliticized feminism" that is a market strategy rather than a praxis-driven process (Goldman, Heath, and Smith 1991).

In carrying out this work, our analysis underscores several key debates that center on the intersection of feminism and consumer culture and highlight the problems engendered by commodity feminism. These debates include: How does one market an ethic of feminist liberation? Can an ethic of feminist liberation actually be "bought" and "sold"? What does a bodily discourse of feminist liberation promote and what does it mask? Who benefits? How does one reconcile the tyranny of bodily ideals alongside the empowering aspects of self-construction? How does one reconcile the feminist gains of Western, white, middle-class women (the target audience in Nike ads, e.g., "Just Do It") being predicated on growing inequality among women in the United States and worldwide?

In 2000, *Women's Sports & Fitness* was discontinued and subscribers were sent a Condé Nast replacement, *Self*—along with a letter explaining that *Women's Sports & Fitness* was defunct. Replacing a magazine that covered women's sports with one that focused on fit aesthetics raises a number of broader cultural questions and reflects contemporary societal currents. Given the growing consumer power of female athletes,[2] and the potential value of the niche market (as evidenced by the wide range of attempts to capture this market),[3] one might think that a magazine such as *Women's Sports & Fitness* could survive. The demise of *Women's Sports & Fitness* therefore sheds light not only on the trials of a particular magazine, but on the struggle to redefine feminism in consumer culture. We begin by tracing the history of the magazine. We then analyze the content and covers during different periods to note changes over time. We conclude with an assessment of the transitions we observed.

Women's Sports & Fitness: *A Brief History*

Originally titled *Women's Sports, Women's Sports & Fitness* was a product of the second-wave feminist movement. In 1974, tennis luminary and feminist advocate Billie Jean King concurrently founded both the magazine *Women's Sports* and the Women's Sports Foundation. This followed in the wake of Title IX, which states, "No person in the United States shall, on the basis of sex, be excluded from participation in, be denied the benefits of, or be subjected to discrimination under any education program or activity receiving Federal financial assistance."[4] This act has had a significant impact on the opportunities for female athletes. Hence, both the magazine and this organization heralded a time of tremendous change for women's athletics.

After successfully campaigning for pay equity in tennis, King worked ardently to promote sports for and by women. The Women's Sports Foundation and its official publication, *Women's Sports*, were both uncompromisingly feminist in mission and content, reflecting the changing status of women. The magazine focused on improving women's access to sport, providing equal opportunities, profiling female athletes, critiquing the quality and quantity of media coverage of women's athletics, marking athletic milestones, and highlighting the achievements of women in sport. As women's gains into sport were continually challenged, the magazine worked hard to defend women's entrance into sports. For example, *Women's Sports* assiduously defended Title IX while numerous opponents attempted to undermine and weaken the ruling and few demanded enforcement.[5] By the mid-1970s, a base rate of 210,000 subscribers indicated that the magazine was fairly successful.[6] At the end of 1978, the magazine went into a 10-month hiatus as publishers debated its future.

When the magazine re-emerged, only about 50,000 of its 200,000+ subscribers remained and it then became the official publication of the Women's Sports Foundation, later to be replaced by the *Women's Sports Foundation Newsletter*.[7] As the official publication of the WSF, the magazine was linked to a nonprofit organization with a proactive mission, giving it a different status than a purely for-profit magazine. Most commercial magazines are "for profit," meaning the success or failure of these magazines hinges on the ability to generate a growing target demographic that can lure advertisers. By contrast, *Women's Sports* was linked to the nonprofit Women's Sports Foundation, giving it a base readership and funding not reliant entirely on advertising sales. As we will note later in the chapter, this helps the magazine to be able to produce "risky" or "progressive" content without concerns that advertisers might become alienated and pull financial support.

The new *Women's Sports* premiered in January 1979. The "Premier" issue included articles on top U.S. athletes like squash phenom Barbara Maltby, basketball star Carol "The Blaze" Blazejowski, coverage of the first women to top Anapurna (one of the top mountain climbing spots in the Himalayas), provided tips on how to get started in cross-country skiing, and offered an update on the enforcement of Title IX. The cover featured a woman cross-country skiing–shot from a distance, with mountains in the background, a track stretching out in front . . . she glides confidently toward the camera, grinning broadly.

With a name change to *Women's Sports & Fitness* in 1986, and a new positioning toward fitness as well as sports,[8] the magazine experienced growth in circulation and advertising revenues. By January 1987, readership had recovered from an initial dip to an advertising guarantee of 300,000 (Dougherty 1986, June 30). Throughout this time period, the magazine remained dedicated to a specific niche market—the female athlete. With the advent of the 1990s, the magazine saw a small decline in readership. In 1991, editor Marjorie McCloy argued that despite a loss in circulation, the magazine was "healthy." She asserted, "Our readers enjoy athletics for the sake of athletics. Getting thin is just a happy byproduct. Most of the other fitness magazines for women are how-to-catch-a-guy publications." She forecast a successful future for the magazine as "Equipment manufacturers are realizing the potential of the women's market. Our market surveys show women buy more than half the equipment such as shoes, bikes, etc. We have an active, well-educated and affluent readership" (Davidson 1991, August 24).

As the magazine grew, the profit potential became very apparent. To maximize this potential, in 1990, the magazine went from being published by World Publications for the Women's Sports Foundation to being published by a small independent publishing company, Sports & Fitness, based out of Boulder, Colorado. Although the magazine remained affiliated with the WSF, the Foundation took a much less active role in the production and content of the magazine from this point onward. The focus of the magazine was expressed by then editor Dagny Scott as follows: "Our original mission was to be a lifestyle magazine for women who are passionate about athletics and outdoor activities." Scott noted changes wrought by the success of second wave feminism in creating increased opportunities for girls and women in sports:

> Back then, it was really a crusade, It had this "yes, we can" tone. But now, that has changed. We're done proving ourselves. Women are out there living it and doing it . . . It's oriented for the real serious woman athlete, for the woman who is passionate about her involvement. Our readers can vary by age and level; sports is a big part of her life and who she is, but we're not elitist.[9]

Certainly, privileged women could be conceived as successfully carving out a space in women's athletics. The value of their dollar in the athletic equipment, clothing, travel and media markets promised a host of new opportunities that would continue to be offered to those who had the capital to participate. But as social barriers for some disappeared, and indeed were even replaced by injunctions to participate, economic barriers remain salient for most. Sport and fitness participation has become a sign of the successful woman. But for most of the world's women, participation in this process means making the high-end sportswear and equipment used by the privileged few.[10] For economically privileged feminist sports and

outdoor activities enthusiasts, *Women's Sports & Fitness* was the best option available. This was not lost on others in the field, as *Women's Sports
& Fitness* was reviewed by others as having a feminist slant. For example,
in 1996, the *Atlanta Journal Constitution* highlighted different publications
that featured profiles of Olympians and writes of WSF, "For feminists, the
July-August Issue of *Women's Sports & Fitness* focuses on women athletes
in the games" (Jensen 1992, July 7).

In January 1998, *Women's Sports & Fitness* was acquired by Condé
Nast for an estimated $7 million (Kelly 1998, January 13). Condé Nast's
magazine empire already consisted of a number of successful publications, including *Self, Glamour, Vanity Fair, Allure, GQ, The New Yorker,*
and *Lucky.* Commenting on the sale, John T. Winsor, then chairman of
Sports & Fitness Publishing, the former publisher of *Women's Sport & Fitness,* stated, "We look at our publications as a portfolio, and each magazine has a lifespan. . . . Our job is to do the best job we can for our
readers and advertisers and to maximize the value to the shareholders"
(Romero 1998, January 17; Jhally 1987). Under Condé Nast, the magazine
was merged with an existing Condé Nast publication, *Condé Nast's Sport
for Women,* in 1998. Condé Nast took only the name and the subscriber
list, but brought in its own staff to run the publication. Prior to the sale,
the paid circulation of *Women's Sports & Fitness* was almost 220,000, and
the Condé Nast title immediately improved to 350,000 with the merger.
During this time, the magazine also went from publishing 10 issues a year
to bi-monthly. As the magazine became a Condé Nast creation, the tenor
of the magazine shifted. The magazine moved away from sports coverage
toward fitness. Some lamented these changes. As John Moore of the *Denver Post* noted:

> While S+F just kept producing authentic news for the female athlete,
> *Sports Illustrated's* Women/Sport test issue included an article by a writer
> who had developed a crush on Grant Hill. *Condé Nast for Women* made
> a similarly embarrassing splash with advice on how women can go about
> picking up a millionaire on the golf course. Clearly, different purposes
> were being served.[11]

During the ensuing period, there was a great deal of confusion about
the identity of the magazine as it vacillated between a fashion magazine
with fitness and a fitness magazine with fashion. The role that women's
sports and athletes would play in the magazine remained undefined. Did

the magazine want to foreground women's sports and women athletes, or did it want to promote the aesthetic aspects of fitness? With features on athlete-models like Gabrielle Reece and Lisa Leslie, the magazine tried to walk a fine line between the two.

In 1999, the magazine announced a 37 percent increase in its advertising rate base, the largest percentage jump for any Condé Nast title in the previous eight years (Rose 1999, September 23). Despite these gains, the magazine failed to meet Condé Nast's "projected targets."[12] Though it was named *Min Magazine*'s "Most Improved Magazine" in 2000,[13] Condé Nast discontinued *Women's Sports & Fitness*. Subscribers were offered *Self* magazine as a substitute. At the time of discontinuation in 2000, *Women's Sports & Fitness* had a circulation of over 650,000, and advertising pages were up by about 41.9 percent. However, Condé Nast had promised advertisers an ad base of 1 million, which would have been an unprecedented increase at the time this promise was made.

Some critics speculated whether the goal was to eliminate the competition. Some asserted that the readership of *Women's Sports & Fitness* overlapped with the more successful *Self* magazine, which boasted a readership of 1,149,506 (in 1999). The *New York Daily News* asserted that an industry insider reported: "It was just a slightly more brutish version of *Self*, and it was competing with *Self*" (Staff and Wire Reports 2000, June 28). Ignoring the implications of the word "brutish," certainly *Women's Sports & Fitness* was a direct competitor with *Self*, and offered an alternative that many found more appealing. The *New York Daily News* reports, "It's a common strategy for Condé Nast chairman Si Newhouse," said Steve Cohn, editor of Media Industry Newsletter. "They have the checkbook to buy out the competition" (Kelly 1998, January 13). The merger was finally completed when Lucy Danziger, the former editor of *Condé Nast's Women's Sports & Fitness*, was hired as the editor-in-chief of *Self* in June 2001 (Colford 2001, June 7).

Responses to the demise of *Women's Sports & Fitness* were varied. Critics questioned the focus of the Condé Nast's version of *Women's Sports & Fitness*. An article in the *Chicago Sun-Times* noted the demise of the magazine by sarcastically lamenting, "Which means no more articles such as the informative 'Which Body Do You Want? . . . And Who's Got It?' in the latest issue" (Harris 2000, July 19). Others suggested that the niche market which such magazines formerly served were being integrated into the larger world of sports magazines such as *Sports Illustrated* or *ESPN*. It was alleged that as mainstream coverage of women's sports and female athletes increases, magazines such as *Women's Sports & Fitness* have less relevance. Further, the growth in specialty publications, such as those aimed at mountain bikers, runners, skiers, snowboarders, fitness participants, and so forth, had siphoned off a share of the market. These trends made publications that attempt to cover all of these activities less competitive. The subsequent failure of *Sports Illustrated for Women* in October 2002 could support such arguments. At the same time, however, a slate of new magazines and websites continue to vie for market dominance, and to court the over 55 million women who participate in sports at some level. Recent arrivals included magazines and webzines like *Her Sports, Wsports,* and *Real Sports. Her Sports* debuted in the spring of 2004 with a circulation of 50,000 and is carried at several national retail chains, including Barnes and Noble, B. Dalton, and REI (Arrington and Thurston 2004, February 18). Moreover, an ongoing longitudinal study conducted by the LA 84 Foundation in conjunction with Margaret Carlise Duncan and Michael Alan Messner et al., has demonstrated only small improvements in the quantity and quality of media coverage of women's athletics over the last 25 years, indicating that there is still a shortage of quality news coverage of women's sports (Duncan, Messner, and Williams 2005; Duncan, Messner, and Cooky 2000; Duncan, Messner, Wachs, and Jensen 1994).

The Times, They Were A-Changing: Contextualizing the Shifting Marketplace

Throughout the 26-year lifespan of *Women's Sports & Fitness,* feminism was undergoing significant transformation. Arriving with a host of opportunities earned by the activism of the second wave feminist and Civil Rights movements, women encountered an array of new social opportunities and witnessed significant alterations in relations of power and privilege. Despite a vitriolic backlash against women entering a wider range of sports, notable progress continued throughout the 1970s and 1980s, as evidenced by the vast number of firsts covered by the magazine: the first woman to climb Anapurna in 1979, the first women's Olympic Marathon in 1984, the first woman to win the Iditarod in 1987, new Olympic events throughout, combined with a plethora of new records. This coverage shattered conceptions about the limitations of female bodies. The passage of Title IX in 1972, which mandated equality of opportunity in all educational and federally funded institutions, opened the door for demands for equitable opportunities for women in a multitude of areas, including women's athletics. As a result, the ratio of girls' participating high school athletics as compared to boys improved from 17:1 in 1975 to 3:2 in 1984 (Women's Sports Foundation 1985). By 1995, Mediamark research reported that over 20 million women aged 24–54 in the United States actively participated in three or more sports/activities. That was a threefold increase from 1985 (Feitalberg, May 1996).

Despite these gains, the Women's Sports Foundation reported in 2003 that while 49.1 percent of all high school students are female, girls comprise only 42 percent of all high school athletes, receiving 1.1 million fewer opportunities to play. Moreover, though women now comprise the majority of college students (55 percent), female athletes still receive less than half of the operating expenditures (36 percent), scholarship opportunities (43 percent), and participation opportunities (42 percent) offered at universities.[14] Recent research by Michael Messner suggests that significant institutional change is still required to produce gender equity in sports (Messner 2002). This is hardly surprising given the lack of enforcement and compliance mechanisms and the systematic weakening of the provisions of the amendment under the Reagan and both Bush administrations.[15] Assaults continue as the Supreme Court recently made it more difficult to bring lawsuits against the NCAA. Though individual women have successfully sued for compliance, a systematic means for enforcing the law remains a problematic omission.[16]

The larger social and political climate for women similarly improved. During this time period, date rape became a punishable offense, sexual harassment began to be taken seriously as a social problem, and though representation in government remains poor, it certainly improved. In 2004, 14 women sat on the Senate, compared to 0 in 1976. Indeed, only four women served during the 1970s—three were elected to replace spouses who had died in office. Sixty-eight women served in the House of Representatives in 2004, whereas only 23 served during the entire decade of the 1970s. More women than men now graduate from college, though given the continuing wage gap, and declining real wages, the payoff is comparatively less than in the past, and than the wages of men of the same ethnic group and education level. The battles of the Second Wave had made a dent in gender relations and had offered a somewhat successful start. Unfortunately, as feminist analysis has shown, improvements have disproportionately benefited the most privileged groups of women (white, economically advantaged, Western) whose massive gains have obscured the growing poverty and poor health of many women and their children during this same time period (Sidel 1996).

Despite the many gains that women experienced throughout this time period, many feminist issues remain. In a worldwide context, the continuing exploitation of an increasingly female workforce, the proliferation of sexual slavery, rising HIV/AIDS rates (the face of HIV/AIDS is now a woman from the Global South) (Dworkin and Ehrhardt 2007), lack of access to health care, and the continued impoverishment of women and their dependent children inhibit the ability for many to have a reasonable quality of life. And, while women's newfound strength is celebrated on the ball fields, domestic violence remains a critical threat to women worldwide and is a leading cause of injury to women under the age of 30 nationally. Still, some women's powerful sporting performances and strength on (and off) the playing fields was increasingly celebrated, and the popularity of female athletes continued to soar.

From the Second to the Third Wave: Feminism in Transition

Marsha Lear coined the term "second wave" to describe the notable increase in feminist activity in Western nations that began during the 1960s in concert with other key social movements. Just as the discrimination women faced in the abolitionist movement helped spawn the suffrage movement of the first wave, the discrimination women faced in the Civil Rights and antiwar movements fueled the burgeoning second wave and solidified a passionate connected network of activist women. Despite fractures within the movement along the lines of race, class, or sexuality, second wave feminists shared a common concern with the expansion of equal rights in all areas of life and the recognition of the intersections between "public" and "private" problems. The gains made during the rise of the movement, such as the reduction of the wage gap, family-friendly work-family policies, victims' rights, increased awareness of domestic violence, were achieved in a climate of ongoing activism. Seeking to unite women to achieve positive social action, the movement is sometimes criticized for promoting the existence of a unifying experience that reifies a universal category of woman (Ortner 1997). Creating this category often meant essentializing cultural/experiential differences between men and women, while obscuring differences among women.[17]

Some argue that with the advent of consumer culture, neoliberal politics, and postmodern sensibilities, a host of contradictions arise that have changed the ways in which identity politics and social movements operate. In this view, a new wave of feminism is in effect. Third wave feminism builds upon the insights of second wave feminism. Despite the perceived generational conflict between second- and third wave feminists, it is imperative that third wave feminism not be confused with post-feminist positions. Post-feminists "characterize a group of young, conservative feminists who explicitly define themselves against and criticize feminists of the Second Wave" (Heywood and Drake 1997). Individual improvement replaces collective improvement, while the results of the collective action of the second wave movement are taken as a given (Cole and Hribar 1995, pp. 347–69).

While post-feminists set up a dichotomy between the feminist victimization view of the second wave, and the current attitude of empowerment, third wavers recognize the "false polarity of this position" (Heywood and Drake 1997). Drawing on insights from multiracial feminism, the third wave conceptualizes structures of privilege and oppression as creating contexts in which some people have more and better options than others, not that any particular single identity category (e.g., gender, race) is unified or over-determined as victim or oppressor. Rather, it is understood that a potentially contradictory position may arise out of different identity categories (Collins 1990; McIntosh 1988). At the same time, identity may not function to adequately capture social practices—perhaps a sense of cumulative experiences gets at the issue more than did second wave claims of identity.

Third wave feminism problematizes that the ways that some women work to acquire privilege can be part of a system that oppresses others. This type of insight is critical—it does not undermine calls for gender equity (although this is how some frame the result), but rather, broadens the fight to recognize that equity is a multifaceted problem. By framing privilege and oppression around options or issues (or experiences, rather than identity), the false polarity of unified identity categories is exposed (Heywood and Dworkin 2003). This moves the focus of study from the individual to the availability of options and the cultural legitimacy of these options for those in different subject locations or with different experiences.

Combining insights from multiracial feminism, queer theory, poststructuralism, and postmodernism, third wave feminists acknowledge that the social locations of individuals are shaped by a matrix of domination (Collins 2000). In other words, though everyone has to contend with privilege and oppression, they manifest in very different ways depending on one's intersecting social locations. This means that women's liberation is complicated. The liberatory potential opened up to first world women by consumer culture may in fact rest, in part, on the disenfranchisement and, in some cases, virtual enslavement of women in other regions of the world. Within the Western world, the lifestyle promoted for successful women is contingent upon low-wage service work performed primarily by working-class women. In the cities and suburbs of the United States, immigrant women of color are paid to take care of white, middle-class children while middle-class mothers sneak off to the gym to find "time for themselves" that offers the liberatory potential of getting one step closer to an ideal body. Building on second wave politicization of "personal" issues, third wave feminists problematize quality-of-life issues faced by women at different social locations.

The third wave recognizes that lived experience is contradictory, paradoxical, and that one can be at cross-purposes. For example, the eroticization of feminine subordination means that one can experience pleasure in submission, recast it for instrumental purposes, use it as camp or parody, sell it to make money to build a shelter for battered women, or queer the discourse in a same-sex relationship to enact the semiotics of play. This doesn't mean the individual wants to be underpaid, exploited, or assaulted. It also doesn't necessarily mean the individual is a "traitor to a cause," or needs to be "fixed." These contradictions must be politicized as part of an ongoing struggle to improve quality of life and experience (Heywood and Drake 1997). A third wave perspective on the modern sports scene is one that engages directly with these complications. As women's market power grows, middle-class women gain social power and prestige, but this is a small subset of women. As shifting market relations saddled these women with a second shift of household labor and childcare, to legitimate women's subset and membership within it, a "third shift" of body maintenance became essential (Dworkin 2001; also see Dworkin and Messner 1999). As will be explained below, the marketplace, the relationship between sport and fitness, feminism, and consumer culture intersected in new and different ways. The rise of commodity feminism is a critical feature that defines the challenge for the third wave—it also structures the possibilities for health.

Consumer Culture, Commodity Feminism, and the Third Wave

Goldman, Heath, and Smith used the term commodity feminism to describe how the culture industry had appropriated the concepts of feminism and femininity as a "range of strategies for capturing market share" (1991, p. 333). An effectively aesthetically depoliticized feminism ensues such that feminism largely means associating with a range of commodities tied to feminist imagery, rather than praxis. Moreover, individualism is bolstered as energies are focused entirely on the project of the self and goals are limited to personal lifestyle goals. The authors further argue that a contradiction ensues as a result of advertiser efforts to merge feminism and femininity. This effectively focuses one's action on the body as a means to liberation (ibid.). Commodity feminism reifies the power of femininity and the arbiters of beauty (such as these magazines), masking how these processes reinforce other sets of social relations, for example, class. Such trends have been present since the inception of the magazine.

The magazine industry began mass marketing in the 1800s. Magazines dependent on advertising revenues are a product of the ascendancy of consumer culture and played a critical role in the veneration of the lifestyle associated with consumer society (Garvey 1996; Scanlon 2000), and in the production of consumers.[18] Through articles, advertisements, and fiction, the gendered consumer was defined and linked to a host of products and services. For example, the image of the new woman of the first wave feminist movement became a key means to reach increasingly affluent female consumers. Stories that featured women riding bicycles began to appear in the late 1800s. Though such stories subverted dominant views of appropriate feminine behavior, this element could be used as a marketing point for women. Readers could vicariously experience the empowerment of being a "new woman," and were encouraged to reap the benefits of the best experiences available to modern women.

These types of experiences required the consumption of products or leisure activities, and stories tended to reaffirm many aspects of standard middle-class life, despite the aura of rebellion cultivated by the authors and publishers (Garvey 1996). Readers could become part of a progressive social movement when they purchased and enjoyed their new bicycles. By living the life of the "new woman" featured in stories and articles, readers would become a part of expanding women's liberation. This repackaging of dominant ideologies as "rebellious" and "progressive" obscures

Left: This image represents a woman of the past and her vulnerable/submissive position relative to a symbolic, heterosexual, significant other. (*Women's Sports & Fitness*, January 2000). *Right*: Contrast the last image with this one which shows "how far women have come" to become the sporty woman of today. Examine her position relative to a significant other. (*Women's Sports & Fitness*, January 2000)

the manifestations of privilege in consumer culture and demonstrates that commodity feminism is not a new phenomenon.

For the reader, participating in this process may generate some insecurities, but it also opens up a range of pleasures. The gratification readers gained from this process, from learning to read the codes and participating in the system of meanings and signs that arise in consumer culture, demonstrated the empowerment of indoctrination (Garvey 1996). By learning to read cultural codes, consumers could and still do negotiate self-identity through a "reflexive project of the self," something that can be personally empowering. These codes further allowed individuals to situate other individuals in the larger social order, offering information about others (Giddens 2000). Some have argued that this type of project of the self co-opts feminist principles, offering a twisted form of self-empowerment centered on individualized consumption (Eskes, Duncan, and Miller 1998). Though one cannot deny that achieving the aesthetically fit body brings with it privileges and benefits ideologically supported by discourses of healthism, critics point to the ways the proliferation of these beliefs reinforces the dominant social order and offers opportunities for resistance (for some).

Women's Sports & Fitness presents a fascinating case not only because of the ways in which it rode the cusp of the transition from the second to the third wave, but also because the magazine evolved from being part of the nonprofit Women's Sports Foundation (though the magazine was a commercial venture) to a small, independent publishing company to being part of the Condé Nast empire. In many ways, this transition further reflects the re-appropriation of feminist principles by the marketplace and the ubiquity of commodity feminism. As noted by Samantha King, the shift in responsibility for activism from public and nonprofit resources to private corporations has effectively undermined the critical efficacy of

Here, the model wears boxing gloves and a lace-trimmed bustier. Exemplifying post-feminist ideals, the "Knock 'em Out" caption refers to the simultaneity of her smouldering appearance and her sport performance. One could argue that we also see the feminization of a traditionally male activity. The strikingly feminine appearance of the model reminds the reader she should be strong (but not big) and beautiful. (*Ms. Fitness*, Summer 2001)

such movements (King 2006). For many, this shift, and the contradictions engendered by the rise of neoliberal consumer culture, mark the transition to the third wave. Feminists in the third wave may simultaneously participate in consumer displays and critique the limitations of consumer culture. Hence, female athletes challenge perceptions of women as physically inferior through their physical performances, and middle-class women's athletic endeavors further mark women's advancements in Western society. At the same time, global relations of power are reproduced as some women perform their challenges in athletic wear made by women in the sweatshops of developing nations.

In order to examine what specific contextual shifts meant for the life of the magazine, the analysis divides the lifespan of the magazine into five periods. The analysis begins with the Women's Sports Foundation period (1979–1989).[19] This time period is characterized by the magazine's affiliation with the nonprofit Women's Sports Foundation. During this time, the close relationship to the Foundation is evident—the foundation is referenced frequently, as are issues of importance to the foundation. The second era examined below is the Independent era, which ran from 1990 to 1997. During this time, the magazine was published by a small independent press that specialized in sports and fitness magazines aimed at outdoor enthusiasts. Though the magazine remained the "Official Publication of the Women's Sports Foundation," the foundation took a much less visible role with the change of publisher. The third era examined was the Condé Nast era, which ran from 1998 to 2000, when the magazine was bought out and managed by the media giant. Finally, *Self* absorbed *Women's Sports & Fitness*, during the final period of analysis (2001–2005).

TABLE 5.1
Timeline: From Women's Sports & Fitness *to* Self

Era of Analysis	Years	Characterized By
Early Period	1974–1978	Difficult to obtain. Omitted from study.
Women's Sports Foundation	1979–1989	Close relationship between the magazine and the Nonprofit Women's Sports Foundation. Published 10–12 times a year.
Independent	1990–1997	Published independently, though relationship with WSF still maintained. The magazine is published 8 times a year.
Condé Nast	1998–2000	Magazine bought out by Condé Nast empire. Published 6–10 times a year.
Self	2001–2005	Magazine folds. Subscribers receive *Self* magazine instead. Published monthly.

Feminism in Transition: From Collective Concerns to Individual Issues

Late consumer culture and post-feminism are critiqued for the conflation of a free market with "freedom" and individual success with the advancement of social equity (Bordo 1997). Commodity feminism is similarly critiqued for conflating feminine with feminist, and personal improvement with praxis (Goldman, Heath, and Smith 1991). As the magazine transitioned from *Women's Sports & Fitness* to *Self*, the content shifted from a balance between individual and collective concerns to a focus on strictly individualized issues, reflecting a move from second- and third wave, to commodity feminist content. During the Women's Sports Foundation era, *Women's Sports & Fitness* retained a focus on collective action as fundamental to creating and preserving equal opportunity for women in the field of sports. The magazine operated as an advocate for change in gender relations at sport at three different levels (e.g., individual, cultural/symbolic, and institutional/structural). Michael Messner identifies all three of these realms as critical to challenging gender regimes and achieving equity.[20] During the Women's Sports Foundation era, the magazine contains numerous articles and columns that highlight the importance of improving gender equity at all three levels.

First, at the structural level, the magazine demanded institutional change that challenged structured rules and hierarchies in sport. The magazine repeatedly called for the enforcement of Title IX, debated control over women's sporting leagues, and examined controversies in the field. Strides, a regular column from 1979 to 1987, documented progress and opportunities for women in sports and acted as the mouthpiece for the Women's Sports Foundation. For example, the August 1982 column covered Avon's sponsorship of the Women's Sports Hall of Fame. The regular column, Arena, provided commentary on institutional access issues such as "Title IX Is a Civil Rights Issue" (July 1979); "Getting Your Act Together," which discussed the lack of professional opportunities for women (August 1980); "A Kick in the Right Direction" (October 1981), which covered the battle to achieve funding of girls' soccer programs in New York City public schools; "Requiem for the WBL" (January 1982) lamented the demise of the Women's Basketball League (WBL); "Aspire Higher!" (August 1986) offered scholarships for female athletes and teams and solicited support of the scholarship fund; and "National Girls and Women in Sports Day" promoted celebration of the day (February 1987).

In addition to the regular columns, feature articles routinely covered issues of institutional access for girls and women in sports. The inaugural issue of the new version of *Women's Sports,* in January 1979, featured several pieces that endorsed stricter enforcement of Title IX. Taking a resoundingly clear and consistent position, the magazine noted successes, failures, and the absence of sufficient enforcement mechanisms for Title IX. The magazine recognized women's sports as contested terrain, and took a clear stance on key events. For example, the magazine lamented, "Diamonds Aren't Forever: Women's Professional Softball Strikes Out" (August 1980), it critiqued the NCAA usurpation of the AIAW in the June 1981 issue,[21] and covered the end of the WBL in the January 1982 issue. The magazine further celebrated expanding opportunities. "Ladies Day in Dublin" (September 1984) examined the largest women's 10K in the world, including logistical information for potential participants (airfares, hotels, tourist attractions).

In addition to issues of institutional access and enforcement, other articles centered on a plethora of institutional issues such as recruitment, coverage of women who gained access to and experienced success within male-dominated sports, and scholarship information. For example, an article from the September 1984 issue titled "Recruiting Nancy Reno" examined the effects of recruiting on young athletes. "A Day at the Races" (August 1980) examined the experiences of female jockey Karen Rogers, while the February 1987 issue offered coverage of Libby Riddles and featured her on the cover as the first woman to win the Iditarod. Another article, "On the Road Again (January 1982), covered the career of drag racer Shirley Muldowney. The magazine also published annual scholarship guides, and included advice for young athletes, such as providing a list of questions they should ask about scholarship offers.

At the second level of dominant cultural symbols and beliefs, the magazine was critical of media coverage of female athletes, and provided a vehicle to rectify these trends and offered alternative coverage. During the initial period, *Women's Sports & Fitness* critiqued sexist coverage of female athletes, debated key issues in media coverage, and provided an alternative for those who sought serious coverage of female athletes and their accomplishments. The January 1982 issue critiqued coverage of the New York City Marathon with "You've Come a Long Way, Maybe." "When Allison Roe neared the finish of the New York Marathon, she was running in a small group of men. Commentator Jim McKay noted that the attractive woman was probably accustomed to being surrounded by men. Funny, he never mentioned that men's winner Alberto Salazar rates high in the good looks department" (January 1982). The January 1982 issue also noted that the magazine *Inside Sports*, which had once claimed "We cover the big spectator sports, and women are not competitive in them. They can't be; their bodies aren't built for it," was now featuring a piece on Martina Navratilova. Speed Skater Beth Heiden is featured on the cover of the May 1980 issue after blasting the media for asking insensitive questions following a subpar performance at a press conference during the Lake Placid Olympics. During this early period, *Women's Sports & Fitness* played an important role of being both a media watch dog and a media product. The affiliation with the WSF gave the magazine a readership base that was not market-dependent, and hence, the magazine could afford critical coverage likely to please readers, without worrying about alienating advertisers.

In addition to critiquing mainstream coverage that tended to erase or trivialize women's sports and female athletes, the magazine provided alternative and positive coverage, featuring profiles of women athletes in a multitude of sports. The regular feature "Sidelines" noted achievements of all types from the success of ultra marathoner March Schwam (October 1981) to the state of rhythmic gymnastics. The regular feature "Up & Coming" covered young stars and was billed as featuring "Women to Watch." Coverage of women's college sports, international sports, and professional leagues made up regular features. Features on runners Grete Waitz, Joan Benoit (who appeared several times), field hockey sensation Nancy White, rockclimber Stephanie Atwood, runner Alison Roe, Melanie Smith (Olympic Equestrian participant), tennis phenom Martina Navratalova, and a host of others covered traditional sports and a wide range of sports that often received little or no coverage in mainstream sports magazines (such as squash, racquetball, and rugby).

Not only are the athletes covered in articles, but they are also sometimes authors. Margo Oberg described critical moments in her career and the joy of surfing in the August 1980 issue. Volleyball sensation Nancy Reno shared her recruitment diary (September 1984). It is not simply that meaningful coverage of women's sports occurred, but also that women's sports was presented as a serious endeavor backed by the legitimacy of star experience, with a long and storied history worth celebrating and recognizing. Because of its association with the Women's Sports Foundation, the magazine had occasion to highlight events celebrating women's achievements in sports, such as the Women's Sports Hall of Fame inductees (October 1981). Hence, the magazine provided an alternative to media coverage that erased or trivialized women's sports and aggressively critiqued such coverage.

Third, the magazine advocated changes in women's day-to-day sporting practices. It promoted being involved in sports and fitness activities at a wide range of levels from recreational to competitive. Adult participatory sport was stressed, encouraging participation in sports and fitness "after college." A lifestyle of fitness was advocated with many articles and features covering a myriad of new adventures. For example, "Two Wheeled Travels" opens with the inspiring tale of a woman who biked from Chicago to San Francisco in 1896 (September 1984) and then provided information on bike tours, and offered tips for different tour levels. Product recommendations focused on the pros and cons of different gear types/styles, rather than emphasizing specific brands or models. In the same issue, a women's-only 10K race is covered, and readers are encouraged to get involved in similar local events. "In Deep Water" provided an insider's account of overcoming fear to learn scuba diving. Readers were encouraged to try golf with "Ms. Duffer's Guide to Life on the Links," a golf etiquette guide for newbies that encouraged us to "get yourself a visor and go for it." Throughout this time period, readers were encouraged to try skiing, snowboarding, running, marathoning, working out, tennis, bicycling, softball, rugby and more. Stories tended to be written from the point of view of a newbie, inviting the reader to try it out, or offering advice from a well-known athlete. Every issue advocated participation in a host of events and sports. The focus on participation provided an alternative model to the traditional limitations on women's involvement in athletics.[22]

Being involved in sports manifested not only in the form of workout and training regimes, but also in calls for women to take a more active role as leaders in sports organizations. For example, "Wanted: Coaches" by Mariah Burton Nelson (May 1988) encouraged women to become coaches for local girls' teams, and included steps for locating local leagues. Coaching was billed as a two-way street, since coaches would acquire leadership skills, learn about kids, spend time with friends and family, and enjoy the intangible elements of sharing something you love with young people.

An interesting tension or contradiction emerged as women were encouraged to attack very specific institutional barriers to participation, especially at the professional and amateur levels. Outside of sexism, the myriad of issues that may prevent women from participating informally went largely unexplored. Indeed, at the informal level, this lack of participation was more often framed as an issue of women making time for themselves than demands for safe spaces, community resources, reasonable accommodations, childcare, and so forth. For example, the piece "Sports After College" featured three individuals who explained their participation in sports and fitness and how they managed to fit it into their lives. "All three came to their sports as adults and elected to pursue them despite—or because of—an already full life" (August 1980). Across all eras, the image of the busy, successful person, who just needed to make time for sports and fitness, and the fact that this is a necessary activity for self-actualization, was advocated.[23]

Of interest is the fact that there were almost no workouts in the early issues—only four appeared in the 22 issues studied in this period. Three workouts cited strength and toning as the key goal, while the fourth was linked to sports performance. The text of these workouts mentioned performance and health as key goals. For example, "Stretch Yourself" (August 1982) encouraged design of a stretching routine that matched the sports that the reader preferred. The necessary infrastructure, a safe environment, minimal equipment (shoes, appropriate clothing), and child/elder care was generally presumed and few critical reflections emerged on social class or arrangements necessary to enjoy activities. However, a wide range of sports and activities were advocated, along with social activism. As the magazine transitions to a commercial venture, it must meet a different set of interests and needs.

Liberation and Consumer Culture in the Early Years

Certainly, *Women's Sports & Fitness* had a consumption imperative from the start. Trying new things also meant trying new equipment. Indeed, a large proportion of advertisements in earlier issues are for sporting goods and performance athletic wear. For example, almost half of the advertisements in the 1979 issues coded were for athletic wear and sports equipment. Overall, however, during this era, a much smaller proportion of the magazine was taken up with advertising (as will be discussed in the next section), and the overwhelming aura of consumption that pervades *Self* and the Condé Nast version of the magazine was not yet present. Given the paucity of sporting goods available to female athletes, meeting consumer demands does carry with it a certain liberatory potential. Having come of age in this era, both authors remember wearing boys' sporting gear for years because there were few affordable options for women. Just being able to finally buy a pair of cleats or running shorts that really fit well did feel like a triumph of sorts.

Transitions from the Independent Era to Self

Just as the Lucy Danzinger quote provided earlier suggests, during the independent era, the new publishers of the magazine clearly perceived the struggle for women's acceptance into sport as largely over, or a matter of celebrating individual achievements. Two of three of Messner's identified areas disappear as institutional and cultural calls for gender equity were effectively eliminated, and individual action is reframed as physical self-improvement. Overall, there is a change toward total individualization in the framing of issues surrounding women's sports and fitness. What went along with these changes was a sharp increase in the price of advertising, while advertising itself came to infiltrate and eventually saturate every aspect of the magazine. Ads were even merged with the content of feature articles, making it difficult to ascertain when the magazine was purporting an ideology of health or fitness and when it was selling products. Ultimately, the goals of each became inextricably intertwined and blurred in this era. Finally, what occurred along with this shift was a transition in emphasis from sports to fitness.

The Ubiquity of Advertising—The Growing Consumption Imperative

Over the course of the publication, advertisements and articles increasingly merged seamlessly into a phalanx of lifestyle necessities. Earlier issues, however, were less advertising saturated. The January 1979 issue offered four articles on top female athletes, one on female sports reporters, an update on Title IX, a directory of athletic scholarships, and an article on the Women's Basketball League among its feature articles. However, there were three additional featured articles—one on how to start cross-country skiing, one on the best cross-country ski equipment, and one on the best places to visit for cross-country skiing. This trend of merging advertising with content expanded as the magazine transitioned.

There are a number of ways these sorts of mergers between content and advertising proliferated during the independent era, and such trends continued through the transition to *Self*. First, there was a rapid increase in what we call "the snippet." As defined earlier, snippets are regular columns with short news and informational items. During this time period, focused regular columns were decreasing in number, while snippets were becoming ubiquitous.[24] A large proportion of snippets related directly to the availability of new products, services, or trends. In some cases, the entire snippet was devoted to new products. For example, the column "Marketplace" emerged during the transition to the independent era. This column was described as a "product potpourri" and featured images and short comments on new products and activities. "Great Gear" became a regular feature during the independent era. The May/June 1990 "Great Gear" snippet featured sunscreen-on-a-string, fitness mats, glitter oils, bike brake levers designed for women, sunglasses, dog life vests, and sports tea. July/August 1991 featured new jump ropes, chalk bags for rock climbers, reflective gear for nighttime runners and dogs, a waterproof runner's pack, and the new Saucony G.R.I.D. running shoes. In each case, readers were informed as to who made the products, how much they cost, and where to purchase them. Once the magazine was usurped by *Self*, a large portion of the magazine was made up of snippets. *Self* featured a number of sections, each containing several pages of snippets (Self Beauty, Fitness, Health & Happiness, Nutrition, and Style).

It is not surprising that during this time there is a dearth of articles that focus on institutional and cultural calls for change, as there was less space devoted to articles at all. Rather, there was an enormous increase in the amount of paid advertising featured in the magazine when it entered the independent era, a trend that continued. During the Women's Sports Foundation era, approximately 25 percent of magazine page space was allotted to advertisements. In the Independent era, advertising pages increased to about a third of the magazine, while in the Condé Nast era, 40 percent of the magazine is advertisements. *Self* magazine dedicates over 40 percent of its pages to advertising, and at times, up to one-half of the magazine is advertisements.[25] Summaries of the advertising codes can be found in the appendix.

In addition to direct advertising, there was a sharp increase in other forms of content that merge advertising and articles. Buyers' guides and recommendations for specific brands (rather than general products) and photo essays exemplify this trend and emerged during the independent era. The eventually ubiquitous "Buyer's Guide" began to appear in the 1980s, usually as a 4–6 page article that marketed the product on the basis of the practicalities for the athlete. During the Women's Sports Foundation era, product recommendations only accompanied articles that covered trying out new sports. In the early 1990s, a "Great Gear" column became a regular feature, along with articles on fashion.[26] In addition, during this time period, the traditional photo essays that had featured athletes disappeared, while photo essays that showcased fashionable clothing and accessories worn in exotic settings became a regular feature. The use of photo spreads as a means to map out social spaces that readers are likely to find attractive and desirable and the link between this and the growth of advertising has been well documented. Specifically, the photo essay encourages readers to visualize themselves in the scene. The wider context of the lifestyle involved in such a scene operates to socially locate the audience.[27] Carrying the veneer of information, images and text combine to normalize a lifestyle and the requisite accouterments.

From Sports to Fitness

Finally, during the independent era and continuing through the transition, there was a shift away from sport to aesthetic fitness. As a result, calls for institutional access and cultural critiques disappeared and were replaced by advice about individualized fitness. This trend was exemplified by the sharp increase in the total number of workouts in the magazines.[28] By the Condé Nast era, the majority of the magazine consisted of photo spreads, snippets, and pieces on celebrities.

Self, the replacement magazine for subscribers to *Women's Sports & Fitness,* rarely covered female athletes, and given the subject matter it purported to cover, the magazine had no obligation to cover sports or athletics. While specific workouts were almost entirely absent from the earliest period, *Self* has 2–6 workouts per issue. By contrast, many more articles on sports participation appeared in the WSF era of *Women's Sports & Fitness,* than in later eras and *Self.* It seems that over time the meaning of participation was narrowing from a variety of sports and activities to a more limited fitness and leisure/travel-oriented list of activities. Certainly, such changes are consistent with the increasing commercialization of the magazine. Commercial magazines are guided by market analyses and corporate interests centered on constructing a desirable audience that can be marketed to advertisers.[29]

Because the markers of fitness are generally presented as appearance, rather than achievement-oriented, these tie more centrally to individualized consumption imperatives (Featherstone 1982). In chapter 2, we discussed how sports became a trope used to validate masculine bodywork as men's bodies are increasingly objectified in consumer culture. By contrast, because women have long been expected to experience the objectified aspects of subjectivity, fitness has been normalized as appropriately feminine behavior. At the same time, fitness as presented in these magazines centers on appearance rather than health- or performance-related goals. This is not surprising, as appearance-based goals can more easily be tied to the consumption of a host of ever-changing products. Both shifts were reflected in two related trends—the shift in the status of cover models, and the activities or lack thereof, in which they are shown engaging.

As noted by Leath and Lumpkin (1992), the magazine changed its emphasis from coverage of sports to fitness activities between 1974 and 1989. We found this shift further perpetuated in the change in status of cover models. Comparing the status of the cover models across time periods, during the WSF era 14 of 22 cover models were athletes, 1 was a fitness expert, only 6 were models, and the one remaining cover featured a river rafting guide. Hence, almost 82 percent of the covers featured athletes, fitness experts, or someone employed in an athletic job. In the Independent era, nine athletes, one fitness expert, and two women who are both models and athletes were featured on covers. Hence, 75 percent of the covers presented athletes or fitness experts. The Condé Nast era featured three athletes, two models, and one model athlete. Finally, *Self* magazine showed no athletes or fitness experts and only models on the covers. The steady shift from featuring athletes, to fitness, to models indicates a shift in the self-presentation of the magazine. It goes from selling itself around sports, to fitness, to idealized images of appearance. These transitions are shown in table. 5.2.

It was not simply that the covers shifted away from featuring athletes, but also that the photos and poses shifted from active to passive. Just as in chapter 2, we coded according to whether the cover models were shown posing passively, or engaged in an activity (see table 5.3).

During the WSF era, models were posed in active poses in 12 out of 22 covers, and only 3 were passive. Hence, 86 percent of the covers in this era featured active or action implied poses. By contrast, *Self* featured entirely passive posses. The Condé Nast era similarly featured no action

TABLE 5.2
Cover Model Status

	Athlete	Fitness Expert	Model	Supermodel— Named Model	Actress/ Entertainer	Other	Total Number of Covers
Self 2000–2004	0	0	2 (25%)	1 (12.5%) (noted for famous mother— Jane Seymour)	5 (62.5%) (3 actress, 1 model actress, 1 singer)		8
Women's Sports & Fitness 1979–1989	14 (63.6%)	1 (4.5%)	6 (27.3%)	0	0	1 (4.5%) river guide	22
Women's Sports & Fitness 1990–1997	9 (56.3%)	1 (6.3%)	4 (25.0%)	0	0	2 (12.5%) model/ athletes	16
Women's Sports & Fitness— Condé Nast years, 1998–2000	3 (50%)	0	2 (33.3%)	0	0	1 (16.7%) model/ athlete	6
Women's Sports & Fitness Total	25 (56.8%)	2 (4.5%)	14 (31.8%)	0	0	3 (6.8%)	44

Note: Two models appeared on three covers. In one case, a wife-husband team is featured, with the woman featured more prominently. Two athletes are featured on one cover, and two models on another. Since the status of each was the same, each was counted as one for the cover code.

TABLE 5.3
Cover Model Poses

	Active	Action Implied	Passive	Total
Self 2000–2004	0	0	8 (100%)	8
Women's Sports & Fitness 1979–1989	12 (54.5%)	7 (31.8%)	3 (13.6%)	22
Women's Sports & Fitness 1990–1997	10 (62.5%)	3 (18.8%)	3 (18.8%)	16
Women's Sports & Fitness— Condé Nast years, 1998–2000	0	3 (50.0%)	3 (50.0%)	6
Women's Sports & Fitness Total	22 (50.0%)	13 (29.5%)	9 (20.5%)	44

Note: Two models appeared on three covers. In one case, a wife-husband team is featured, with the woman featured more prominently. Two athletes are featured on one cover, and two models on another. Since the status of each was the same, each was counted as one for the cover code.

shots, though half of the covers were action implied. During the independent era, 10 covers were active, while 3 were action implied and three were passive. A similar study by Hardin et al. (2005) noted that images in magazines such as *Shape* are largely passive and reinforce stereotypical sex differences, while *Women's Sports & Fitness* featured women in at least as many active and passive shots.

Why is fitness more appealing to consumer culture than sports? How is continued consumption facilitated by the shift in focus from sports to fitness? Applying Foucault's concept of docile bodies helps to explain this trend. As he noted, part of the production of docile bodies is self-analysis in a quest for self-improvement (Foucault 1979). Technologies of the self such as self-help magazines shape this question and redefine appropriate self-governance (Giulianotti 2005). The creation of a passive subject focused on display is part of this process. An active subject can be without lack, and the activity in which the person engages is the focus of the display. The active subject becomes a feminist by engaging in political, personal, and/or social struggles. By contrast, the passive object is always already being evaluated as one who will inevitably come up short, if for no other reason than that styles and fashions will change. The passive object is framed as a subject who becomes a feminist by wearing products associated with the image of the new, modern, and successful woman.

As was previously noted, the "subjective aspects within-being-as-object" means that one can experience an empowering and pleasurable form of self in the construction of the self as an object (Haug et al. 1987). As this sort of empowerment is largely commodified, it is intimately related to market concerns. Fitness needs to be understood as a product of the commodified construction of the self, rather than entirely related to the dictums of health. The possibilities for meaningful social action are largely limited to personal physical self-improvement.

Individualized Problems

During this transition, demands for change within sports institutions and local communities disappeared, while a focus on the day-to-day activities of individuals, and issues relating to the experiences of specific individuals within sports media, replaced the broader demands advocated in the previous era. The magazine does still advocate for protection for individual athletes. For example, it takes a strong stance in favor of protecting the rights of individual athletes involved in high-risk sports, defending the rights of mothers to participate in sports like mountain climbing.[30]

While in the Women's Sports Foundation era, the magazine demanded changes in the way media covered female athletes, in the independent era and through the transition to *Self,* the magazines focused on the individual's responsibility for managing her image. "Hard Bodies, Soft Sell" (November/December 1990) addressed the issue of images of strong athletic women in the media. The piece discussed marketing, what men and women consumers respond to, and ads that have succeeded and failed. The article focuses on what makes a successful advertisement, and the debate over whether or not successful women make good copy. This focused the debate centrally on getting women into advertisements and into the media, regardless of text or content. The Condé Nast era and *Self* magazine confine discussions of women in the media to coverage of stars and the self-management of appearance. It is the responsibility of the individual to create an image that can be promoted positively in the media.

The Consumption Conundrum—Feminism and the Marketed Self

Following the transitions of *Women's Sports & Fitness* over the lifespan of the magazine highlights a parallel set of conundrums faced in consumer culture. Achieving success in the neoliberal marketplace means exclusively individual responsibility for personal success. While the magazine once provided advocacy for women on all three levels identified by Messner as necessary for achieving gender equity in sport—institutional, cultural, and individual—once the magazine goes from being affiliated with the Women's Sports Foundation, institutional and cultural demands disappear and individual improvement becomes self-improvement.

According to Jennifer Scanlon, women's "inarticulate longings" for "personal autonomy, economic independence, intimacy, sensuality, self-worth, and social recognition" are linked to the marketing of products and lifestyles of the new woman (1995). Scanlon notes that the new womanhood promised by advertising corresponded to some degree with women's changing economic power. Products were marketed as representative of liberation, for example, the aforementioned bicycle. Called "an implement of power" by feminist Frances Willard, the bicycle emerged as a symbol of women's growing freedom (Garvey 1996).

Similar tendencies emerge in the recent upsurge in the marketing of the female athletes today such that fit and sexy forms and engagement in a sporting lifestyle are emblematic of success. As noted by Eskes, Duncan, and Miller (1998), "It is now much easier for women at least to entertain goals and lifestyles that are not specifically 'gender appropriate.'" This can almost certainly be in part attributed to the success of the feminist movement.

Sports and fitness have been part of these changes in a myriad of ways. Certainly, participation in sport and fitness in and of itself could be resistant, but by the same token, fitness can also be an "implement of power."[31] In referring to racial politics, bell hooks (1992) notes the "way meaningless commodification strips these (signs of resistance and power, i.e., raised fist) signs of political integrity and meaning, denying the possibility that they can serve as a catalyst for concrete political action." Goldman, Heath, and Smith (1991) noted the conflation of femininity and feminine in consumer culture. Commodity feminism repackages feminism as feminine displays, rather than in social or political action. The emerging contradictions are evident in the female athlete. The commodified image of the female athlete simultaneously reflects some women's growing market power while undermining the political salience of sport, masking the ways the market system (in which sport is embedded) disenfranchises other women.

What inarticulate longings emerge in the marketing of the fit woman today? In the Women's Sports Foundation era, participation in a wide range of activities is offered; however, as the magazine transitions, these "longings" overwhelmingly relate to bodywork enacted in a quest to achieve gendered bodily ideals. Individualized problems, personal health, injury, eating disorders, all come to be framed as within the agentic control of the "progressive" individual (see Lupton 1995). By educating herself with the help of texts such as this magazine, the progressive individual is framed as being able to conquer many if not all of her problems and look good doing it (as noted in chapter 4). Indeed, looking good is central to the "empowering" solutions. By bringing up controversial topics such as eating disorders, the text appears to be engaged in a critical assessment. However, controversy remains individualized as critical assessment is limited to pleas to readers to conquer such issues by being informed and vigilant. The structural facets of social problems, participation in sport and fitness, and health are rendered invisible. How is feminism to respond? We argue that combining second wave feminist attention to structural and institutional inequality, multiracial feminist understandings of intersectionality, and third wave critiques of consumer culture/commodity feminism can provide a means to address these issues. That is one of several topics to be examined in the final chapter as we further consider the emancipatory potential of the consumption imperative and body panic.

6

Emancipatory Potential, Social Justice, and the Consumption Imperative

In 1993, William Solomon and Michael Messner published a journal article in the *Sociology of Sport Journal* titled "Outside the Frame: Newspaper Coverage of the Sugar Ray Leonard Wife Abuse Story." In this analysis, the authors split the types of newspaper coverage of this famous abuse case into two categories. Themes that dominated print media coverage of the case were said to be "inside the frame" (in this instance, stories of drug abuse and alcohol use, and individualized stories of sin and redemption from starting/stopping drugs and alcohol), while other themes remained wholly "outside" of the print media framings of the event (analysis about wife abuse) (Messner and Solomon 1993). When we originally began working on this book together, we were discussing the conceptual work in this analysis, and during the course of our conversation, we linked Messner and Solomon's concept of "outside the media frame" with a term known as the "realm of the unfathomable." The phrase the "realm of the unfathomable" was coined by the French philosopher Michel Foucault to highlight how particular configurations of power and knowledge intersect to produce a preponderance of certain types of knowledge claims while others are wholly unthinkable, or left out (e.g., outside the frame).

In Messner and Solomon's analysis, the "wholly unthinkable" themes stood on the side of social justice frames. Here, the authors recognized the paradoxes associated with limiting the print media coverage about a domestic violence case between a (famous male athlete) husband and wife to themes of drug and alcohol abuse (and themes of individual morality/sin/redemption associated with drugs/alcohol), without discussing masculinity, sport, violence, or gender inequality. Not all scholars would agree with this interpretation, of course. For example, in Darnell Hunt's book,

OJ Simpson Fact and Fiction: News Rituals in the Construction of Reality (1999), that examined print media coverage of the O.J. Simpson murder trial, he underscored how race should be central to any analysis of what is or is not inside of media frames. Some researchers would therefore argue that negative media attention is in fact disproportionately cast upon sports stars, particularly African-American athletes. Given the ways in which media focuses attention on the "bad behavior" of such celebrities, it frames their guilt as predetermined due to racialized and racist notions of crime in U.S. society, foreclosing discussions of possible innocence.

Nonetheless, similar conceptual work on what is included or excluded from analytical framings of events was offered by Karin Lutzen, in her 1995 published work titled "La mise en discours and silences in research on the history of sexuality." In this work, she highlights how certain deviant sexual acts were not marked as such during the 1800s. Individuals who carried out what many would clearly call sexually deviant acts in contemporary culture were not arrested for sexual deviance at that time, but rather, were arrested for "pathological obsessions"[1] Her chapter highlights that it is analytically important to examine not only what history says about sexuality—but also what it does not say. She notes that "with silence as a track, one must reconstruct the attitude causing the refusal to talk" (p. 23). Throughout Lutzen's work, silences and omissions are indirectly linked to social justice, as her central concerns are linked to the ways in which history is often unable to constitute the discursive logic associated with recognition of the sensual, erotic, or sexual.

By "studying up" on dominant health and fitness ideals and by extension examining the politics of inclusion and omission in our own relational coverage of women's and men's health and fitness magazines in *Body Panic*, we took a similar analytical approach. We carried out an analysis of what is included inside the frame of health and fitness media texts concerning gender and bodies—and also examined what remains external to or outside of imagery and text. Despite the common analyses of the past within an academic sociology of sport, fitness, and media that often report men as subjects and women as objects,[2] our own analysis did not solely uncover a simple, traditional female object/male subject dichotomy. Rather, for the most privileged bodies, the convergence of experiences by gender makes objecthood for both men and women a sign of status and part of the experience of idealized subjecthood in consumer culture.

In this work, we combined a number of approaches to generate a new analysis of gender and the body in consumer culture. First, we carried out

longitudinal analysis of media materials instead of using the more typical cross-sectional analysis that examines one snapshot in time. Second,
instead of focusing on a woman-centered or male-centered analysis, we
carried out a relational analysis of both women's and men's fitness media
texts. Through these two analytic strategies, we've attempted to uncover
a more thorough analysis not only of gender relations and the body, but
of an intersectional analysis of race, class, sexuality, and the body as well.
We met these goals first through much needed empirical recognition of
a gendered bodily continuum of prescribed goals and practices (e.g., to
produce low body fat), body poses, facial expressions, and bodily positioning by gender. Our work might therefore be considered an empirical
examination of Mary Jo Kane's useful theoretical frame proposed in the
1990s and known as "a continuum of overlapping size, strength, and performances" across genders. Typically, Kane had found that media (in her
analysis, sports media) had reproduced cultural mechanisms that erase or
trivialize female athletes while featuring men in ways that helped to produce an ongoing myth of dichotomous gender difference that reaffirmed
natural male physical superiority. As was underscored in chapter 1, Kane
argued that an analysis of sport and fitness media clearly revealed a gap
between reality and media coverage, where material experience offers evidence of a continuum of overlap.

In the case of our analysis of women's and men's health and fitness
magazines, we did in fact uncover some innovative findings concerning
the tendency toward convergence and overlap by gender over time in
media trends (body fat, head shots, facial expressions, hand positionings,
active/passive poses) and prescribed fashion, grooming, and leisure products (chapter 2). Note, however, that we *only* saw this overlap in terms of
certain domains. In a few areas, "natural gender difference" was assiduously constructed. Physical size and sexuality were two key areas in which
men and women were exhorted to work to achieve their "true" natures.

Recognizing the profitability of the difference market is critical to understanding how gender has been framed in consumer culture. It is only
by purchasing gendered grooming products that simultaneously converge
in function, engaging the proper services (again, services that are largely
converging, but are marked with titles that insist on gender difference,
i.e., Mani-cures), and through displays of the appropriate products and
styles that the idealized male or female body is marked. The sheer volume
of bodywork and maintenance necessary to do this makes the endeavor
seem like a truly meaningful project of the self. Such individualized body

projects take on the moral equivalent of the projects of the soul that were so popular in the nineteenth century. The necessity of consumption to being a good citizen has been called into question by scholars as underscoring a neoliberal agenda and benefiting multinationals as social programs that benefit the multitudes erode (Baudrillard 1998; also see Klein 2002; Landau 2004; Crawshaw 2007). Both women and men are subject to these trends, although some important differences were also uncovered, particularly in chapter 3.

In chapter 3, we argued that bodily trends for women and men were not just converging and men in fitness media are not only constituted as having objective aspects within being-as-subject. Through the analysis, we argued that men's objectified status still offers powerful forms of subjecthood, which were not included inside the frame of women's fitness magazines. These forms of subjecthood, we showed, are linked to the display and actualization of hegemonic masculinity through a large physical size, the placement of muscle on certain parts of the body over others, and institutionalized links to sport, the military, and police work. Chapter 3 also underscored the ways in which the idealized male body was accompanied by a "third wave" crisis of masculinity through themes of masculinism, fears of social feminism, and a backlash to feminism that were constructed and partly resolved through male body panic.

The findings from men's magazines differed somewhat from women's magazines, which did not tend to feature or prescribe upper body strength, focusing instead on lower body "moves," toning, and light weights. Functionality, or the type of bodily practice that women and men were supposed to enact, further differentiated men and women. Although men's and women's workouts were shown to converge to some extent, men's workouts were more often linked to athletic or sports performance than women's, and professional fitness contests were more likely to constitute an entire women's magazine (e.g., *Ms. Fitness*) versus the occasional presence of these experts within men's fitness magazines. Furthermore, chapter 4 revealed the tendency for white, heterosexual, middle-class notions of fit family values and domesticity to triumph in the case of pregnant women. Hence, magazines overall were quite centered on the constitution of "emphasized femininity," which is defined as the form of femininity that is dominant in a given era: white, middle class, and heterosexual, shaped in relation to hegemonic masculinity (Connell 1987).

At the same time that chapters 2 and 3 partly challenged and reinforced a gendered bodily subject/object dichotomy, they also underscored the importance of intersecting relations of power that stretch beyond gender to include race and sexuality. These intersections highlight another key flaw in the main claims of work that relies on the subject/object dichotomy in sport and fitness media—or even for those authors who claim that the dichotomy has been flipped (Heywood and Dworkin 2003). Adding race and sexuality to the analysis of media frames uncovered that a range of races were featured in ads (chapter 2), but the race of cover models and those demonstrating workouts in the magazines was overwhelmingly white. The same trend was found in chapters 4 and 5. We also found the tendency to only feature "lighter" skinned models with "European" facial features and straightened hair in both men's and women's health and fitness magazines. Nonwhite individuals were not featured much at all, and thus their inclusion almost solely in ads therefore plays a very particular role within health and fitness magazines—that of featuring the progressiveness of the advertisers or the consumers of the products being marketed while the key players in the magazines remained a clear white majority.

In chapter 3, race and class relations were also built into the connections made between concerns for physical fitness, restoring force, re-energizing masculinity, and reaffirmations of control during times of war, revealing similarities to other historical calls for physical fitness that circulated widely in public during times of war. The specificity of signifiers of size and protection that emerged in fitness magazines during times of war corresponds to new forms of societal uncertainty and assists with the production of a moral order based on gender, race, class, and nation. That is, we highlighted that actual men in hegemonic sports and the military are disproportionately men of color and working-class men, while models in the magazines depicted as moral, fit, and responsible for national protection were overwhelmingly white and middle class. The magazines target a demographic of readers who are largely middle class, while the "enemies" (e.g., "criminals," "terrorists") loom large and readers must build themselves up to protect against a perceived enemy, largely marked with tropes signaling that they are disproportionately of lower socioeconomic status. When one expands this analysis to an international context and considers the disparities between the "deserving" haves who must be protected from the "immoral" have-nots, this reinforces the necessity of critical media analysis.

The resultant effect of our combined analysis of materials leads us to form conclusions based not only on gender but also pertaining to race, nation, and socioeconomic status. We conclude that when media offer limited inclusion of images of the healthy ideal, and overlook numerous nonwhite bodies, this produces a situation in which people of color are, by extension, left out of the frame and are associated with the negative stigmas tied to unhealthy bodies. Dominant bodies are in the center of the frame, to be linked to the moral signifiers afforded to bodies that meet the ideal. This analysis represents the flip side of a long history of social analysis on media content that has tended to include people of color in the frame while erroneously conflating these groups with a lack of morality. Such omissions also offer the opportunity to reinforce contemporary race and class relations in such a way that "terrorists" and "criminals" remain external to the frame, inadvertently reinforcing atavistic notions of people of color, the underclass, Middle Eastern populations, and the poor. These frames serve very specific purposes in terms of reconfiguring a masculinist national identity post-9/11, and such tactics are consistent with those who note that the East is viewed as "the site of passivity and irrationality awaiting the conquest by the masculine and rational West" (Volpp 2003, p. 154, as cited in Takacs 2005, p. 300).

Including people of color sparsely in the main content (in terms of "terror," the East is never in the frame) while including them in numerous advertisements allows for media audiences to consume the "other" while working to reduce feelings or racism, "providing the guise that one is not racist," "viewers can feel as if their consumption and appropriation of the other is a sign of respect of the other rather than a sign of disrespect or exploitation" (see hooks 2000; Smith and Beal 2007). As was noted in chapter 2, through the process of buying magazines, gazing at the imagery, text, and ads, consumers can be associated with many different positive antiracist imaginings through which one can avoid the appearance of direct participation in racist and classist social structures. This underscores bell hooks' observations regarding the use of the "other" as a panacea for guilt, creating the impression that racism is a thing of the past, while obscuring and partly reproducing its continual manifestation (hooks 1992).

These findings are consistent with those of other researchers who argue that the ways in which people of color have been packaged in America have long aided white and middle-class consumers in thinking that they are embracing the "messy problems of actually distributing resources," or "living the effects of affirmative action" (Banet-Weiser 1999; Gray 1992). Framing the solutions in individualized prescriptions for health and fitness is the way that healthism operates to displace blame for structural scenarios that leave marginalized individuals with fewer and qualitatively worse options onto their assumed-to-be less moral actions or individual bodies. The process within the magazines simultaneously reinforces and justifies the privileging of some bodies while reinforcing the stigma of oppression[3] by marking some bodies as inherently flawed, immoral, or unwilling to do the work necessary to obtain a "better" form. As noted in chapter 1, health discourse frequently operates, similar to medicine, to situate the problem of health and disease at the level of the individual. Within such a system, a lack of health begins to be associated with individual "moral laxity."[4] By framing the maintenance of health as the responsibility of all individuals, the "person is the victim of her/his health turned nasty, but also the agency responsible for this state of affairs" (Fox 1993 as cited in Lupton 1995, p. 70). Reinforcing neoliberal conceptions of individual responsibility, it is largely through individualized solutions employed in the project of the self that one displays personal commitments to healthism (Cranshaw 2007).

The above comments are important to consider because tropes of guilt or failure reaffirm narratives of race and class (Jhally 1987), and undergird the myth of meritocracy central to notions of the American dream. These points also raise larger questions about whether magazines are in fact deploying the status of experts to prescribe fitness practices/products to constitute narratives about *health*. That is, given the critically important role that race and socioeconomic status play in the actual health of bodies, omissions about these links and health raise fundamental questions about what is actually for sale in the magazines. While the marketplace increasingly becomes a source of expert advice, it creates a "moralism that is extended to people who become ill because they have allowed themselves to be . . . by failing to regulate their 'lifestyle' with sufficient discipline" (Lupton 1995, p. 75).

As we progressed through this work, it became clear that an analysis of bodies that examined the politics of inclusion and exclusion requires a sociological social justice analysis, an analysis centered on media and consumer culture, and a medical sociological one, too. Such an analysis holds not only for gender, race, and class issues but also certainly for sexuality. Some might argue that the tendency to include "gay vague" (chapter 2) (which acknowledges the "gay gaze" for men in some small segment of men's health and fitness magazines that are sold largely to heterosexual men) is simply a strategic marketing tactic endorsed to please a growing target demographic of increasingly dollared (and fit) gay and middle-/ upper-middle-class men. However, it is also important to underscore that such cultural alterations reformulate the subject/object metaphor in another important way. For example, as Dowsett argued, societal norms have now shifted and it

> becomes publicly permissible for men to be passively gazed upon and desired. Consequently, this can apply to all men, and that historic achievement is a dangerous and destabilizing shift in Western sexual formations, for it blurs the generally accepted gender distinctions between men and women, and generates uncertainty as to what appropriately constitutes the masculine and the feminine. (1994, p. 73)

Thus, in chapter 3, when media imagery and content relied on the link between fitness and social responsibility through the deployment of iconography from the military, firefighters, and police officers, this is not

Evidence that contemporary culture offers an increased allowance for men to be passively gazed upon and desired. This has historically been the subjsect position for women in media imagery. (*Exercise & Health*, Fall 2001)

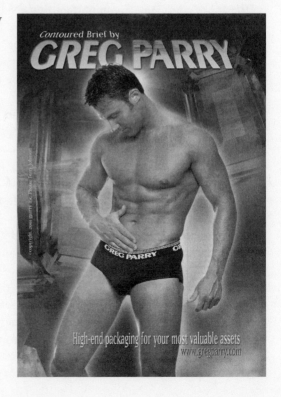

Contoured Brief by

GREG PARRY

GREG PARRY

High-end packaging for your most valuable assets
www.gregparry.com

simply about creating gender difference or reaffirmations or the reproduction of hegemonic masculinity. Instead of a desiring young woman gazing at marines displaying ripped abs under their flight suits, it would be male readers who often gazed upon these forms. These facts destabilize the traditional relationship between subjectivity and gender, and undermine traditional notions of masculinity, making men into desired objects to be gazed at by other men, no matter what their sexuality.

However, as we've noted, there isn't anything close to offering equal-opportunity consideration of a parallel range of sexualities for audiences of women reading women's magazines. Within chapters 2–5, in the case of sexuality, heterosexuality is repeatedly reinvoked across both women's and men's magazines. For men, sexual success with women was a nearly omnipresent theme. While the women's magazines were devoid of any references to alternative family forms or relationships, or gay vague in advertisements, men's magazines did not contain explicit references to sexuality, but several of the magazines met the criteria for "gay vague." That is, while presenting a dominant text that appeared to be unambiguously heterosexual, advertisements, articles, and images presented a fairly ambiguous context. A further ambiguity about male sexuality is also created by the cultural move to present male bodies more generally as objects to be gazed upon. Given that women have long been presented in this way, recent presentations of men as objects carry some semblance of feminine connotations.

The producers of the magazine may not explicitly wish to mark the main magazine content as being willing to court alternative sexualities which might alienate heterosexual readers, given the stigma of homosexuality. However, gay vague is a very effective indirect alternative since the "use of implicit gay and lesbian imagery such as gay and lesbian iconography and symbolism may allow marketers to effectively target the gay and lesbian consumers who will recognize the symbolism . . . while posing far less risk of offending heterosexual consumers, who may be unaware of the content" (Oakenfull et al. 2005). The strategy of gay vague has also been termed a dual marketing strategy known as "gay window advertising" (Stabiner 1982). Exploring this concept in her analysis of "commodity lesbianism," Danae Clark underscores that "gays and lesbians can read into an ad certain subtextual elements that correspond to experiences with or representations of gay/lesbian subculture. If heterosexual consumers do not notice these subtexts or subcultural codes, then advertisers are able to reach the homosexual market along with the heterosexual market without ever revealing their aim" (1993). At the same time that androgyny in women has become more commonplace in fashion and advertising, it is interesting to note the ways in which fitness in particular has played a role in constructing emphasized femininity, or the most dominant form of femininity in a given period. As underscored by other researchers who examine the ways in which sexuality symbolism is carefully cross-coded (or excluded) by media producers, "care must be taken not to appease one audience while forsaking another" (Oakenfull et al. 2005).

The ways in which media imagery and text offer the opportunity for different audiences (or the same person to occupy several different audiences) to bring varied readings to imagery and text offers what some would call emancipatory potential through fluidity in the gender and sexuality order (Dowsett 1994; Miller 2001; Griggers 1994). Similar to the situation with race, ads appeared to offer more progressive content than the main articles. One need only consider the Snickers commercial of two men kissing during the most recent (2007) Super Bowl to understand the varied audiences that advertising can cater to in a more playful manner than is often offered in the main content of a program. Simultaneously, however, there were literally no ads and very rare references directed overtly toward lesbian or bisexual women in any women's fitness magazines. Part of the reason for this may be because there is no agreed upon singular female bodily ideal that might overlap across sexual identity categories, whereas there may be an agreed upon and valorized hegemonic male form that overlaps across sexual identity categories (large, muscular, cut). Nevertheless, the lack of gay vague in the women's magazines coupled with its frequent inclusion in men's magazines is an important gender difference that needs to be fleshed out further, for it represents what Lutzen would term a particularly strong silence.

Given the long history of associations between corporeality, masculinity, femininity, and sexuality and the prominence of sexuality in recent political debates over GLBT rights, the lack of acknowledgment of a range of sexualities affirms heteronormativity. This is especially the case for *Women's Sports & Fitness*, which explicitly recognized feminist issues in sport, issues of gender inequality and distributive justice, and yet an analysis of sexuality and sport was almost entirely mute during our study period. This is the case despite the historical recognition that women of alternative sexualities flock to sport for safety, validation, and camaraderie (Cahn 1994; Griffin 1998; Nelson 1995).

Of importance was the fact that cross-coding to nonheterosexual women was equally invisible in the realm of fitness, and despite a very large demographic of non heterosexual women who are having children and who could be catered to in the "shape fit motherhood" market, there were no mentions of same-sex families, relationships, or fitness needs for two mothers within that publication ("Families that stay/play together"). In chapter 4, in our analysis of *Shape Fit Pregnancy*, we highlighted how contemporary fitness discourse for mothers only deployed sports analogies to train women before, during, and after labor, while "getting your body back" with the baby normalized women's responsibility for domestic heterosexual motherhood[5] at home. Additionally, we previously noted how contemporary fit motherhood eased fears of a loss of femininity from weight work with feminized baby barbells at home. The fact that our relational analysis of men's and women's magazines uncovered a strong link between men's magazines and sports and women's magazines and fitness may be telling in this regard.

Why might these trends hold when carrying out a relational analysis of male and female sexuality in health and fitness magazines? In 1994, Sheila Jeffreys wrote an important and relatively contentious piece in *Women's Studies International Forum* titled "The Queer Disappearance of Lesbians: Sexuality in the Academy." In it, she noted that queer theory, with its emphasis on the performative aspects of sexuality and gender, was an inadequate political tool for those who are concerned about equity and distributive justice for women and female sexuality minorities. She argued that when queer theory would take force, it would do so by erasing lesbians and featuring gay men. She considers this inevitable given "an economically powerful commercial gay male culture." This trend was first noted in a 1982 review in the *New York Times Magazine* called "Tapping the Homosexual Market" where top advertisers were said to be interested in "wooing . . . the white, single, well educated, well paid man who happens to be homosexual" (see Clark 1993, p. 187). At the same time that Jeffreys could have argued that queer theory might seem well positioned to recognize the multiplicity of signifiers that can apply across sexual identities (Griggers 1994), she argues that queer theory is "feminism free" and queer has come to symbolize "white gay male" while masquerading as "new and uniquely liberating" (p. 469). While we want to make clear that no fitness magazine explicitly contained any analysis of sexuality, gay and lesbian liberationism, or queer theory, the concept of "gay vague" and the content in ads lent themselves to the use of queer theory as an analytical frame more easily than did the disappearance of sexual minority women from the magazines.

We recognize that Jeffreys' analysis has been criticized in a number of ways, one of which is for its "misreadings" of queer theory. In this work, we do not suggest that queer theory is responsible for the trends that omit recognition of lesbian or marginalized female sexualities in health and fitness magazines. However, we do highlight that both of these trends that Jeffreys notes took place in our sample—the queering of gender and sexuality for men and the erasure of non-heterosexual women. One could argue (as some of our readers will) that the producers of content within corporate media and magazine operations are only meeting the demographic needs of their markets, or that gay men are a more powerfully dollared demographic to contend with than are lesbians. However, the production of media content cannot be viewed solely as an issue of meeting the needs of a target demographic for many reasons—one of which is that bodily signifiers have increasingly merged across gender, age, class, sexuality, and race/ethnicity (Griggers 1997) and another involves the ability for advertisers to "cross-code" across populations.

Why bodily signifiers would increasingly merge for gay and heterosexual men in fitness magazines, queering men's sexuality and not women's—when there is a growing demographic of lesbian and bisexual women who can spend cash on advertisers' products and who might clearly enjoy such recognition (and sports and fitness bodily ideals)—is not entirely clear. In short, this cannot simply be an issue of fearing the alienation of audiences who occupy dominant sexualities as men's magazines code for gay vague quite directly while women's fitness magazines do not. And, while it may be true that hegemonic male bodily ideals have been more commodified within the gay male community, there are many ways for media to effectively cross-code to nonheterosexual women that are not deployed in the magazines.[6] This omission is particularly problematic given the history of sports and the acknowledgment of lesbians and marginalized female sexualities in the history of sport.[7] Indeed, this may be another instance of how previous researchers have found that "gay imagery" is more popularly deployed than lesbian imagery in media, "mirroring the enormous bias toward male-oriented advertising in gay and lesbian media" (Oakenfull et al. 2005). This is so despite the fact that heterosexuals overall have more positive attitudes toward lesbians than they do toward gay males (ibid.), and women have more permissive attitudes toward minority sexualities than do men (see Herek 2000, 2000a).

One possible response to these debates is the issue of whether media creates or reflects "demand" for fitness products, practices, and services. Clearly, the easier position is to suggest the media only reflects current demands of the target demographic. However, it is vitally important to recognize that producers of media texts also create it. It would seem the producers of magazines spent a great deal of space constructing the needs of readers while failing in crucial ways to meet the needs of their target demographic, even when they knew what these needs were. For example, in our analysis of *Shape Fit Pregnancy* magazine, we noted that 62 percent of the readership held full-time jobs, yet little mention was made of women getting back to work in the text of the magazine—particularly in the earlier issues of our sample.

Similar analyses of the gap between the demand for certain types of media content and its (lack of) supply have been abundant around the issue of media coverage of women in sport. For instance, during the 1996 Olympics, stadiums were sold out for women's soccer events. However, print media analysis revealed that media coverage disproportionately featured those Olympic events that involved individualized sports that best characterize the qualities of emphasized femininity of grace, slenderness, and lack of contact with others (e.g., gymnastics). And, despite dramatic increases in interest for women's sports, very recent analyses now show that sports media has made miserable progress concerning the proportion of attention given to women's events. An ongoing study sponsored by the LA 84 Foundation (previously the Amateur Athletic Foundation) in Los Angeles, led by Margaret Carlisle Duncan and Michael Alan Messner, uncovered that between 1989 and 2005, there was little improvement in the quantity of print and televised media coverage of women's sports relative to men's, and in some cases, there was actually a decrease in some types of reporting on women's sports in terms of the proportion of airtime on several major network news stations. Women's sports continue to lack commensurate audience-building activities relative to men's sports (Messner, Duncan, and Wachs 1996), and newsroom work routines disadvantage women's sports (Theberge and Cronk 1986; also see Hunt 1999). As a result, women's sports and athletics are not imbued with the same importance and prominence as men's events.

Our analysis also points to the need to consider the pastiche of signifiers that producers of media texts use to seek profit and disseminate notions of health. These ranged from the strategic deployment of "just do it" commodity feminism to produce fit mothers in the name of getting their bodies back, reaffirmations of hegemonic masculinity, the commodification of signifiers from progressive social movements to sell products and bodily norms, the destabilization of men as subjects through the gay gaze, the deployment of a discourse of "science" and "health" to sell idealized gendered bodily norms, and the erasure of lesbians, transgenders, and racial/ethnic minorities. What is left inside the frame is a consumer-based project of the self which is validated while personal physical investments are imbued with health and morality. Communal concerns and public responsibility continue to form a major "silence." Commodity feminism further demonstrates the silence of communal concerns with its merger of style and identity such that femininity and feminism are conflated for readers who are encouraged to engage in social action exclusively through marketplace purchases (Goldman, Heath, and Smith 1991).

What are the implications of the very real tensions we've raised in the uncomfortable juncture between emancipatory potential, the consumption imperative, and social justice? In chapter 5, we noted that the rise of commodity feminism has left individual readers of media texts in a consumption conundrum—one that sold the liberatory potential of products, services, and practices to the individualized self while literally erasing more structural and collective forms of distributive and social justice. This was reflected not only in the content analysis but in the literal structural closing down of a women's sport and fitness media text that emphasized institutional aspects of justice which was replaced by the more individualist *Self*. We argued that by combining second wave feminist attention to structural and institutional inequality, multiracial feminist intersectionality, and third wave critiques of consumer culture, both the "liberatory potential" and the new forms of inequity engendered simultaneously, might offer solid insights.

This approach is particularly necessary given that achieving success in the neoliberal marketplace disproportionately means individual responsibility for personal success. Discourses of health, and the legitimation of magazines as sources of information regarding the science of health, produce areas of expertise that are viewed as essential. Through a process of dedifferentiation, healthism comes to permeate all aspects of advice,[8] merging consumer and health concerns seamlessly as the style of health, and lifestyles become synonymous with actual health. Over time, individual improvement becomes self-improvement and the neoliberal marketplace becomes an imperative part of the construction of the healthy self. At the same time, blame for the negative aspects of consumer culture or social injustices found within social structures is systematically displaced. The next section examines these forces in greater depth.

Displacement of Blame

Both men and women's fitness magazines displaced blame for the negative aspects of consumer culture onto marginalized groups and individualized bodies (Duncan 1994). This occurred in a number of ways. First, a displacement of the negative aspects of consumer culture was accomplished through the stigmatization of those not succeeding in consumer displays (some of whom were inside the frame, and others who were outside of the frame). Outside the frame were a mythic group of (less progressive) others who didn't carry out what the more up to date or progressive reader might enact. The use of text and image implied that participation in dominant privileged lifestyles is a resistant activity. That is, when readers engaged in the activities, practices, or lifestyles that are espoused by magazines as "new" or "current," they were framed as resistant and standing in brave opposition to a mythical set of others who spouted outdated philosophies that threaten to hold them back (Garvey 1996).

By creating "new" practices, products, and services and attaching signifiers of morality, health, or public citizenship to bodily ideals within the frame, those who stand inside of the frame are paradoxically rendered "resistant" to an out-of-date past right at the moment in which he or she may be most complicit in maintaining the status quo. Just as early magazines equated buying "modern" conveniences like bicycles with being the new woman (Garvey 1996), readers of today's health and fitness magazines are led to believe that using the latest health and fitness products makes them and their bodies signifiers of an exclusive or more moral group. In various chapters and in our summary at the beginning of this chapter, we have alluded to how these signifiers work to reinforce various classed, racialized, sexualized, and gendered relations of power, including designations of morality, health, citizenship, and more.

Second, many of the injunctions and negative aspects of a consumer culture of lack were displaced onto the dictums of natural gender difference. As this occurs, the parameters of natural difference are reinvoked and then called up and then tautologically used to justify engagement in consumer culture. For example, in our analysis of men's magazines in chapter 3, male body panic was rife with fears of social feminization, and groups that dared to challenge notions about the real nature of men or gender differences between men and women were called up as a source of humor and derision. Paradoxically resolving body panic through a better tie or more muscle offers the impression that men's problems reside in the region of style. Only by restyling masculinity, specifically around men's appearance and sexual prowess, can gender wars that are rooted in complex structural changes be solved. In short, the magazines offered bodily and consumption-based solutions that relied on tropes of gender and nature to solve complex, global structural social problems.

Note that the texts failed to highlight how men's experiences are contextualized within an arena of increasing global inequality, declining real wages, the rise of the urban underclass, domestic shifts in race, class, and gender inequality, or an exportation of jobs to Third World countries and peripheral nations. Rather, when men's careers were described as faltering, it was the wrong shirt, abs, hair, or tie that defined (and solved) the problem. Men who were constructed as "slipping behind" on the job were framed as failing to consume the appropriate array of goods and services that were solutions to becoming the "right" kind of successful man. Just as for women, becoming a successful object resolves the tensions and displaces the blame associated with broader forces that shape health and fitness.

Furthermore, processes of inclusion and exclusion within media frames and processes of blame obscure the relationship between gendered bodily practices and health. That is, what is being sold or promoted within the health and fitness industry is not necessarily a healthy body, but a body that looks and enacts gendered "health" through sufficiently gendered signifiers. Using Haug's subjective aspects within being-as-object and objective aspects within being-as-subject, we argued that gendered bodily ideals became tied not solely to health, but to what type of object and subjecthood are available to women and men in postmodern consumer culture. Our analysis revealed that despite recent trends to objectify both men and women, men's objectification was more often tied to the maintenance of male-dominated institutional privileges (sport, military, police work) and demonstrated taking up space through powerful action, while women's objectification tended to remain tied to decreased body mass and service to others (second and third shifts, and having less leisure time).

Third, along these lines, the negative aspects of consumer culture were redefined as fundamental flaws that lie within men and women (and their failure to attain idealized natural gender differences, primarily of physical appearance). We have previously discussed how women have long measured their worth in culture through their success at being the right kind of object. Building on this, women's power within many media frames comes to mean not just competency, but superiority at this task. While it is true that both women's and men's magazines portray women's power as situated in their ability to master objecthood, sexuality in particular was differentially constructed for women and men. Men's success with women was predicated not only on appearance, but on sexual performance, something that is done to women. Women's power as her sexual allure for men reaffirms women's experience of the subjective aspects within being-as-object, but in somewhat problematic ways.

Note the contrast between men's power over women as coming from what they can do to women, while women's power over men comes from self-presentation. While post-feminists have continued to maintain that women's beauty operates as a form of social and cultural power, third wave feminism has painted a far more complicated picture. Popular culture offers women limited access to power by becoming the right kind of object; however, some women are advantaged in developing beauty as capital. In this way, relations of privilege that center around race, class, and sexuality are obfuscated behind "natural beauty." Paradoxically, readers are led to believe that beauty is open to any woman willing to succumb to a series of rigors (dieting, exercise, fashion, grooming), and that it is "natural." Hence, anyone who is not deemed beautiful and granted the concomitant advantages is further stigmatized as failing to put forth the requisite effort to succeed. Our findings reinforce what other researchers have observed concerning the relationship between public health, consumer culture, and beauty ideals. For example, according to Alan Petersen and Deborah Lupton, "the feminine 'healthy' citizen, it is suggested, should seek both soundness of body and physical allure . . . in these discourses there is an elision between the ideal of commodity culture and public health, for both promote the slim, attractive, physically fit, youthful body as that which women should seek to attain" (1996).

Fourth, the magazines "talk out of both sides of their mouths," simultaneously extolling and critiquing participation in consumer culture. In this way, the negative aspects of consumer culture can be simultaneously reinvigorated and critiqued, making the magazines seem resistant, when they are generally reproductive of dominant cultural norms.[9] Moreover, the magazines have a tendency to critically analyze trends within the system, while avoiding larger critiques of the system itself. For example, magazines often mocked the frantic weight loss and dieting generated by images of perfection while simultaneously acting as a vehicle to display these same images. The use of humor to mock the overcommitted is similar to the ways that early magazines poked fun at those who absorbed the messages of advertising completely.[10] By publishing content that is critical of consumer culture, and by using humor to indicate that extreme adherence is foolish, the magazines deflect criticism from themselves and most of the tenets of consumer culture.

These types of tactics are consistent with the ways in which magazines and advertisers are "able to assimilate feminist criticisms . . . as well as elements of progressive social change" (Lazar 2006). Such tactics are also consistent with "the trend towards critical engagement in consumer health cultures" which is "mobilized by a perceived democratic right to question normative beliefs" (Newman 2007). Some argue that simply by providing multiple competing alternatives that offer the illusion of choice, magazine content again reinforces contemporary neoliberalism that promotes the concept that individuals are simply free to choose and can liberate themselves from constraints if they put their minds to it and decide to.[11] Once again, however, "the idea that women have only to make the right health 'choices' ignores both the complex range of determinants which shape health outcomes and the rapidly shifting boundaries between convention and critique in consumer health politics" (Dworkin and Messner 1999, p. 165).

Finally, consumer culture is presented as the solution to the very problems it engenders. The presumption of the necessity of presenting a certain image of the new contemporary individual operates as a fundamental assumption that reinforces consumer culture. The magazines offer readers the ability to reaffirm their good citizenry and moral natures by participating in the "right kind of consumption." Moreover, the problems of a "project of the self" conducted through practices shaped primarily by market forces are solved through finding the "right" ways to consume. Rather than the more radical solutions offered by the critiques we've raised or by the anticonsumer movement, consumers can displace the negative effects of consumer culture by simply self-constituting in pleasurable and lifestyle-validating ways. Certainly, the failure to consider meaningful alternatives structures (some of) the parameters for social change in the contemporary era. As public responsibility and accountability erode in the face of neoliberal assaults, one of the main legitimate means to enact social, political, and cultural change that appears to remain is participation in the marketplace.

Gender, Bodies, Power, Nature, and Culture

As we have been describing in this chapter, one key means to reinvigorate consumer culture is to displace the blame for its negative consequences onto natural difference. These claims require more careful examination. Because the body is largely situated in the realm of the natural, and U.S. society goes to great lengths to argue that beauty and bodies are "natural" and innate, when one transgresses the "natural" with the body, one has not only transgressed or sinned, but has sinned against nature.[12] This demonstrates the difficulty of understanding gender and the body within fitness media frames, because one is essentially asked to choose between studying bodies as a product of nature or culture, when they are always both. What is so ironic is that the magazines insist that bodies are simultaneously "natural" but also requiring constant interference. By following the prescriptions provided by the magazines, one can uncover or achieve a better "natural" body through individual effort. As a result, the body is paradoxically presumed to be natural and the result of individual effort. Failure to properly invest in the body is viewed as a failure to make the most of the natural. In other words, underneath it all, a "natural" exists, and bodies must work hard to maximize the "natural" while minimizing other unnatural manifestations.

Unpacking this complexity requires a closer theoretical examination of the nexus of nature and culture. Latour notes the differentiation of these poles is at the crux of relations of power (1993). In other words, by designating some bodily forms and practices as "natural" for those at certain social locations, power is manifest. It is precisely by defining concerns as natural, health-related, or as seamlessly merged with issues of medicalization that consumer culture and its concomitant practices are protected from critical scrutiny. At the same time, those in specific subject locations are legitimated (included in the frame) or stigmatized (left outside of the frame). The specific ways in which the poles of nature, culture, and the body come together within media texts form a body/consumer matrix that will be described next. The body/consumer is a fertile route through which to examine the ways in which domestic and global relations of power are disseminated, defined, modified, and deployed.

Social Justice and the Body/Consumer Matrix

On July 14, 2005, the lead story of the *Los Angeles Times* covers the governor of California (former Mr. Universe and film star) Arnold Schwarzenegger. He has accepted an estimated $8 million in consulting fees from a fitness magazine to "further the business objectives" of the publisher of several health and fitness magazines. In an unrelated news story, he also vetoed legislation that would have imposed government regulation on the supplement industry, an industry on which these magazines rely heavily for advertising (Nicholas and Salladay 2005, July 14). Consistent with healthism, a discussion of the role and responsibilities of the state in promoting health and fitness is virtually ignored by media. For example, while government at all levels laments the obesity crisis, it is generally framed as an individual failure, and the structural factors that contribute to obesity are largely ignored.[13] With the speed-up in work, declining real wages, shortages of affordable childcare, and availability of fast food, it is not surprising that people are out of shape. Providing safe, available, and attractive places in which to work out is difficult since the funding for parks, after-school programs, and community centers continues to erode.

One of the most striking features of our analysis is the abdication of public responsibility for providing and protecting individuals' abilities to engage in health and fitness practices, and the ascendancy of individual responsibility for such endeavors. After examining all of the magazines, we were struck by Judith Williamson's observation that advertising perpetuates the idea that we are free to choose (Williamson 1986). In this view, (much of) our power is carefully repackaged to us as the power to choose between a range of similar options. If these magazines are construed as advertisements for privileged lifestyles in the new millennium, the reader is offered a variety of choices that amount to engagement in a similar consumerist lifestyle. Since most media are dependent on advertising, media which stimulates aesthetically oriented consumption is more desirable for advertisers. The usurpation of texts which do not reinvigorate consumption-oriented content, as discussed in chapter 5 with the demise of *Women's Sports & Fitness* (or dominant ideals of gender, race, class, and sexuality), demonstrates the pervasiveness of a body/consumption matrix.

Public responsibility to the citizenry to assist in the process of obtaining health has been largely abdicated, as citizenship has been replaced by consumerism (Landau 2004). Progress moves out of the realm of the advancement of society to refer explicitly to individual improvement. Baudrillard similarly notes the rise of a dominant mythology of the individual pleasure seeker, whose enjoyment is limited to consuming a wide range of goods and services (Baudrillard 1998). Even altruism, according to some scholars, becomes primarily a consumerist practice, as charity comes to mean buying products adorned with pink ribbons, mailing in yogurt caps, or participating in often costly walks, runs, or bike rides (King 2006). This means that the basic things necessary for health and fitness, such as health care, usable open spaces, affordable quality food, are not inside of the media frame of free market concerns in the body/consumer matrix.

It must be acknowledged that the democratic possibilities of the project of the self in consumer culture are far greater than in many societies of the past and present. Negotiating identity through display allows many more the possibility of advancement in the social order (Giddens 1991, 2000). At the same time, it is impossible to ignore the advantages some bodies have, both in terms of the ability to engage in practices, and the ascribed characteristics that are made meaningful given the unique historical moment of a given society. Race, sexuality, class, and gender are all critical master statuses that significantly affect the body one is encourage to develop, how one's body is read, and to what type of scrutiny one's body is subjected. Foucault's distinction between the docile bodies of the poor and disenfranchised, subject to panoptic scrutiny and the confessional body of the privileged (subject to self-scrutiny), highlights this distinction (Foucault 1979). While privileged bodies bemoan the size of their bodies (depending on their gender, as discussed in chapter 2), their body fat percentage, and more, a host of bodies toil in sweatshops, work as domestics, and clean the gym equipment of the privileged. Interestingly, while these bodies are subject to panoptic scrutiny as labor, they are largely invisible to the confessional bodies reaping the benefits of their labor. Thus, structural realities intersect with media in important ways to produce differentially valued forms of cultural capital whose values inhere in the body. Cultural capital acquired and deployed as a resource through the body is called bodily capital. Bodily capital is something that can be selectively deployed, as was noted in chapter 3, as a type of "mobile resource" (Skeggs 2004) that is used by more privileged individuals for their benefit, or it can be overdetermined among the bodies of the marginalized and used as evidence of their sense of "lack."[14]

How do individuals reconcile their participation in a body/consumer matrix that has contributed to—and is part of—a changing social landscape that is redefining the parameters of social justice toward more consumption-based individualism? And what types of research should gender, body, and health/fitness scholars engage in to press beyond the constraints we've found within such a matrix? Certainly, coming to question these dictums and to consider and participate in meaningful alternatives is the first step toward positive social change. Additionally, continuing to describe, analyze, and then place pressure on media to expand upon the range of imagery for both women and men beyond powerful male subjects and domestic and sexualized female objects is needed. While some positive changes were seen in these trends over time, more of this trend would lead to better representation of an actual continuum of overlapping bodies and performances by gender. It would also open up the possibility to make critical challenges as to whether it is health or gender (a racialized, classed, sexualized one) for sale in magazines.

Additionally, improving the quantity and quality of inclusion of minorities and a wider range of sexualities would provide important cultural work that would minimize displacements of blame for poor health onto disenfranchised groups, reshaping ideologies that are frequently used to justify differences in access to resources and along lines of distributive justice. Similar to other social movements that include the voices of the affected,[15] it would certainly be novel to include voices of discontent and represent the needs of more than a narrow target demographic. While not necessarily a popular concept, important collaborations can take place between academic, corporate, and community-based groups dedicated to corporate social responsibility. Here, collaborations that take social justice stances while using media imagery and text to further many of its causes are one promising avenue for social change.[16] Those campaigns that move beyond "corporate social responsibility" philanthropic stances to form truly collaborative relationships across stakeholders to define, identify, and solve social problems using the creativity and appeal of media and branding is certainly one such possibility (Bruns 2006).

And finally, in order for Sociology and Cultural Studies to advance analysis on the tensions between the consumption imperative, producers of media texts, and emancipatory potential—which seem to keep cropping up repeatedly over time—it would be helpful to press for further interdisciplinary analysis. These different fields—and Medical Sociology and Public Health—could increasingly join forces in future analyses.

Here, the relationship between profit imperatives, media content, social justice, and how these factors are linked to bodies and health needs to be better understood. As Messner suggests, the cultural/symbolic realm is one of three key areas critical to challenging gender regimes and achieving equity. Extending analyses of gender, bodies, and media to reach the inner workings of media organizations is a necessary collaboration not only to unravel the black box of daily operations, but also to find new areas of overlap between the goals of profit, the imperative of social justice, the need to reduce health disparities, and positive social change.

Finding (and taking) space to do just that is all the more necessary in an environment in which government spending wanes in most areas of distributive justice while war funds dominate. Participation in health and fitness as prescribed in consumer culture need not structure frames where size matters so narrowly in the ways we have highlighted. Rather, the size and space of representational frames can stretch beyond size matters to fill in the silences and omissions, and to include justice—distributive, corporeal, and health-related—concerning race, class, gender, and sexuality.

Appendix

Our initial coding consisted of seven men's and seven women's health and fitness magazines. We coded three issues in 1997–1998, selected at random (seasons were separated so that all issues did not come from a particular time of year).

Magazine	Issue Dates
Exercise for Men Only	February 1998, December 1997, August 1997
Exercise & Health	Spring 1998, Winter 1997, Fall 1997
Fitness Plus	January 1998, November 1997, March 1997
Men's Exercise	March 1998, January 1998, November 1997
Men's Fitness	December 1997, November 1997, September 1997
Men's Health	December 1997, November 1997, September 1997
Prime Health & Fitness	Fall 1998, Spring 1998, Winter 1997
Fit	January/February 1998, November/December 1997, September 1997
Fitness	November 1997, October 1997, September 1997
Living Fit	January/February 1998, November/December 1997, September 1997
Ms. Fitness	Fall 1998, Fall 1997, Summer 1997
Shape	November 1998, October 1997, September 1997
Women's Fitness	November 1997, August 1997, June 1997
Women's Sports & Fitness	November/December 1998, March/April 1998, January/February 1998

Final codings involved selecting two issues a year from the following magazines. Cover codes involved selecting a random sample from the magazines, though we did not limit ourselves to only two a year as we did for the workout codes.

	Magazines from Which Sample Was Selected
Men's Magazines	*Exercise for Men Only, Exercise & Health, Men's Exercise, Men's Fitness, Men's Health*
Women's Magazines	*Fit, Fitness, Living Fit, Ms. Fitness, Shape, Women's Sports & Fitness/Self*

Date	Total Pages	Pages of Ads	Ratio of Ads: Total (%)
January 1979	71	18	25.0
July 1979	68	23	34.0
May 1980	70	20	28.6
August 1980	68	13	19.0
October 1981	67	19	28.0
June 1981	68	15	22.0
August 1982	62	14	22.0
January 1982	70	22	31.4
December 1983	78	15	19.2
May 1983	62	14	22.5
March 1984	62	18	29.0
September 1984	62	18	29.0
August 1985	62	21	34.0
January/February 1985	78	23	32.0
August 1986	64	20	31.0
November 1986	72	24	33.0
February 1987	80	28	35.0
July 1987	70	21	30.0
December 1988	60	17	28.0
May 1988	84	23	27.0
June 1989	68	15	22.0
October 1989	68	16	24.0
June 1990	84	34	40.0
November/December 1990	64	15	23.0
January/February 1991	66	13	20.0
August 1991	72	24	33.0
October 1992	72	25	35.0
June 1992	116	33	28.0
November 1993	88	32	36.0
March 1993	88	32	36.0
June 1994	104	45	43.0
September 1994	84	25	30.0
August 1995	100	36	36.0
April 1996	100	37	37.0
December 1996	84	39	46.0
April 1997	98	41	42.0
June 1998	130	50	38.0
November/December 1998	141	39	28.0
July/August 1999	141	44	31.0
March 2000	134	47	35.0
September 2000	150	49	33.0
December 2002	184	93	51.0
August 2002	168	78	46.0

Workout Code Summary

Date	Number of Workouts	Body Area	Type (cardio, tone, sport-specific)
January 1979	0		
July 1979	1	Total	Sport-specific: Tennis work-out—Strength
May 1980	1	Legs	Tone and strengthen
October 1981	0		
June 1981	0		
January 1982	0		
August 1982	1	Hips and thighs	Stretch and tone
December 1983	0		
May 1983	0		
March 1984	0		
September 1984	0		
January/February 1985	0		
August 1985	0		
August 1986	0		
November 1986	0		
July 1987	1	Upper body	Strength and tone
February 1987	0		
December 1988	0		
October 1989	0		
June 1989	0		
November 1990	0		
June 1990	0		
Jan/Feb 1991	0		
August 1991	0		
June 1992	0		
October 1992	0		
March 1993	1	Upper body	Strength for sport
November 1993	1	Total body	Strength training for skiing
June 1994	1	Abdominals	Tone/strength
September 1994	2	Cardio, total body	Cardio, strength/tone
August 1995	2	Total body, shoulder	Cardio training for performance, strengthen/injury prevention
April 1996	0		
December 1996	0		
April 1997	0		
September 1997	0		
October 1997	0		
July/August 1998	3	Abs, lower body and abs, total body	Strengthen/tone, tone, cardio/strength 30-minute workout
January/February 1998	0		
June 1998	1	Total body	Yoga
July/August 1999	2	Total body, glutes	Tone: linked to beach sports, tone
March 2000	5	back, total body, legs/cardio abs, total body/yoga	Strengthen/tone, falun gong, cardio, strengthen/tone, yoga
September 2000	5	Lower body, lower body, torso, total body (cardio), total body	Soccer workout: strength and agility, increase speed, torso training for swimming, cardio—stamina, strength/tone/stretch

(continued)

Workout Code Summary (*continued*)

Date	Number of Workouts	Body Area	Type (cardio, tone, sport-specific)
Self, August 2002	4	Total body (cardio, tone and stretch), lower body, total body, Total body	Burn fat/tone body, tone, tone, pilates
Self, December 2002	3	Total body, total body/ yoga, abs	Strength/tone, yoga, strength tone

Notes

1. See Brownell and Napolitano (1995) and unpublished work by Wayne Phillips at Stanford University.

2. See Gillett and White (1992). At the same time, this may indicate that those men who were previously left out of dominant bodily ideals began to carry signifiers of them (e.g., gay men).

3. Please see Cahn (1994). Anne Bolin (1996) puts forward that the sex-gender-sexuality triad in Western cultures is another explanation for why women and men are being constituted as distinct creatures.

4. Please see Whitson (1990); Burstyn (1999). Works on homophobia rely on this too, such as Blinde and Taub (1992); Blinde and Taub (1992a); Griffin (1998).

5. There is some contestation to these beliefs of course, as evidenced by the increasing overlap between heterosexual, bi-, and gay men's signifiers (e.g., the metrosexual), and increasing overlap in the signs and symbolism of femininity/masculinity across heterosexual, bi-, and lesbian women. For example, see Griggers (1994).

6. Fiske (1994); Heywood and Dworkin (2003); Griggers (1994); Halberstam (1998). Still, researchers find the trend of assumptions of lesbianism when women play male-dominated sports. See Harris (2005).

7. Even children are said to be subject to sexualization and objectification. See American Psychological Association, Task Force on the Sexualization of Girls (2007a).

8. It is important to note that some work reports that while both women and men have distorted views of their body, white women have the most distorted view of their own body. African-American women appear to have the most accurate perception. Please see Demarest and Alien (2000).

9. Tensions in the literature range from fitness ideals not speaking to the majority of working-class women or women of color to fitness messages being increasingly internalized across all social locations. For the former, see Hargreaves (1994). For the latter, see Bordo (1993).

10. Bartky (1988). Others note the seemingly private nature of this struggle that is internalized as moral failure instead of leading to cultural critique. While

we will examine the moral nature of bodily failure or success, we find one work particularly instructive. Please see Duncan (1994).

11. Positions such as Kilbourne (1999); Garvey (1996). Note that magazines and advertisements encourage self-surveillance and that the reader will come up lacking. This lack can be assuaged with purchasing and making use of the right set of goods and services.

12. For a discussion of the emergence of healthism, its links to shifting forms of power in capitalist society, its links to themes of morality, and its larger relationship to acritical assertions about the role of social structures in reproducing health disparities, see Kirk and Colquhoun (1989). Also see Lupton (1995).

13. While Kirk and Colquhoun (1989) underscore this point, few have carried out an empirical analysis over a ten-year period to show precisely which bodies are included and which are left out in the most popularly read health and fitness magazines.

14. See Featherstone (1991a). Featherstone notes the link between the healthy and moral body. Since the Victorian era, external appearance has been conflated with morality. Modern manifestations make fitness a moral imperative, and the privileged few who have the option of participation are deemed worthy of redemption. By extension, those who lack the time, resources, wherewithal, or body habitus to participate are unable to achieve redemption.

15. For further understanding on the relationship between what is inside and outside of media frames, see Stuart Hall's seminal work titled *Representation* (1997).

16. In chapter 3, a distinction will be made between Stanley Cohen's concept of moral panics of the past and processes associated with contemporary body panic that we arrive at through an analysis of the relationship between who is inside the media frame and who is left out. In this way, body panic is constructed within media through the attachment of signifiers to what is inside the frame—and by extension what is left out. The moral panics of the past were derived through an analysis of the marginalized who were stigmatized. In the current analysis of contemporary body panic, the moral panic is around the types of women, men, citizens, mothers, etc., people have access to becoming.

17. Spitzack's 1990 work is an innovative examination of the ways in which women internalize panoptic power, confess to reveal "the truth" about women's "sinful" "excesses" of the flesh. This concept will be revisited in chapter 4 of this text, "Getting Your Body Back," which is an empirical examination of the ways in which feminist ideals are sold to pregnant women as empowerment when in fact these discourses are also rife with confessions of excess and bodily surveillance.

18. Polysemy refers to multiple meanings that individuals interpret out of texts. For an excellent overview, see Fiske's 1994 work, *Media Matters*.

19. Linguist Ferdinand de Saussere breaks the sign into two components, the signified and the signifier. The signifier refers to the actual word, and the signified

to what it represents. The signifier is not necessarily only a word, but any system of representation that refers to a signifier. For a fuller explanation, see: Saussure ([1916] 1983); Fiske (1982), (1987).

20. See Markula (1996); Dworkin (2001). "Nondominant" or "othered bodies" are rendered invisible, undersirable, and affixed with markers of stigma. The under-representation of and limited roles given to people of color in the mass media demonstrates invisibility, while the common conflation of gay and AIDS provides an example of stigma. See Dworkin and Wachs (1998).

21. According to Goldman, "The pun commodity feminism is a reminder that commodity relations turn the relations of active subjects into the relations between objects. The process of turning feminism into sign values fetishizes feminism into an iconography of things." " 'Commodity feminism' represents the process of punning used to double and join the meanings of feminism and femininity." In this view the sign of feminism and not feminism itself is manipulated by women's magazines in an effort to market to women. In this view feminism is reduced to a mere sign. Goldman (1993, p. 131). See also Cole and Hribar (1995).

22. The matrix of domination was coined by Patricia Hill Collins in her 1990 work titled *Black Feminist Thought*. In it, she underscores the intersectional nature of oppression according to race, class, gender, and sexuality.

23. Wachs (2005) demonstrates how coed sport provides the ability for viewers to witness a side-by-side performance challenge to traditional gender ideologies. The lack of coed depictions of health and fitness, except for a few "heterosexy" images, necessarily reinforces ideologies of difference.

NOTES TO CHAPTER 2

1. For an example of the continuing trend toward media blame and overdetermined arguments about media and sexual objectification, see the American Psychological Association, Task Force on the Sexualization of Girls (2007a). Or, see the American Psychological Association, Task Force on the Sexualization of Girls (2007b).

2. This is exemplified by the classic difference between male-appropriate and female-appropriate sports. While male-appropriate sports tend to require achieving an objective goal, female-appropriate sports such as gymnastics and figure skating include judged scores for which appearance is a critical component.

3. See chapter 4 and excellent work carried out by Carole Spitzack (1990) for an analysis of how women's bodily narratives are rife with ideologies of sin and redemption in the confessional process.

4. Given the implications of the large obese body, it is not surprising that American women fear becoming fat more than they fear death. And, the designation of a body as "overweight" or "obese" places it under the control of medical professionals and marks it with a very specific stigma; Campos (2004).

5. Duncan (1994) discusses how these magazines contain two "panoptic mechanisms" that operate to impose self-surveillance of women's bodies. She ties this surveillance to a conflation of public and private concerns. Spitzack (1990) also discusses the politics of the confessional process and self-surveillance related to morality, health, and the female body. She argues that the confessional makes one right with "humility and graciousness" (p. 59) "precisely when women are most actively involved with a questioning of, and potential resistance to, dominant representations" (p. 62).

6. Bourdieu raises the concept of capital being physical and embedded in the body as a result of a lifetime of practices that are in part determined by class status (1984). Wacquant further develops these ideas into the concept of physical capital, and specifically addresses how the muscular body is a valuable form of capital for men; see Wacquant (1995) and (1995a).

7. The authors are not qualified to offer a Freudian analysis of this trend, though we found this rather tempting. We suspected that part of the prevalence of pools, oceans, and lakes was designed to explain the attire of the cover models (swimsuits, etc.).

8. AP Press Wire Service (2007, January 9), Business News. "Clive Owen tapped as 'face' for Lancôme's ad campaigns for new men's grooming products. Owen is marketing a line of anti-aging products, skin care products, and fragrances."

9. Soshnick and Sessa (2005, September 20): "Mr. Womack, 35, who gets as many as three hand and foot treatments a month, isn't the only professional athlete taking a cue from England's soccer captain, David Beckham, who pampers himself with manicures and eye cream. From Ray Allen of basketball's Seattle SuperSonics to Charles Woodson of football's Oakland Raiders, spa treatments have become de rigueur among athletes no longer concerned with being ridiculed for showing concern for their cuticles."

10. *EMO* is a fairly homoerotic magazine, featuring ads clearly aimed at a gay readership. It is interesting that many of the articles implied heterosexuality, despite imagery and advertisements that suggested otherwise. One student assistant asked in confusion if the magazine was intended only for gay men.

11. The U.S. census reports higher median incomes for Asian families than white families during our period of analysis. Census.gov: http://www.census.gov/Press-Release/www/releases/archives/income_wealth/002484.html. However, it is crucial to note that there are vast disparities in income among different groups lumped under the heading of Asian. While for Asian Indians the median income in 2004 was $68,771, for Vietnamese Americans, it was $45,980 (Source: American FactFinder), http://www.census.gov/Press-Release/www/releases/archives/facts_for_features_special_editions/006587.html.

12. Race was determined by inspection and using the name of the cover

model. Certainly, the authors concede that race may be misidentified in this way, but we concluded that what viewers perceive a cover model to be is more salient than how he or she self-identifies. In case of any doubt, we coded the person as other, but we were probably fairly generous in this designation, and most likely these models were white.

13. We found only one professional reference to her online; however, given that she hailed from pre-Internet days, it was difficult to gauge how well known she was.

14. E. Anderson, Personal correspondence (2006, November 7). When I queried Eric Anderson as to how he would describe the images presented in *Men's Health & Fitness* magazines, he used the term "gay vague." Kate Clinton also uses the term in her piece, "Unplugged: Tastefully Gay," *The Progressive*, (2000, September). Also see a similar discussion using a different term known as "gay window advertising" by Clark (1993).

15. Chris Haines posts his views that *Men's Health* is aimed at a gay male audience: "Launched in 1988 as a spinoff of *Prevention*, the magazine has a subscription base that has ballooned like a steroid-juiced biceps in the past decade—from 90,000 to 1.45 million. Half of its readers earn more than $50,000 annually; 43 percent top $60,000. The target audience, according to its press office, is 'upscale young men, guys who are in their 30s. Maybe they're married but they don't have any kids yet.' The target audience, according to me, may indeed be upscale, but they're definitely not married. Let's come back to that one." "Why else publish an 'AIDS Update' column with breaking news about HIV? Could it be that this column is written for all those IV drug users who pull down more than $60K? And why would Merck (never a company to squander its advertising dollars) hawk Crixivan, a protease inhibitor, if the circulation was so relentlessly straight?" http://www.salon.com/media/1998/01/05media.html.

16. Applying Latour (1993) to this example, how the use of the poles of nature and culture to rearticulate power relations becomes apparent.

NOTES TO CHAPTER 3

1. As cited in McRobbie and Thornton (1995). They argue that, "As Watney puts it, the theory of moral panic is unable to conceptualize the mass media as an industry instrinsically involved with excess, with the voracious appetite and capacity for substitutions, displacements, repetitions, and signifying absences. Moral panic theory is always obliged in the final instance to refer and contrast 'representation' to the arbitration of 'the real' and hence it is unable to develop a full theory concerning the operations of ideology within all representational systems. Moral panics seem to appear and disappear, as if representation were not the site of permanent struggle of the meaning of signs" (563–64).

2. The "folk devil" refers to the "demonized" within moral panics, which are described extensively in McRobbie and Thornton's analysis of media and moral panics (1995).

3. Special thanks go to Kari Lerum, Ph.D., a professor at the University of Washington at Bothell, for our conversations on this topic. She argues that the folk devil cannot be created without its counterpart, the folk angel. In this instance, there is no tangible folk devil, but the emphasis on the folk angel helps to reiterate forms of social control on the marginalized.

4. Campos (2004). Also see page 53 in Saltman (2005), who notes that "in a society driven by the imperative for consumption and growth one of the biggest taboos remains on obesity." Also see Monaghan (2005), for coverage of some unique aspects of masculinity and fat male embodiment in U.S. culture.

5. It is interesting to note that discourses on women's need for protection hinges on women's smaller stature, and how this results in victimization. Yet, instead of encouraging women to get quite strong and lift plenty of weights, men are told to strive for size and strength and women are mostly cautioned to watch strength gains.

6. For media analysis that considers how media helps to produce acritical individualized situations of blame without broader consideration for the production of cultural norms, please see Duncan (1994). For analysis of the way in which the citizenry does not necessarily critically evaluate how the military needs of the state inculcate the individuals with fit disciplinary practices, see Saltman (2005), and Montez de Oca (2005).

7. Montez de Oca (2005); Gorn and Goldstein (1993). Also see notions of the "militarized body" as it links to fitness in the war on terror (Armitage 2005). Also see Saltman (2005).

8. Hegemonic sports tend to be violent, competitive team sports, though some individual sports, the martial sports, in particular are also coded as male. See Burstyn (1999), and Gorn and Goldstein (1993).

9. For excellent discussions on the effects of what is "inside" versus "outside" the frame in media analysis, especially see Lutzen (1995); Messner and Solomon (1993); Dworkin and Wachs (2004).

10. For a discussion of the relationship between muscular nationalism and feminized Muslims, see Jasbir Puar's work titled "Queer Narratives of U.S. Exceptionalism" in the 2005 issue of *Social Texts*.

11. For an analysis of pugilistic capital, and the relationship between bodily capital and occupational capital for boxers, see Wacquant (1995).

12. For good critical discussions of how seemingly objective scientific endeavors are shaped by cultural discourses of gender, see Van De Wingaard (1997); Fausto-Sterling (1985). Also see Fausto-Sterling (2000). The same can be said for race and sexuality, and there is a long list of works for these types of manuscripts as well.

13. The end of the chapter explains this historical pattern in greater depth; for more in-depth work, please see Kimmel (2000).

14. For arguments around the way in which advertisers and magazines may in fact be capitalizing on "vague" signifiers that draw in a gay gaze, please see Oakenfull et al. (2005). Also see R. Martin (1995); and see Ebencamp (2005). According to a Harris study, GLBT consumers have $600 million worth of buying power and are more likely to make purchases from companies who have actively reached out to the GLBT market.

15. Puar (2005). Also see Eng, Halberstam, and Munoz (2005), who underscore Lee's work on the "politics of racial castration in the place of an anxious phallic restoration of whiteness." They note that "Lee asserts that racial castration preserves a space of alterity to embrace "femininity as race" and "race as femininity." See Lee (2005).

16. For discussions of capital and how to extend notions of economic capital to include "social" capital, please see P. Bourdieu (1984). Also see Shilling (1991). For extensions of the concept of capital to the development of the concept of bodily capital, please see Wacquant (1995).

17. See Messner (1992). For discussions of how disenfranchised men may experience a different transferability of bodily capital to workplace opportunities than more privileged men, see Messner (2002), p. 150. For work on how disenfranchised men intensively rely on and develop bodily capital in sport, see Wacquant (1995).

18. For more details on the hazards of work in male-dominated occupations, see Harrison, Chin, and Ficarrotto (1995). Also see Messner (1992).

NOTES TO CHAPTER 4

A previously published version of this chapter appeared in *Gender & Society:* S. L. Dworkin and F. L. Wachs (2004), "Getting Your Body Back:" Post-Industrial Fit Motherhood in Shape Fit Pregnancy Magazine. *Gender & Society 18*, 610–24.

1. To reiterate, preferred meanings are the message that the producer of the text wants to convey to the audience.

2. For an excellent discussion of Foucault, surveillance, confessions of bodily excess, women, and femininity, please see Spitzack (1990).

3. On this point, there is excellent work that shows the co-optation of feminist principles for the purpose of the sell in consumer markets, such as Cole and Hribar (1995). Also see Scott (2000). For perspectives that offer more integration of these ideas with health and economic perspectives, see Stratigaki (2004). Also see Jan Thomas and Mary Zimmerman's work on the strategic deployment of feminism and the transformation of women's health centers over time (2007).

4. For more on these arguments, see hooks (1992) and King (2006). Also see Lazar (2006).

5. For a strong theoretical analysis of healthism, public health, and the maintenance of health in everyday life, see Lupton (1995).

NOTES TO CHAPTER 5

1. AIAW, the Association of Intercollegiate Athletics for Women, was founded in 1971 to replace three different governing agencies that oversaw women's collegiate athletics. The AIAW was usurped by the NCAA, as discussed in note 21.

2. Heywood and Dworkin (2003). The authors note the growing marketability of female athletes and women's sports.

3. Hardin, Lynn, and Walsdorf (2005). The authors discuss the increase in the number and circulation of a host of magazines and e-magazines for women that focus on sports and fitness.

4. Title IX of the Educational Amendment of 1972, 20 U.S.C. §§ 1681–1688. Title 20—Education, Chapter 38—Discrimination Based on Sex or Blindness.

5. Federal rulings undermined Title IX, by limiting to whom it applied. Further, the lack of enforcement mechanisms meant it could largely be ignored. Regular columns in *Women's Sports* vociferously critiqued attempts to weaken it and the lack of enforcement mechanism. This is discussed later in the chapter.

6. Dougherty (1977, October 18). Philip H. Dougherty reports the establishment of ad credibility and the circulation of *Women's Sports* since single-copy distribution was curtailed. Subscriptions then accounted for 185,000 copies and new rate base of 210,000 copies was effective as of January 1978.

7. Up until 1979, though Billy Jean King controlled both ventures, the two were not officially linked. In 1979, *Women's Sports*, later renamed *Women's Sports & Fitness*, became the official publication of the Women's Sports Foundation.

8. *Women's Sports & Fitness* expanded its coverage to appeal to the growing number of women interested in fitness in addition to sport. It is a bit ironic that fitness is viewed as a move forward for women, when culturally, fitness has long been offered to women as a more acceptable corollary to sports. See Cahn (1994); Hargreaves (1994).

9. Hainer (1997, April 8). The author explores new arrivals *Sports Illustrated for Women* and Condé Nast's *Sports for Women*.

10. Cole and Hribar (1995). Cole and Hribar critique the exploitation of female labor worldwide in the sports industry.

11. Moore (1998, February 10). Moore laments the demise of *Women's Sports & Fitness* and notes, "As anyone who has been on the losing end of a newspaper war can tell you, the surviving paper is not necessarily the better paper." He notes that Condé Nast's *Women's Sports* had a circulation of only 350,000 and lacked the athlete legitimacy that *Women's Sports & Fitness* had.

12. Moreover, it was known that many subscriptions had been connected to off price subscription offers and might not be reliable future sources of income.

13. Along with the publication *Roads and Bridges*, *Women's Sports & Fitness* was named the most improved magazine just as plans for its termination were finalized.

14. Women's Sports Foundation Press Release, March 6, 2003. Fifty-five percent of all college students (women) receive only 42 percent of all participation opportunities, 36 percent of all operating expenditures, 43 percent of all college athletic scholarship money, and 32 percent of all college athlete recruitment. The information on college athletics was cited from the NCAA.

15. Insufficient mechanisms for enforcement remain a problem. Further, under the Reagan administration the provisions of Title IX were weakened to no longer include schools that receive only indirect federal funding rather than direct funding.

16. For example, a Minnesota girls' hockey team sued for the provision of venues equivalent to their male counterparts in State Tournament play in 2003, and in 1999, parents of athletes in Michigan sued the state, alleging MHSAA does not provide female athletes with the treatment and benefits it provides for males. It alleges that girls often must compete during nontraditional and shortened seasons and play events, including championship games, in inferior facilities. In 2006, the city of Alhambra, California was cited for building a brand new multimillion-dollar stadium for boys' baseball, that included concessions, locker rooms, and bleachers, while the girls' softball teams played on a grassless field that lacked water fountains and bathrooms, let alone locker rooms and bleachers. Despite repeated warnings that the city was in violation of Title IX, rather than coming into compliance voluntarily, the city is retrofitting the stadium to allow both baseball and softball—only after losing a multimillion-dollar lawsuit.

17. Working-class women and women of color often take issue with the idea that there can be a single unifying women's experience given the intersection of other axes of power like race, class, and sexual orientation. See Collins (2000; first published 1990); hooks (2000; first published 1984); Spelman (1988). Assuming a common experience has been a tool of oppression; see de Beauvoir (1952); Tong (1998).

18. Early magazines operated to inculcate consumerist values and instruct in the art of consumption. By creating a consumerist aura around self-identity, readers were given a series of codes to interpret, reconstruct, and employ in multiple ways. Gender identity was a key part of this process (Garvey 1996).

19. The first period, from 1974 to 1979, is excluded from the analysis due to the difficulty in obtaining back issues.

20. Messner argues that to improve the current inequitable situation, changes need to occur on the level of individual day-to-day practices, institutional structured rules and hierarchies, and dominant cultural symbols and belief systems as manifest in the media (Messner 2002).

21. AIAW was founded in 1971 to replace three different governing agencies

that oversaw women's collegiate athletics. The organization operated the national championships for women's collegiate athletics. The NCAA showed little interest in women's sports until the 1980s, when it began to offer competing championships. The NCAA used its television broadcast contracts as a means to lure the top women's programs to its events, rendering the AIAW effectively obsolete.

22. As noted by a multitude of scholars, including Cahn (1994) and Hargreaves (1994), access to sports and fitness is the result of a history of struggle for access by advocates of women's sports.

23. While one cannot dispute the health benefits of sports participation, the individual responsibility for "making time" ignores the sheer impossibility of doing just that for most. Further, one cannot ignore the cultural context that makes fitness an activity that conforms to dominant notions of femininity, while sport carries with it stigmatizations of otherness, specifically centered around sexuality (Shakib 2003).

24. Snippets are informational columns, such as "Men's Health Malegrams," or Fit's "Activefile." Snippets may be one page, or several pages, and each has a theme that relates to something topical, such as the season, the Olympic games, or a featured activity like mountain biking. A series of visuals and graphics accompany each piece.

25. The pervasiveness of calls for consumption is underestimated by the increase in advertising alone. It is an increase in advertising that comes along with a shift in the other areas of the magazine toward covering only individualized issues centered around consumption. In addition, the type of products advertized shifts from sports equipment, to more beauty-oriented products, though alcohol and cigarette advertisements also disappear from the magazine during this time period (Kilbourne 1999).

26. The December 1983 issue features a four-page "Winter Wear Buyer's Guide" that offers outdoor wear for winter with the focus on "warm and dry." December 1988 features the four-page "Home Workout Equipment Guide" that provides general information on options and lists multiple manufacturers for each product. "Splash Dance" (May 1988) features summer's hottest swim wear modeled by athletes. An increase in the amount of space devoted to product guides occurs over time. The January/February 1998 issue is devoted entirely to what the magazine rates as "The best bikes, hiking boots, backpacks, running shoes, swimwear, trail runners, climbing gear, walking shoes, inline skates, home fitness equipment, camping gear, jackets." The link between "new" and advertising, even when "new" is not so new, has long been discussed. The sense of urgency engendered is reinforced by larger cultural notions of progress and modernity (Slater 1997).

27. Garvey (1996); Ohmann (1996). By 1980, the lifestyle photo essay was becoming a prominent feature, as the May 1980 issue invites readers to "Be a hit on the court" with the Tennis Fashions. The spread includes sources for fashions and athletic equipment. Still, many issues, such as August 1980, do not contain

such spreads. Moreover, they are clearly marked as fashion pieces. The August 1982 issue invites readers to participate in Pool Masters, marketing recreational sport for adults. This trend continues for most of the 1980s, with magazines featuring an occasional photo spread, but focusing primarily on women's sports and athletics. By the 1990s, the photo spread appears in every magazine and the products are becoming more and more central. A typical photo essay is "Dress for Excess" featured in the October 1992 issue. This seven-page spread features "technical outerwear" being worn in a variety of outdoor settings. Manufacturer and price are included in the write-up. The essays further play on the "new," "hip" nature of the appeal. Later issues continue this trend, for example, during the final year of production, the April 2000 photo essay, "SkateStyle," features photos of the hottest/latest street wear modeled on the style of skaters. "SoCal is ground zero for the latest streetwear, Pay close attention: What these boarders are wearing today, you'll have on tomorrow." Referencing the street for hip and current, the styles for sale with the price included in the essay are made more tantalizing by the prospect that others will wear tomorrow what you own today. Most issues featured similar photo essays, usually eight pages. *Self* magazine features photo essays in every issue as well. These essays are the ultimate in advertising.

28. We considered any demonstration of a specific exercise to constitute a workout; however, general information about working out or health and fitness did not.

29. Goldman (1993). Goldman is specifically referring to Condé Nast, the publisher of *Self*, in these observations.

30. A December 1995 piece, "On Her Own Terms," profiles Allison Hargreaves, who died on K2 on August 13, 1995. The article defended Hargreaves from criticism for attempting K2, a mountain that claims one in three climbers. Hargreaves had already been the subject of controversy when she climbed Eiger while five months pregnant and because Hargreaves's husband cares for her children when she climbs. *Women's Sports & Fitness* defends Hargreaves decision with a host of admiring quotes, and quotes that focus on not condemning her more than male climbers.

31. Frances Willard's comments on the bicycle as cited in Garvey (1996).

NOTES TO CHAPTER 6

1. Lutzen (1995), p. 20. For example, she offers the historical story of a man who liked to cut off girls' pigtails (66 in total) and collect them. Once collected, he tended to rub the pigtails against his genitals to experience "lively sensations." She argues that such acts were not conceived of as sexual deviance until the turn of the twentieth century, when "the focus soon shifted from a pathological obsession to the fact that erection and ejaculation were always part of the acts. Around

the turn of the century, these acts were isolated from other obsessions and were classified as sexual perversions."

2. Harding (1986), (1991), (1998); Harding and Hintikka (1983); Hartsock (1998); Hekman (1990). However, Heywood and Dworkin (2003) are a notable exception who point to the power, pleasure, and resistance in objecthood that makes it part and parcel of subjecthood in the consumer society. In addition, they note the increasing objectification of the male body, something we discussed at length in chapter 3.

3. We are using oppression in the multiracial feminist sense of the term to refer to a limiting of options (McIntosh 1988); Collins (2000).

4. For a discussion of the emergence of healthism, its links to shifting forms of power in capitlist society, its links to themes of morality, and its larger relationship to acritical assertions about the role of social structures in reproducing health disparities, see Kirk and Colquhoun (1989).

5. Or bisexual motherhood for bisexual women who are married to men.

6. This discussion is effectively carried out by Oakenfull and Greenlee et al. (2005), who argue that there are many ways to market advertising or other content to gay and lesbian consumers without alienating heterosexual consumers. Our findings are especially intriguing given that "heterosexuals tend to have a more negative response to gay males than they do lesbians" (p. 423).

7. The relationship of gender and sexuality to sport or fitness is different for women and men. In the case of women, fitness is viewed as more feminizing and as heterosexualized space. In the case of men, sport is viewed generally as unquestionably masculine and heterosexual (in hegemonic team sports). Fitness for men is viewed as more feminizing than sport. Perhaps the more feminizing spaces of fitness allowed for alternative constructions of masculinity, while the more feminizing space of fitness for women erases more masculinized bodily ideals. Why women's sports magazines would not allow for the inclusion of more muscular ideals that are cross-coded for alternative sexualities is still a conundrum. See Nelson (1995) (on the screaming silence of lesbians in sport).

8. Crawshaw (2007). Dedifferentiation refers to the blurring of boundaries between spheres that were thought of as mutually exclusive. When this process occurs, roles and responsibilities for individuals become more diffuse. For example, currently, there is a process of dedifferentiation in women's and men's roles that is the focus of chapter 2.

9. As noted by Eskes, Duncan, and Miller (1998), fitness magazines simultaneously critique the pressures put upon individuals and reinforce these pressures.

10. Garvey (1996). For example, the Pears Soap slogan, "Good Morning, Have you used Pears Soap this morning?" became a source of humor and joking in popular culture, as viewers would state this phrase to one another, and then jokes arose among social groups around the response. In this way, an advertising slogan became a part of cultural discourse, such that people would use the slogan as a

way to inject humor into a situation. What underlies this is the idea that the ubiquity of advertising became a joke.

11. This is similar to Dworkin and Messner's analysis of "Just Do It" feminism. See Dworkin and Messner (1999).

12. (2004, May 5). "Barbie-shaped Women Are More Fertile: Study," *London Times*, p. A9. This story reports a recent study that shows women's hip-to-waist ratio reveals their fertility, "according to new research that helps unravel the biological origins of feminine beauty." Similar arguments are found throughout the academic literature. For examples, see Singh and Young (1995), and Singh (2002). Other researchers have used other biological markers to make similar arguments about desirability for the purposes of reproduction. There are many, but for one example, please see Lay-Smith et al. (2006). While certainly there may be a natural component, and individual taste is not purely a product of culture, it is impossible to separate out the effects of socialization and culture on individual definitions of beauty. Given the variability of fashion and body type over time, it seems intriguing that individuals cling to this myth.

13. Vertinsky notes this trend for women as the social and systematic barriers that limit women's ability to achieve a healthy lifestyle are generally ignored (1998).

14. Clearly, these are dichotomized a bit much—but this is the general conclusion we come to given our particular results in this particular sample of magazines over the ten-year period.

15. The voice of civil society is fairly regularly integrated into government policy formation or corporate social responsibility, for example, including even the most contentious issues such as HIV/AIDS.

16. Promising examples include the MAC AIDS Fund Viva Glam lipstick campaign which contributes 100 percent of the selling price to the MAC AIDS Fund, the second largest corporate foundation for the purposes of fighting HIV/AIDS in the country. This was the first example of a "purpose-built consumer brand aimed at raising funds to combat HIV/AIDS." See Bruns (2006, April 28). Other examples include Levi's corporate efforts to engage in a highly visible branded condom distribution and safe-sex awareness campaign. Corporate collaborations need not be so highly and commonly criticized, as corporations are paradoxically stepping in to meet social justice needs at a time when the state is backing off on funds. While it is important to maintain critical analysis on the role of corporations in processes of justice, automatically assuming that such projects or collaborations are detrimental to and not consistent with the goals of social justice is not the answer.

Bibliography

Acosta R. V., and L. J. Carpenter. (1996). *Women in Intercollegiate Sport: A Longitudinal Study—Nineteen Year Update, 1977–1996*. Brooklyn: Department of P.E., Brooklyn College.

Alexander, K. (2000, July 3). "'Women's Sports' Folds and Niche Gets Redefined." *USA Today*, 8B.

American Psychological Association, Task Force on the Sexualization of Girls. (2007a). *Report of the APA Task Force on the Sexualization of Girls*. Washington, DC: American Psychological Association. Retrieved from www.apa.org/pi/wpo/sexualization.html.

———. (2007b). *Report of the APA Task Force on the Sexualization of Girls: Executive Summary*. Washington, DC: American Psychological Association. Retrieved from www.apa.org/pi/wpo/sexualization.html.

Anderson, E. (2005). *In the Game: Gay Athletes and the Cult of Masculinity*. Albany: SUNY Press.

———. (2006, November 7). Personal correspondence.

Anzaldua, G. (1987). *Borderlands/La frontera: The New Mestiza*. San Francisco: Aunt Lute Books.

AP Press Wire Service. (2007, January 9). "Clive Owen Tapped as 'Face' for Lancome's Ad Campaigns for New Men's Grooming Products." *Business News*.

Armitage, J. (2005). "Militarized Bodies: An Introduction." *Body and Society* 9:1–12.

Arrington, D., and D. Thurston. (2004, February 18). "In Focus." *Sacramento Bee*, p. C7.

Baca-Zinn, M., and B. Dill. (1994). "Difference and Domination." In *Women of Color in U.S. Society*, ed. M. Baca-Zinn and B. Thornton, 2–12. Philadelphia: Temple University Press.

Baer, J. (2005, May 17). "Obese Workers Have Higher Med Costs, Lower Pay." *Stanford Daily*.

Bailey, L. (2001). "Gender Shows: First-time Mothers and Embodied Selves." *Gender & Society* 15:110–29.

Balsamo, A. (1994). "Feminist Bodybuilding." In *Women, Sport, and Culture*, ed. S. Birrell and C. Cole, 341–54. Champaign, IL: Human Kinetics.

Banet-Weiser, S. (1999). *The Most Beautiful Girl in the World: Beauty Pageants and National Identity.* Berkeley: University of California Press.

Bartky, S. L. (1988). "Foucault, Femininity, and the Modernization of Patriarchal Power." In *Feminism and Foucault: Reflections on Resistance,* ed. I. Diamond and L. Quinby, 61–85. Boston: Northeastern University Press.

———. (1990). *Femininity and Domination: Studies in the Phenomenology of Oppression.* New York: Routledge.

Baudrillard, J. (1975). *The Mirror of Production.* St. Louis, MO: Telos.

———. (1998). *The Consumer Society: Myths and Structures.* Thousand Oaks, CA: Sage.

Baumann, Z. (1999). *In Search of Politics.* Cambridge, UK: Polity.

Beauvoir, S. de. (1952). *The Second Sex.* New York: Vintage.

Berger, J. (1972). *Ways of Seeing.* London: Penguin.

Birrell, S., and C. L. Cole. (1990). "Double Fault: Renee Richards and the Construction and Naturalization of Difference." *Sociology of Sport Journal* 7:1–21.

Birrell, S., and M. McDonald, eds. (2000). *Reading Sport: Critical Essays on Power and Representation.* Boston: Northeastern University Press.

Blinde, E. M., and D. E. Taub. (1992). "Women Athletes as Falsely Accused Deviants: Managing the Lesbian Stigma." *Sociological Quarterly* 4:521–33.

———. (1992a). "Homophobia and Women's Sport: The Disempowerment of Athletes." *Sociological Focus* 2:151–66.

Blum, L. (1999). *At the Breast: Ideologies of Breastfeeding and Motherhood in the Contemporary United States.* Boston: Beacon.

Bolin, A. (1992). "Flex Appeal, Food, and Fat: Competitive Bodybuilding, Gender, and Diet." *Play & Culture* 5:378–400.

———. (1996). "Traversing Gender: Cultural Context and Gender Practice." In *Gender Reversals and Gender Cultures: Anthropological and Historical Perspectives,* ed. S. P. Ramet, 22–51. New York: Routledge.

Bordo, S. (1993). *Unbearable Weight: Feminism, Western Culture, and the Body.* Berkeley: University of California Press.

———. 1997. *Twilight Zones: The Hidden Life of Cultural Images from Plato to O.J.* Berkeley: University of California Press.

———. 1999. *The Male Body: A New Look at Men in Public and Private.* New York: Farrar, Straus, and Giroux.

Bordowitz, G. (1994). *American Imago.* Baltimore: Johns Hopkins University Press.

Bourdieu, P. (1984). *Distinction: A Social Critique of the Judgment of Taste.* Cambridge, MA: Harvard University Press.

———. (1998). *Acts of Resistance: Against the Tyranny of the Market.* New York: New Press.

———. (2001). *Masculine Domination.* Stanford, CA: Stanford University Press.

Boutilier, M. A., and L. F. SanGiovanni. (1994). "Politics, Public Policy, and Title

IX: Some Limitations of Liberal Feminism." In *Women, Sport, and Culture*, ed. S. Birrell and C. Cole, 97–110. Champaign, IL: Human Kinetics.

Breward, C. (1995). *The Culture of Fashion*. Manchester, UK: Manchester University Press.

Brownell, K., and M. Napolitano. (1995). "Distorting Reality for Children: Body Size Proportions of Barbie and Ken Dolls." *International Journal of Eating Disorders* 18:295–98.

Brumberg, J. J. (1997). *The Body Project: An Intimate History of American Girls*. New York: Vintage.

Bruns, C. (2006, April 28). "Harnessing Brands." *Mail & Guardian*, Supplement B, 8.

Burstyn, V. (1999). *The Rites of Men: Manhood, Politics, and the Culture of Sport*. Toronto: University of Toronto Press.

Bush, G. (2001). "Address to a Joint Session of Congress and the American People." Retrieved on June 10, 2007 from www.whitehouse.gov/news/releases/2001/09/print/20010922.html.

Butler, J. (1990). *Gender Trouble: Feminism and the Subversion of Identity*. New York: Routledge.

———. (1993). *Bodies that Matter: On the Discursive Limits of "Sex."* New York: Routledge.

———. (1996). "Performativity's Social Magic." In *The Social and Political Body*, ed. T. R. Schatzki and W. Natter, 29–48. New York: Guilford.

Cahn, S. K. (1994). *Coming on Strong: Gender and Sexuality in Twentieth Century Women's Sport*. New York: Free Press.

Campos, P. (2004). *The Obesity Myth: Why America's Obsession with Weight Is Hazardous to Your Health*. New York: Gotham.

Chanter, T. (1999). "Beyond Sex and Gender: On Luce Irigaray's 'This Sex Which Is Not One.'" In *The Body*, ed. D. Welton, 361–75. Malden, MA: Blackwell.

Clark, D. (1993). "Commodity Lesbianism." In *The Lesbian and Gay Studies Reader*, ed. H. Abelove, M. Aine Barale, and D. M. Halperin, 186–201. New York: Routledge.

Clinton, K. (2000, September). "Unplugged: Tastefully Gay." *Progressive*.

Cohen, S. (2002). *Folk Devils and Moral Panics*. 3rd ed. New York: Routledge.

Cole, C. L., and D. Andrews. (1996). "'Look—It's NBA Showtime!' Visions of Race in the Popular Imaginary." In *Cultural Studies: A Research Annual*, vol. 1, ed. N. Denzin. New York: Jai.

Cole, C. L., and A. Hribar. (1995). "Celebrity Feminism: Nike Style Post-Fordism, Transcendence, and Consumer Power." *Sociology of Sport Journal* 12:347–69.

Colford, P. D. (2001, June 7). "Condé Nast Hires Top Editor for Self Magazine." *New York Daily News*, 33.

Collins, P. H. (1990). *Black Feminist Thought: Knowledge, Consciousness, and the Politics of Empowerment*. Boston: Unwin Hyman.

Collins, P. H. (1999). "Shifting the Center: Race, Class, and Feminist Theorizing about Motherhood." In *American Families: A Multicultural Reader*, ed. S. Coontz, 197–217. New York: Routledge.

Connell, R. W. (1987). *Gender and Power*. Stanford, CA: Stanford University Press.

———. (1995). *Masculinities*. Berkeley: University of California Press.

Crawford, R. (1980). "Healthism and the Medicalization of Everyday Life." *International Journal of Health Services* 10:365–88.

Crawshaw, P. (2007). "Governing the Healthy Male Citizen: Men, Masculinity and Popular Health in *Men's Health* Magazine." *Social Science & Medicine* 65:1606–18.

Creedon, P. J. (1994). "Women, Media, and Sport: Creating and Reflecting Gender Values." In *Women, Media and Sport: Challenging Gender Values*, ed. P. Creedon, 3–27. Thousand Oaks, CA: Sage.

Crosset, T. (1990). "Masculinity, Sexuality, and the Development of Early Modern Sport." In *Sport, Men and the Gender Order*, ed. M. A. Messner and D. F. Sabo, 45–54. Champaign, IL: Human Kinetics.

Daniels, D. B. (1992). "Gender (body) Verification (building)." *Play & Culture* 5:378–400.

Davidson, D. (1991, August 24). "Business News: Fitness Publication for Women Refines Its Target Audience." *Atlanta Journal-Constitution*, D2.

Davis, L. (1997). *The Swimsuit Issue and Sport: Hegemonic Masculinity in Sports Illustrated*. Albany: SUNY Press.

Davis-Floyd, R. (1993). *Birth as an American Rite of Passage*. Berkeley: University of California Press.

Demarest, J., and R. Alien. (2000). "Body Image: Gender, Ethnic, and Age Differences." *Journal of Social Psychology* 140:465–73.

Domhoff, G. W. (1998). *Who Rules America? Power and Politics in the Year 2000*. Mountain View, CA: Mayfield.

Dotson, E. W. (1999). *Behold the Man: The Hype and Selling of Male Beauty in Media and Culture*. New York: Haworth.

Dougherty, P. H. (1977, October 18). "Advertising Setting New Goals for Women's Sports." *New York Times*, 60.

———. (1986, June 30). "Advertising; New name, New Hope for Women's Sports." *New York Times*, D11.

Dowling, C. (2000). *The Frailty Myth: Women Approaching Physical Equality*. New York: Random House.

Dowsett, G. W. (1994). Baring Essentials: Science as Desire. *Sexuality Research and Social Policy: Journal of NSRC* 1:69–82.

Dresang, J. (2005, December 25). "Unhealthy Discrimination? Overweight Workers May Hit More Obstacles on the Job." *Milwaukee Journal Sentinel*, D1.

Duncan, M. C. (1990). "Sports Photographs and Sexual Difference—Images of

Women and Men in the 1984 and 1988 Olympics Games." *Sociology of Sport Journal* 7:22–32.

——. (1993). Beyond Analyses of Sport Media Texts: An Argument for Formal Analysis of Institutional Structures. *Sociology of Sport Journal* 10:353–72.

——. (1994). "The Politics of Women's Body Images and Practices: Foucault, the Panopticon, and Shape Magazine." *Journal of Sport and Social Issues* 18: 40–65.

Duncan, M. C., and B. Brummett. (1993). Liberal and Radical Sources of Female Empowerment in Sport Media. *Sociology of Sport Journal* 10:57–72.

Duncan, M. C., and C. A. Hasbrook. (1988). "Denial of Power in Televised Women's Sports." *Sociology of Sport Journal* 5:1–21.

Duncan, M. C., M. Messner, and C. Cooky. (2000). *Gender in Televised Sports: 1989, 1993 and 1999*. Amateur Athletic Foundation Report, Los Angeles.

Duncan, M. C., M. A. Messner, F. L. Wachs, and K. Jensen. (1994, July). *Gender Stereotyping in Televised Sports: A Follow-Up to the 1989 Study*. Amateur Athletic Foundation Report, Los Angeles.

Duncan, M. C., M. A. Messner, and N. Williams. (2005). *Gender in Televised Sports: News and Highlight Shows 1989-2004*. Amateur Athletic Foundation Report, Los Angeles.

Dutton, K. (1995). *The Perfectible Body*. New York: Continuum.

Dworkin, S. L. (2001). "'Holding Back': Negotiating a Glass Ceiling on Women's Strength." *Sociological Perspectives* 44:333–50.

——. (2003). "A Woman's Place Is in the . . . Cardiovascular Room? Gender Relations, the Body and the Gym." In *Athletic Intruders: Ethnographic Research on Women, Culture, and Exercise*, ed. A. Bolin and J. Granskog, 131–58. Albany: SUNY Press.

Dworkin, S. L., and A. A. Ehrhardt. (2007). "Going beyond ABC (Abstinence, Be Faithful, Condom Use) to Include GEM (Gender Relations, Economic Contexts, and Migration Movements): Critical Reflections on Progress in the HIV/AIDS Epidemic." *American Journal of Public Health* 97:13–16.

Dworkin, S. L., and M. A. Messner. (1999). "'Just Do' What? Sport, Bodies, Gender." In *Revisioning Gender*, ed. J. Lorber, B. Hess, and M. M. Ferree, 341–64. Thousand Oaks, CA: Sage.

Dworkin, S. L., and F. L. Wachs. (1998). "Disciplining the Body: HIV Positive Male Athletes, Media Surveillance and the Policing of Sexuality." *Sociology of Sport Journal* 15:1–20.

——. (2000). "The Morality/Manhood Paradox: Masculinity, Sport, and the Media." In *Masculinities, Gender Relations, and Sport*, ed. M. A. Messner, D. Sabo, and J. McKay, 469–79. Thousand Oaks, CA: Sage.

——. (2000a). "Gender for Sale: Consumption and Constructions of Difference in Mainstream Health and Fitness Magazines." Unpublished paper presented at the 2000 North American Society for Sociologists in Sport (NASSS) Annual Meetings, held in Colorado Springs, Colorado.

Dworkin, S. L., and F. L. Wachs. (2004). "Getting Your Body Back: Post-Industrial Fit Motherhood and the Merger of the Second and Third Shifts." *Gender & Society* 18:610–24.

Ebencamp, R. (ed.) (2005, November 7). "Queer Eye for the Best Buy." *Brandweek*, 20.

Eng, D. L., J. Halberstam, and J. Esteban Munoz. (2005). "What's Queer about Queer Studies Now?" *Social Text* 23:1–17.

Ensemble, C. A. (2005). "Reimagining the War Machine." *Body & Society* 8: 89–91.

Eskes, T. B., M. C. Duncan, and E. M. Miller. (1998). "The Discourse of Empowerment: Foucault, Marcuse, and Women's Fitness Texts." *Journal of Sport and Social Issues* 22:317–44.

Espiritu, Y. (1997). *Asian American Women and Men: Labor, Laws, and Love.* Thousand Oaks, CA: Sage.

———. (1997a). "Race, Gender, and Class in the Lives of Asian Americans." *Race, Gender, and Class* 4:12–19.

Fausto-Sterling, A. (1985). *Myths of Gender: Biological Theories about Women and Men.* New York: Basic Books.

———. (2000). *Sexing the Body: Gender Politics and the Construction of Sexuality.* New York: Basic Books.

Featherstone, M. (1982). The Body in Consumer Culture. *Theory, Culture & Society* 1:18–33.

———. (1991). *Consumer Culture and Postmodernism.* London: Sage.

———. (1991a). The Body in Consumer Culture. In *The Body: Social Process and Cultural Theory,* ed. M. Featherstone, M. Hepworth, and B. S. Turner, 170–96. London: Sage.

Featherstone, M., and B. S. Turner. (1995). "Body & Society: An Introduction." *Body & Society* 1:1–12.

Feitalberg, R. (1996, May). "Courting the Athletic Set." *Women's Wear Daily Marketing,* 10.

Financial Desk. (2007, May 28). "The Male Dieter." *New York Times,* C2.

Financial Desk. (2007, May 28). "The Scent of a Man, Bought by a Woman." *New York Times,* C2.

Fisher, L. A. (1997). "'Building One's Self Up': Bodybuilding and the Construction of Identity among Professional Female Bodybuilders." In *Building Bodies,* ed. P. Moore, 74–86. New Brunswick, NJ: Rutgers University Press.

Fiske, J. (1982). *Introduction to Communication Studies.* London: Routledge.

———. (1987). *Television Culture.* London: Routledge.

———. (1994). *Media Matters: Everyday Culture and Political Change.* Minneapolis: University of Minnesota Press.

Foucault, M. (1978). *The History of Sexuality*. New York: Vintage.

———. (1979). *Discipline and Punish: The Birth of the Prison*. New York: Vintage.

———. (1980). *Power/Knowledge*. Brighton, UK: Harvester.

Fox, N. J. (1993). *Postmodernism, Sociology, and Health*. Buckingham, UK: Open University Press.

Frankenberg, R. (1993). *White Women, Race Matters: The Social Construction of Whiteness*. Minneapolis: University of Minnesota Press.

Frith, H., and K. Gleeson. (2004). "Clothing and Embodiment: Men Managing Body Image and Appearance." *Psychology of Men & Masculinity* 5:40–48.

Garvey, E. G. (1996). *The Adman in the Parlor: Magazines and the Gendering of Consumer Culture, 1880s to 1910s*. New York: Oxford University Press.

Giddens, A. (1991). *Modernity and Self Identity: Self and Society in the Late Modern Age*. Cambridge, UK: Polity.

———. (2000). *The Third Way: The Renewal of Social Democracy*. Cambridge, UK: Polity.

Gillett, J., and P. G. White. (1992). "Male Bodybuilding and the Reassertion of Hegemonic Masculinity." *Play & Culture* 5:358–69.

Gillis, J. (1996). *A World of Their Own Making: Myth, Ritual, and the Quest for Family Values*. New York: Basic Books.

Gimlin, G. (2002). *Body Work: Beauty and Self Image in American Culture*. Berkeley: University of California Press.

Giulianotti, R. (2005). *Sport: A Critical Sociology*. Cambridge, UK: Polity.

Gladwell, M. (2000). "Listening to Khakis: What America's Most Popular Pants Tell Us about the Way Guys Think." In *The Gender and Consumer Culture Reader*, ed. J. Scanlon, 179–91. New York: New York University Press.

Glassner, B. (1990). "Fit for Postmodern Selfhood." In *Symbolic Interaction and Cultural Studies*, ed. H. Becker and M. McCall, 215–43. Chicago: University of Chicago Press.

———. (1992). *Bodies: Overcoming the Tyranny of Perfection*. Los Angeles: Lowell House.

Goffman, E. (1976). "Gender Advertisements." *Studies in the Anthropology of Visual Communication* 3:36–154.

———. (1979). *Gender Advertisements*. New York: Harper.

Goldman, W. (1993). *Reading Ads Socially*. London: Routledge.

Goldman, W., D. Heath, and S. L. Smith (1991). "Commodity Feminism." *Critical Studies in Mass Communication* 8:333–51.

Gorn, W. J., and W. Goldstein. (1993). *A Brief History of American Sports*. New York: Hill and Wang.

Gray, H. (1992). "Television, Black Americans, and the American Dream." *Critical Studies in Mass Communication* 6:376–86.

Greenhalgn, T., and S. Wesselly. (2004). "'Health for Me': A Sociocultural Analysis of Healthism in the Middle Classes." *British Medical Bulletin* 69:201.

Griffin, P. (1998). *Strong Women, Deep Closets: Lesbians and Homophobia in Sport.* Champaign, IL: Human Kinetics.

Griggers, C. (1994). "Lesbian Bodies in the Age of Post-Mechanical Reproduction." In *Fear of a Queer Planet: Queer Politics and Social Theory,* ed. M. Warner, 178–92. Minneapolis: University of Minnesota Press.

———. (1997). *Becoming Woman.* Minneapolis: University of Minnesota Press.

Griswold, R. (1998). "The Flabby American, the Body, and the Cold War." In *A Shared Experience: Men, Women, and the History of Gender,* ed. L. McCall and D. Yacovone, 321–48. New York: New York University Press.

Grogan, S. (1998). *Body Image: Understanding Body Dissatisfaction in Men, Women, and Children.* London: Routledge.

Grogan, S., and H. Richards. (2002). "Body Image: Focus Groups with Boys and Men." *Men and Masculinities* 4:219–32.

Grosz, E. (1994). *Volatile Bodies: Towards a Corporeal Feminism.* Bloomington: Indiana University Press.

Gruneau, R. (1983). *Class, Sports, and Domination.* Amherst: University of Massachusetts Press.

Guthrie, S. R., and S. Castelnuovo. (1998). *Feminism and the Female Body: Liberating the Amazon Within.* Boulder, CO: Lynne Rienner.

Hainer, C. (1997, April 8). "A Burst of Interest in Women's Sports and Fitness." *USA Today,* 10D.

Halberstam, J. (1998). *Female Masculinity.* Durham, NC: Duke University Press.

Hall, A. (1997). *Feminism and Sporting Bodies: Essays on Theory and Practice.* Champaign, IL: Human Kinetics.

Hall, S. (1997). *Representation: Cultural Representations and Signifying Practices.* London: Sage.

Hantover, J. P. (1998). "The Boy Scouts and the Validation of Masculinity." In *Men's Lives,* ed. M. Kimmel and M. A. Messner, 101–8. Boston: Allyn & Bacon.

Hardin, M., S. Lynn, and K. Walsdorf. (2005). "Challenge and Conformity on Contested Terrain: Images of Women in Four Women's Sport/Fitness Magazines." *Sex Roles* 53:105–17.

Harding, S. (1986). *The Science Question in Feminism.* Ithaca, NY: Cornell University Press.

———. (1991). *Whose Science? Whose Knowledge?* Ithaca, NY: Cornell University Press.

———. (1998). *Is Science Multicultural? Postcolonialisms, Feminisms, and Epistemologies.* Bloomington: Indiana University Press.

Harding, S., and Hintikka, M. (Eds.) (1983). *Discovering Reality: Feminist Perspectives in Epistemology, Metaphysics, Methodology and Philosophy of Science.* Dordrecht: D. Reidel.

Hargreaves, J. (1986). "Where's the Virtue? Where's the Grace? A Discussion of the Social Production of Gender Relations through Sport." *Theory, Culture, & Society* 3:110–21.

———. (1994). *Sporting Females: Critical Issues in the History and Sociology of Women's Sport.* New York: Routledge.

———. (2001). *Heroines of Sport: The Politics of Difference and Identity.* London: Taylor & Francis.

Harris, E. (2000, July 19). "Sports: Quick Hits." *Chicago Sun-Times,* 149.

Harris, J. (2005). "The Image Problem in Women's Football." *Journal of Sport and Social Issues* 29:184–97.

Harrison, J., J. Chin, and T. Ficarrotto. (1995). "Warning: Masculinity May Be Dangerous to Your Health." In *Men's Lives,* ed. M. S. Kimmel and M. A. Messner, 296–309. Boston: Allyn & Bacon.

Hartsock, N. (1998). *The Feminist Standpoint Revisited and Other Essays.* Boulder, CO: Westview.

Haug, F. et al. (1987). *Female Sexualization: Questions for Feminism.* London: Verso.

Hekman, S. (1990). *Gender and Knowledge: Elements of a Postmodern Feminism.* Boston: Northeastern University Press.

Henderson, Mark (2004, May 5). "Experts Figure Out Why Men Prefer Marilyn: Barbie-Shaped Women Are More Fertile: Study." *London Times,* A9.

Henley, N. (1977). *Body Politics: Power, Sex, and Nonverbal Communication.* Englewood Cliffs, NJ: Prentice Hall.

Herek, G. (2000). "Sexual Prejudice and Gender: Do Heterosexual Attitudes towards Lesbians and Gay Men Differ?" *Journal of Social Issues* 56:251–66.

———. (2000a). "Gender Gaps in Public Opinion about Lesbians and Gay Men." *Public Opinion Quarterly* 66:40–66.

Herman, E. S., and N. Chomsky. (1988). *Manufacturing Consent: The Political Economy of the Mass Media.* New York: Pantheon Books.

Heywood, L. (1997). "Masculinity Vanishing: Bodybuilding and Contemporary Culture." In *Building Bodies,* ed. P. Moore, 165–83. New Brunswick, NJ: Rutgers University Press.

———. (1998). *Bodymakers: A Cultural Anatomy of Women's Bodybuilding.* New Brunswick, NJ: Rutgers University Press.

Heywood, L., and J. Drake. (1997). *Third Wave Agenda: Being Feminist, Doing Feminism.* Minneapolis: University of Minnesota Press.

Heywood, L., and S. L. Dworkin. (2003). *Built to Win: The Female Athlete as Cultural Icon.* Minneapolis: University of Minnesota Press.

Hilpern, K. (2005, May 16). "Office Hours: Overweight, Underpaid: Sexual, Racial and Age Discrimination Are Outlawed. Are Sizeism and Lookism the Last Prejudices, asks Kate Hilpern." *Guardian Office Hours,* 4.

Hochschild, A. (1989). *The Second Shift.* New York: Avon Books.

Hofmeyr, J. G., E. F. Marcus, and A. M. Butchart. (1990). "Pregnant Women's Perceptions of Themselves: A Survey." *Birth* 17:205–6.

Hondagneu-Sotelo, P., and M. A. Messner. (2000). "Gender Displays and Men's Power: The 'New Man' and the Mexican Immigrant Man." In *Gender through the Prism of Difference*, ed. M. Baca Zinn, P. Hondagneu-Sotelo, and M. A. Messner. Boston: Allyn & Bacon.

hooks, b. (1992). "Eating the Other." In *Black Looks: Race and Representation*, ed. b. hooks, 21–40. Cambridge, MA: South End.

———. (2000). *Feminist Theory: From Margin to Center*. Cambridge, MA: South End.

Hunt, D. (1999). *OJ Simpson Fact and Fiction: News Rituals in the Construction of Reality*. New York: Cambridge University Press.

Jensen, K. (1992, July 7). "The Newsstand: Magazines Go for the Gold with Tie-ins to Olympics." *Atlanta Journal and Constitution*, C3.

Jette, S. (2006). "Fit for Two? A Critical Discourse Analysis of Oxygen Fitness Magazine." *Sociology of Sport Journal* 23:331–51.

Jhally, S. (1987). *The Codes of Advertising: Fetishism and the Political Economy of Meaning in the Consumer Society*. Co-published by St. Martin's Press, New York, and Frances Pinter, London.

———. 1989. "Cultural Studies and the Sports/Media Complex." In *Media, Sports, and Society*, ed. L. A. Wenner, 70–96. London: Sage.

Jhally, S., and J. Lewis. (1992). *Enlightened Racism: The Cosby Show, Audiences, and the Myth of the American Dream*. Boulder, CO: Westview.

Kane, M. J. (1988). "Media Coverage of the Female Athlete before, during and after Title IX: Sports Illustrated Revisited." *Journal of Sport Management* 2:87–99.

———. (1995). "Resistance/Transformation of the Oppositional Binary: Exposing Sport as a Continuum." *Journal of Sport and Social Issues* 19:191–218.

———. (1995a). "Media Coverage of the Post Title IX Female Athlete: A Feminist Analysis of Sport, Gender, and Power." *Duke Journal of Gender Law and Public Policy* 2:21–48.

Kane, M. J., and H. Lenskyj. (1998). "Media Treatment of Female Athletes: Issues of Gender and Sexualities." In *MediaSport: Cultural Sensibilities and Sport in the Media Age*, ed. L. Wenner, 186–201. London: Routledge.

Kane, M. J., and K. Pearce. (2002). "Representations of Female Athletes in Young Adult Sports Fiction: Issues and Intersections of Race and Gender." In *Paradoxes of Youth and Sport*, ed. M. Gatz, M. A. Messner, and S. Ball-Rokeach, 69–92. Albany: SUNY Press.

Kane, M. J., and E. Snyder. (1989). "Sport Typing: The Social 'Containment' of Women in Sport." *Arena Review* 13:77–96.

Katz, J. (1995). *The Invention of Heterosexuality*. New York: Penguin.

Kelly, K. J. (1998, January 13). "Condé Nast Takes Over Competition." *Daily News*, 47.

Kilbourne, J. (1999). *Can't Buy My Love: How Advertising Changes the Way We Think and Feel*. New York: Touchstone.

Kimmel, M. (1990). "Baseball and the Reconstitution of American Masculinity, 1880–1920." In *Sport, Men and the Gender Order: Critical Feminist Perspectives*, ed. M. Messner and D. F. Sabo. Champaign, IL: Human Kinetics.

———. (2000). *Manhood in America: A Cultural History*. Oxford: Oxford University Press.

King, S. (2006). *Pink Ribbons, Inc.: Breast Cancer and the Politics of Philanthropy*. Minneapolis: University of Minnesota Press.

Kirk, D., and D. Colquhoun. (1989) "Healthism and Physical Education." *British Journal of Sociology of Education* 10:417–34.

Klein, A. (1990). "Little Big Man: Hustling, Gender Narcissism, and Bodybuilding Subculture." In *Sport, Men, and the Gender Order: Critical Feminist Perspectives*, ed. M. A. Messner and D. F. Sabo. Champaign, IL: Human Kinetics.

———. (1990). *Little Big Men: Bodybuilding Subculture and Gender Construction*. Albany: SUNY Press.

Klein, N. (2002). *No Logo*. New York: Picador.

Landau, S. (2004). *The Business of America*. New York: Routledge.

Laqueur, T. (1990). *Making Sex: Body and Gender from the Greeks to Freud*. Cambridge, MA: Harvard University Press.

Lasch, C. (1979). *The Culture of Narcissism: American Life in an Age of Diminishing Expectations*. New York: Norton.

Latour, B. (1993). *We Have Never Been Modern*. Cambridge, MA: Harvard University Press.

Lay-Smith, M. J., et al. (2006). "Facial Appearance Is a Cue to Estrogen Levels in Women." *Proceedings of the Royal Society of London* 273:135–40.

Lazar, M. (2006). "'Discover the Power of Femininity!' Analyzing Global 'Power Femininty' in Local Advertising." *Feminist Media Studies* 6:505–17.

Leath, V. M., and A. Lumpkin. (1992). "An Analysis of Sportswomen on the Covers and in the Feature Articles of Women's Sports and Fitness Magazine, 1975–1989." *Journal of Sport and Social Issues* 16:121–26.

Lee, J. O. (2005). "The Joy of the Castrated Boy." *Social Text* 23:35–56.

Leit, R. A., H. G. Pope, and J. J. Grey. (2001). "Cultural Expectations of Muscularity in Men." *International Journal of Eating Disorders* 22:90–93.

Lenskyj, H. (1986). *Out of Bounds: Women, Sport, and Sexuality*. Toronto: Women's Press.

Lloyd, M. (1996). "Feminism, Aerobics, and the Politics of the Body." *Body & Society* 2:79–98.

Lofland, J., and L. H. Lofland. (1995). *Analyzing Social Settings: A Guide to Qualitative Observation and Analysis*. Detroit: Wadsworth.

Lorber, J. (1993). "Believing Is Seeing: Biology as Ideology." *Gender & Society* 4: 568–81.

Lorber, J. (1994). *Paradoxes of Gender.* New Haven, CT: Yale University Press.

———. (1996). "Beyond the Binaries: Depolarizing the Categories of Sex, Sexuality, and Gender." *Sociological Inquiry* 66:143–59.

Lowe, D. M. (1995). *The Body in Late-Capitalist USA.* Durham, NC: Duke University Press.

Lupton, D. (1995). *The Imperative of Health: Public Health and the Regulated Body.* Thousand Oaks, CA: Sage.

Lutzen, K. (1995). "La mise en discours and Silences in Research on the History of Sexuality." In *Conceiving Sexuality: Approaches to Sex Research in a Postmodern World*, ed. R. Parker and J. Gagnon, 19–32. London: Routledge.

MacNeil, M. (1994). "Active Women, Media Representations, and Ideology." In *Women, Sport, and Culture*, ed. S. Birrell and C. Cole, 273–87. Champaign, IL: Human Kinetics.

Markula, P. (1996). "Firm but Shapely, Fit but Sexy, Strong but Thin: The Postmodern Aerobicizing Female Bodies." *Sociology of Sport Journal* 12:424–53.

Martin, E. (1992). *The Woman in the Body: A Cultural Analysis of Reproduction.* Boston: Beacon.

Martin, R. (1995). "Gay Blades: Homoerotic Content in J. C. Leyendecker's Gillette Advertising Images." *Journal of American Culture* 18:75–82.

McCaughy, M. (1997). *Real Knockouts: The Physical Feminism of Women's Self-Defense.* New York: New York University Press.

McDermott, L. (1996). "Towards a Feminist Understanding of Physicality within the Context of Women's Physically Active and Sporting Lives." *Sociology of Sport Journal* 13:12–30.

McIntosh, P. (1988). *White Privilege and Male Privilege: A Personal Account of Coming to See Correspondences through Work in Women's Studies.* Working Paper 189. Wellesley College Center for Research on Women, Wellesley, MA.

McRobbie, A., and S. L. Thornton. (1995). "Rethinking 'Moral Panic' for Multi-Mediated Worlds." *British Journal of Sociology* 46:559–74.

Messner, M. A. (1988). "Sports and Male Domination: The Female Athlete as Contested Ideological Terrain." *Sociology of Sport Journal* 5:197–211.

———. (1989). "Gendered Bodies: Insights from the Feminist Study of Sport." Unpublished paper presented at the North American Society for Sociology of Sport Meetings, Washington, DC.

———. (1992). *Power at Play: Sports and the Problem of Masculinity.* Boston: Beacon.

———. (1995). "Boyhood, Organized Sports, and the Construction of Masculinities." In *Men's Lives*, ed. M. Kimmel and M. A. Messner. Boston: Allyn & Bacon.

———. (1996). "Studying Up on Sex Sociology." *Sociology of Sport Journal* 13: 221–37.

———. (1997). *The Politics of Masculinities: Men in Movements.* Thousand Oaks, CA: Sage.

———. (2000). "Theorizing Gendered Bodies: Beyond the Subject/Object Dichotomy." Paper presented at the Annual Meeting for the North American Society for Sociologists of Sport (NASSS).

———. (2002). *Taking the Field: Women, Men, and Sports.* Minneapolis: University of Minnesota Press.

Messner, M. A., M. C. Duncan, and F. L. Wachs. (1996). "The Gender of Audience-Building: Televised Coverage of Women's and Men's NCAA Basketball." *Sociological Inquiry* 66:422–39. Reprinted in A. Yiannakis and M. Melnick (Eds.), *Sport Sociology: Contemporary Themes,* 5th ed. New York: Kendall-Hunt.

Messner, M. A., and W. S. Solomon. (1993). "Outside the Frame: Newspaper Coverage of the Sugar Ray Leonard Wife Abuse Story." *Sociology of Sport Journal* 10:119–34.

Miller, T. (2001). *SportSex.* Philadelphia: Temple University Press.

Monaghan, L. F. (2001). "Looking Good, Feeling Good: The Embodied Pleasures of Vibrant Physicality." *Sociology of Health and Illness* 23:330–56.

———. (2005). "Big Handsome Men, Beards, and Others: Virtual Constructions of 'Fat Male Embodiment.'" *Body & Society* 11:81–111.

Montez de Oca, J. (2005). "'As Our Muscles Get Softer, Our Missile Race Becomes Harder': Cultural Citizenship and the Muscle Gap." *Journal of Historical Sociology* 18:145–71.

Moor, L. (2007). "Sport and Commodification: A Reflection on Key Concepts." *Journal of Sport and Social Issues* 31:128–42.

Moore, J. (1998, February 10). "S+F Demise No Victory for Women." *Denver Post,* D12.

Morago, G. (2007, April 18). "Skin Care Becomes Masculine; Men Increasingly Turn to Quality Cosmetics Instead of Soap on a Rope." *Hartford Courant,* D1.

Mott, F. L. (1957). *A History of American Magazines, 1885–1905.* Cambridge, MA: Belknap Press of Harvard University Press.

Nelson, M. B. (1995). *The Stronger Women Get the More Men Love Football.* North Yorkshire, UK: Quill.

Newman, C. (2007). "Readers' Letters to *Women's Health* Magazine." *Feminist Media Studies* 7:155–70.

Nicholas, P., and R. Salladay. (2005, July 14). "Gov. to Be Paid $8 Million by Fitness Magazines." *Los Angeles Times,* A1.

Oakenfull, G. K., et al. (2005). "Queer Eye for a Gay Guy: Using Market-Specific Symbols in Advertising to Attract Gay Consumers without Alienating the Mainstream." *Psychology & Marketing* 22:421–23.

Ohmann, R. (1996). *Selling Culture: Magazines, Markets, and Class at the Turn of the Century.* New York: Verso.

Olivardia, R., H. G. Pope, J. J. Borowiecki, and G. H. Cohane. (2004). "Biceps and Body Image: The Relationship between Muscularity and Self-Esteem, Depression, and Eating Disorder Symptoms." *Psychology of Men & Masculinity* 5:112–20.

Omi, M., and H. Winant. (1986). *Racial Formation in the United States: From the 1960s to the 1980s.* New York: Routledge.

Ortner, S. (1997). *The Politics and Erotics of Culture.* Boston: Beacon.

Penaloza, L. (1996). "We're Here, We're Queer, and We're Going Shopping: A Critical Perspective on the Accommodation of Gays and Lesbians in the U.S. Marketplace." In *Gays, Lesbians, and Consumer Behavior: Theory, Practice, and Research Issues in Marketing,* ed. D. L. Wardlow, 9–42. New York: Haworth.

Penniston-Bird, C. (2005). "Classifying the Body in the Second World War: British Men In and Out of Uniform." *Body & Society* 9:31–48.

Petersen, A., and D. Lupton. (1996). *The New Public Health: Health and Self in the Age of Risk.* St. Leonards, Australia: Allen & Unwin.

Phelan, S. (1994). *Getting Specific: Postmodern Lesbian Politics.* Minneapolis: University of Minnesota Press.

Pope, H. G., R. Olivardia, A. Gruber, and J. Borowiecki. (1999). "Evolving Ideals of Male Body Image as Seen through Action Toys." *International Journal of Eating Disorders* 23:65–72.

Pope, H. G., K. Phillips, and R. Olivardia. (2000). *The Adonis Complex: The Secret Crisis of Male Body Obsession.* New York: Free Press.

Posavac, H. D., S. S. Posavac, and E. J. Posavac. (1998). "Exposure to Media Images of Female Attractiveness and Concern with Body Weight among Young Women." *Sex Roles* 38:187–99.

Poster, M. (ed.). (1988). *Jean Baudrillard: Selected Writings.* Stanford, CA: Stanford University Press.

Pronger, B. (1990). *The Arena of Masculinity: Sports, Homosexuality, and the Meaning of Sex.* New York: St. Martin's.

PR Newswire. (2005, March 22). "New Poll: Public Divided on Regulating Appearance—from Weight to Tattoos—in the Workplace."

———. (2006, July 31). http://www.newscom.com/cgi-bin/prnh/20060731/NYM168.

———. (2007, February 7). "2006 Procedural Survey Shows 3 Percent Increase in Men Seeking Cosmetic Surgery."

Puar, J. K. (2005). "Queer Narratives of U.S. Exceptionalism." *Social Text* 23: 122–39.

Quindlen, A. (1999). "Barbie at 35." In *The Barbie Chronicles: A Living Doll Turns 40,* ed. Y. Z. McDonough, 117–20. New York: Touchstone.

Rand, E. (1995). *Barbie's Queer Accessories.* Durham, NC: Duke University Press.

Reiman, J. H. (2000). *The Rich Get Richer and the Poor Get Prison: Ideology, Class, and Criminal Justice.* Boston: Allyn & Bacon.

Reskin, B., and P. Phipps. (1988). "Women in Male-Dominated Professional and

Managerial Occupations." In *Women Working*, ed. A. H. Stromberg and S. Harkess, 190–205. Mountain View, CA: Mayfield.

Rigauer, B. (1981). *Sport and Work*. New York: Columbia University Press.

Ritzer, G. (2004). *The McDonaldization of Society*. 4th ed. Thousand Oaks, CA: Pine Forge.

Romero, C. L. (1998, January 17). "Sports and Fitness of Colorado Sells Flagship Magazine to Condé Nast." *Daily Camera*.

Rose, M. (1999, September 23). "Advertising: Young Condé Nast Title Develops Muscle." *Wall Street Journal*, 14.

Rose, N. (2001). The Politics of Life Itself. *Theory, Culture & Society* 18:1–30.

Rubin, G. (1999). "Thinking Sex: Notes for a Radical Theory of the Politics of Sexuality." In *Culture, Health, and Sexuality: A Reader*, ed. R. Parker and P. Aggleton. Philadelphia: Taylor & Francis.

Saltman, K. J. (2005). "The Strong Arm of the Law." *Body & Society* 9:49–67.

Saussure, F. de. ([1916] 1983). *Course in General Linguistics*. Trans. Roy Harris. London: Duckworth.

Scanlon, J. (1995). *Inarticulate Longings: The Ladies' Home Journal, Gender, and the Promises of Consumer Culture*. New York: Routledge.

———. 2000. "Advertising Women: The J. Walter Thompson's Company Women's Editorial Department." In *The Gender and Consumer Culture Reader*, ed. J. Scanlon, 201–25. New York: New York University Press.

Schulze, L. (1997). "On the Muscle." In *Building Bodies*, ed. P. Moore. New Brunswick, NJ: Rutgers University Press.

Scott, Linda M. (2000). "Market Feminism: The Case for a Paradigm Shift." In *Marketing and Feminism: Current Issues and Research*, ed. M. Catteral, P. MacLaran, and L. Stevens, 16–38. London: Routledge.

Segal, L. (1994). *Straight Sex: Rethinking the Politics of Pleasure*. Berkeley: University of California Press.

Seidman, S. (1992). *Embattled Eros: Sexual Politics and Ethics in Contemporary America*. New York: Routledge.

Sennett, R. (1994). *Flesh and Stone*. New York: Norton.

Shakib, S. (2003). "Female Basketball Participation: Negotiating the Peer Status from Childhood through Puberty." *American Behavioral Scientist* 46:1405–22.

Shilling, C. (1991). "Educating the Body: Physical Capital and the Production of Social Inequalities." *Sociology* 25:653–72.

Sidel, R. (1996). *Keeping Women and Children Last*. New York: Penguin.

Singh, D. (2002). "Female Mate Value at a Glance: Relationship of Waist-to-Hip Ratio to Health, Fecundity, and Attractiveness." *Neuroendocrinology Letters* 23: 81–91.

Singh, D., and R. K. Young. (1995). "Body Weight, Waist-to-Hip Ratio, Breasts, and Hips: Role in Judgments of Attractiveness and Desirability for Relationships." *Ethology and Sociobiology* 16:483–507.

Skeggs, B. (2004). *Class, Self, and Culture*. London: Routledge.

Skolnick, A. (1994). *Embattled Paradise: The American Family in an Age of Uncertainty*. New York: Basic Books.

Slater, D. (1997). *Consumer Culture and Modernity*. Cambridge, UK: Polity.

Smith, M., and B. Beal. (2007). "So You Can See How the Other Half Lives: MTV 'Cribs' Use of the 'Other' in Framing Successful Athletic Masculinities." *Journal of Sport and Social Issues* 31:103–27.

Sobal, J., and D. Maurer. (1999). "Body Weight as a Social Problem." In *Weighty Issues*, ed. J. Sobal and D. Maurer, 1–8. New York: Aldine de Gruyter.

Soshnick, S., and D. Sessa. (2005, September 20). Bloomberg News. *Ottawa Citizen*, D14.

Spelman, E. (1988). *Inessential Woman*. Boston: Beacon.

Spitzack, C. (1990). *Confessing Excess: Women and the Politics of Body Reduction*. Albany: SUNY Press.

Stabiner, K. (1982, May 2). "Tapping the Homosexual Market." *New York Times Magazine*, 80.

Stacey, J. (1996). *In the Name of the Family: Rethinking Family Values in the Postmodern Age*. Boston: Beacon.

Staff and Wire Reports (2000, June 28). "Game Over for 2 Sports Magazines." *New York Daily News*, 33.

Stockdill, B. (2002). *Activism against AIDS: At the Intersections of Sexuality, Race, Gender, and Class*. Boulder, CO: Lynne Rienner.

Stratigaki, M. (2004). "The Cooptation of Gender Concepts in EU Policies." *Social Politics* 11:30–56.

Swiencicki, M. A. (1998). "Consuming Brotherhood: Men's Culture, Style, and Recreation as Consumer Culture, 1880–1930." *Journal of Social History* 31:773–808.

Synnott, A. (1993). *The Body Social*. London: Routledge.

Takacs, S. (2005). "Jessica Lynch and the Regeneration of American Identity and Power Post 9-11." *Feminist Media Studies* 5:297–310.

Theberge, N. (2000). *Higher Goals: Women's Ice Hockey and the Politics of Gender*. Albany: SUNY Press.

Theberge, N., and A. Cronk. (1986). "Work Routines in Newspaper Sports Departments and the Coverage of Women's Sports." *Sociology of Sport Journal* 3:195–203.

Thomas, J. E., and M. K. Zimmerman. (2007). "Feminism and Profit in American Hospitals: The Corporate Construction of Women's Health Centers." *Gender & Society* 21:359–83.

Tolman, D. L. (1994). "Doing Desire: Adolescent Girls' Struggles for/with Sexuality." *Gender & Society* 8:324–42.

Tong, R. (1998). *Feminist Thought*. Boulder, CO: Westview.

Turner, B. (1992). *Regulating Bodies: Essays in Medical Sociology*. London: Routledge.

Van den Wingaard, M. (1997). *Reinventing the Sexes: Biomedical Construction of Masculinity and Femininity.* Bloomington: Indiana University Press.

Vertinsky, P. (1998). "'Run, Jane Run': Central Tensions in the Current Debate about Enhancing Women's Health through Exercise." *Women & Health* 27:81–111.

Wachs, F. L. (2005). "The Boundaries of Difference: Negotiating Gender in Recreational Sport." *Sociological Inquiry* 75:527–47.

Wachs, F. L., and S. L. Dworkin. (1997). "There's No Such Thing as a Gay Hero: Sexual Identity and Media Framing of HIV Positive Athletes." *Journal of Sport and Social Issues* 21:335–55.

Wacquant, L. (1995). "Pugs at Work: Bodily Capital and Bodily Labour among Professional Boxers." *Body & Society* 1:65–94.

———. (1995a). "Why Men Desire Muscles." *Body & Society* 1:163–80.

Walton, A. S. (2006, January 20). "Guy Grooming: More Men Are Taking the Time to Ward Off the Effects of Aging." *Atlanta Journal Constitution*, 1G.

Watney, S. (1987). *Policing Desire: Pornography, AIDS, and the Media.* London: Methuen.

Weeks, J. (1985). *Sexuality and Its Discontents: Meanings, Myths and Modern Sexualities.* New York: Routledge.

West, C., and D. Zimmerman. (1987). "Doing Gender." *Gender & Society* 1:125–51.

Whitson, D. (1990). "Sport in the Social Construction of Masculinity." In *Sport, Men, and the Gender Order*, ed. M. A. Messner and D. F. Sabo, 19–30. Champaign, IL: Human Kinetics.

Williamson, J. (1986). *Consuming Passions: The Dynamics of Popular Culture.* London: Marion Boyars.

Willis, P. (1981). *Learning to Labour.* New York: Columbia University Press.

Winant, M. (1994). *Racial Formation in the United States.* New York: Routledge.

Women's Sports Foundation. (1985). *The Miller Lite Report on Women in Sports.* New York: Women's Sports Foundation.

Young, I. M. (1990). *Throwing Like a Girl and Other Essays in Feminist Philosophy and Social Theory.* Bloomington: Indiana University Press.

WEBSITES

http://www.census.gov
http://www.census.gov/Press-Release/www/releases/archives/income_wealth/002484.html
http://www.census.gov/Press-Release/www/releases/archives/facts_for_features_special_editions/006587.html
http://www.salon.com/media/1998/01/05media.html

Index

snippets, 36, 47, 151, 196n. 24
Sobal, J., 36
social change, 19, 176. *See also* Civil Rights
Movement/issues; consumer culture,
and commodification; feminism; GLBT
communities/issues/rights; social justice;
social movements
social justice, 104–5, 126, 159, 173, 178, 181,
199n. 16; distributive justice, 103, 164,
168–69, 172, 180–81, 199nn. 15–16
social movements, 138–39, 141; and leisure,
141. *See also* Civil Rights Movement/
issues; feminism; GLBT communities/
issues/rights; social change
Solomon, W. S., 126, 159, 192 n9
Soshnick, S., 190n. 9
Spelman, E., 195n. 17
Spitzack, C., 12–15, 39, 108, 118–19, 188n. 17,
189n. 3, 193n. 2
sport, 18, 85, 88–89, 92, 100, 124, 131–36,
140, 147, 152, 157, 163, 171, 198n. 7; as female appropriate, 189n. 2; exploitation
of labor, 194n. 10; and fitness-military
interactions, 85; lesbians, 7, 168, 170, 187n.
5; as masculinizing, 85, 102, 113, 125, 197n.
6 (*see also* masculinities); as signifier
of morality and protectionism, 24, 163;
-military interactions, 24, 66, 73, 82–83,
85–90, 102, 162; participation as a privilege, 133, 138; sport-fitness relationship,
49–50, 92–97, 102, 133, 155, 162, 198n. 7;
Title IX and access to, 18, 130–32, 136–37,
145–46, 148, 159, 194n. 4, 195nn. 14–16,
20, 196n. 22; training for labor, 112–14;
sport and fitness typing, 5; and violence,
85. *See also* gender relations/inequality/
equity; media
Sports Illustrated, 134
Sports Illustrated for Women, 136, 194
Stacey, J., 126
Stabiner, K., 167
Steinbrenner, George, 98
stigma. *See* bodies, body stigma
Stockdill, B., 24
Stratigaki, M., 193n. 3
Swiencicki, M. A., 48
Synott, A., 65

Takacs, S., 164

target demographic. *See* advertising/
advertisers
Theberge, N., 18–19, 27, 109, 171
third wave crisis of masculinity. *See*
masculinities
Thomas, J. E., 193n. 3
Thornton, S. L., 191n. 1, 192n. 2
Title IX. *See* sport
Tolman, D., 31
Tong, R., 195

Van den Wingaard, M., 22, 192n. 12
Vertinsky, P., 199n. 13
violence, 138, 140, 192n. 8; and sexual
assault, 99
Vogue, 130
vulnerability. *See* bodies, body positioning/
presentation/language

Wachs, F. L., vii, 13, 25–26, 44, 67, 136, 171,
189, 192, 193n. 9
Wacquant, L., 85, 190n. 6, 192n. 11, 193n. 16
Walton, A. S., 47–48
Washington Post, 67
Watney, S., 69, 191n. 1
Weeks, J., 67
Weider Corporation, 27, 111
Western world/culture, 27, 80, 89, 107, 131,
138, 140, 144, 187n. 3; dualisms of, 31;
sexual formations of, 166, 187n. 3
Whitson, D., 187n. 4
Wilde, Oscar, 70
Willard, F., 156, 197n. 31
Williamson, J., 178
Women's Basketball League (WBL), 145–46
Women's Fitness, 182
Women's Sports, 131–132, 146, 194nn. 5, 7
Women's Sports & Fitness, 25, 40, 50,
53–54, 61, 129–57, 178, 183, 194nn. 8, 11,
195n. 13
Women's Sports Foundation, 132–33,
144–45, 195; era of, 144–45, 152–53,
156
Women's Sports Hall of Fame, 147
Wsports, 136

Young, I., 30

Zimmermann, M., 193n. 3

About the Authors

SHARI L. DWORKIN is Associate Professor of Medical Sociology in the Department of Social and Behavioral Sciences at the University of California at San Francisco. She is co-author of *Built to Win: The Female Athlete as Cultural Icon.* FAYE LINDA WACHS is Associate Professor of Sociology at California State Polytechnic University, Pomona.